The Critical Shaw

on

Literature

Edited by

Gustavo Rodríguez Martin

The Critical Shaw: On Literature

General Editor's Preface and Chronology © 2016 by L.W. Conolly

Introduction and editorial material © 2016 by Gustavo Rodríguez Martín

Published 2016 by RosettaBooks

ISBN (paperback): 978-0-7953-4893-8

Cover design by David Ter-Avanesyan / Ter33Design

Cover illustration by Shutterstock / Kamenuka

ISBN (EPUB): 978-0-7953-4686-6

ISBN (Kindle): 978-0-7953-4764-1

www.RosettaBooks.com

RosettaBooks®

Contents

Acknowledgements

First of all, I wish to express my gratitude to the general editor of this series, Professor Leonard Conolly, for his continuing guidance and support throughout the process of editing this book.

I would also like to offer my thanks to the rest of the editors in this series (Michel Pharand, Dorothy Hadfield, Christopher Innes, and Brigitte Bogar) for their savvy and professionalism as part of this coordinated collective effort. In particular, I would like to include a special note of gratitude to Professor Pharand, who offered his phenomenal knowledge of Shaw scholarship with the utmost generosity.

General Editor's Preface

Bernard Shaw is not the household name he once was, but in the 1920s and 1930s he was certainly the world's most famous English-language playwright, and arguably one of the most famous people in the world. His plays were internationally performed and acclaimed, his views on matters great and small were relentlessly solicited by the media, he was pursued by paparazzi long before the word was even invented, the biggest names in politics, the arts, entertainment, even sports—Gandhi, Nehru, Churchill, Rodin, Twain, Wells, Lawrence of Arabia, Elgar, Einstein, Garbo, Chaplin, Stalin, Tunney and many more—welcomed his company, and his correspondents in the tens of thousands of letters he wrote during his long lifetime constitute a veritable who's who of world culture and politics. And Shaw remains the only person ever to have been awarded both a Nobel Prize and an Oscar.

Shaw's reputation rests securely not just on his plays, a dozen or so of which have come to be recognized as classics—*Man and Superman*, *Major Barbara*, *Pygmalion*, and *Saint Joan* perhaps now the most familiar of them—but also on his early work as a music, art, literary, and theater critic, and on his lifelong political activism. After he moved to London from his native Dublin in 1876, and after completing five novels, he established himself as one of London's most controversial, feared, and admired critics, and while he eventually retired from earning his living as a critic in order to focus on playwriting, he continued to lecture and write about cultural and other issues—religion, for example—with scorching in-telligence. As for politics, his early commitment to Socialism, and his later expressed admiration for Communism and con-tempt for Capitalism, meant that while his views were relent-lessly refuted by the establishment press they could rarely be ignored—hardly surprising given the logic and passion that underpinned them.

Winston Churchill once declared Shaw to be "the greatest living master of letters in the English-speaking world," and the selections from Shaw's reviews, essays, speeches, and cor-respondence contained in the five volumes of this Critical Shaw series provide abundant evidence to validate Churchill's high regard. Shaw wrote—and spoke—volumi-nously, and his complete works on the topics covered by this series—Literature, Music, Religion, Theater, and Poli-tics—would fill many more than five volumes. The topics reflect Shaw's deepest interests and they inspired some of his most brilliant nondramatic writing. The selections in each volume give a comprehensive and representative survey of his thinking, and show him to be not just the great rhetori-cian that Churchill and others acknowledged, but also one of the great public intellectuals of the twentieth century.

Leonard Conolly
Robinson College, Cambridge
December 2015

Introduction

If one is to name the two qualities that a literary critic must possess, it would be natural to mention a broad knowledge of literature and a sharp critical faculty—if only because these are the semantic concepts involved in the phrase *literary critic*. George Bernard Shaw (1856–1950) had both qualities in large quantities.

Shaw's acquaintance with literature began at a very early age in his native Ireland, when he made up for his scarce formal education with a passion for reading almost anything he could lay his hands on. This bestowed on the young 'Sonny' (as he was known to his family) two characteristics that separated him from the rest: first, he could not "remember any time at which a printed page was unintelligible to me" (*Platform and Pulpit* 277); and second, he knew that his "kingdom was not of this world: I was at home only in the realm of my imagination, and at my ease only with the mighty dead" (*Immaturity* xliii). The scope of these precocious readings expanded during Shaw's early years in London, when he spent much of his time in the Reading Room of the British Museum. At that time, William Archer recalls:

> Bernard Shaw in the Museum as 'a young man of tawny complexion and attire,' assiduous in his attendance and sitting with the same two books in front of him day after day, for weeks at a time. The two books were Karl Marx's *Das Kapital* (in French), and an orchestral score of *Tristan and Isolde*, both of which the

young man studied, according to Archer, 'alternately, if not simultaneously.' (Colbourne 69)

Shaw's critical faculty is inextricably associated with his public persona, especially as a playwright and polymath critic. Many scholars have pointed out his "habit of pouncing on weak points, of finding fault" (*SHAW* 16: 36) However, this habit is complemented by Shaw's conviction that he had mastered the art of "accurate observation," which is "commonly called cynicism by those who have not got it" (*Music in London* 266). After all, one must not lose sight of the fact that Shaw studied and gave serious thought to countless habits, theories, and technical skills; he discussed an array of things that few other men managed to touch upon, let alone master: diet, vaccination, spelling, stage lighting, local government or landscape painting, to mention but a few of them (Palmer 29–30).

But Shaw did not begin reviewing books simply because he had an inborn talent for it. In fact, he resorted to reviewing as a means of remedying his chronic impecuniosity. In Shaw's own words, reviewing was one of "the drudgeries by which the aesthetic professions have to save themselves from starvation" ("Reviewing Reviewed" 71). From the moment he arrived in London, he deemed himself "an incorrigible Unemployable," (Pearson 51) and that condition would not be altered in spite of his strenuous efforts to become a successful novelist. Things took a turn for the worse when Shaw's father, George Carr Shaw, passed away in 1885 and with him the steady—if scanty—money he would regularly send to his emigrated family in London. Luckily for Shaw, William Archer noticed the obvious talents that he possessed—and which were not put to good use simply because Shaw was too sensitive and proud to ask for work. Thus Archer, who was reviewing books for the *Pall Mall Gazette*, gave Shaw a book to review and made up some preposterous excuse to send in "a review written by a deputy who would be glad for more work" (Henderson 165–6). As Shaw's review was appreciated by the literary editor, Shaw would never lack a book to review from then on (at two guineas per thousand words) until his success as a dramatist made him take journalism as a secondary activity. Naturally, Shaw's peculiar initiation as a book reviewer for the *Pall Mall Gazette* explains why several of his reviews appeared unsigned, and only the data in his diaries and a few scrap books he kept with clippings of these pieces attest to their authorship (Laurence 1954).

If we follow the chronology of events in Shaw's career as a book reviewer (he had started ghost-writing music criticism for *The Hornet* in 1876), the first thing to notice is that once he published his first review in 1884, he would never stop writing literary criticism until his death in 1950. The initial milestone would be his first review for *The Christian Socialist*, a review of Hyndman's *The Historical Basis of Socialism in England*. The last one, published in *The Observer*, examined an edited collection of Samuel Butler's works.

Shaw's book reviews, however, were only published regularly in *The Pall Mall Gazette*. There he underwent a steady formative process that marks a turning point in his evolution as a literary critic, particularly because he had to take up reviewing as "mere brute practice with the pen... as a laborer digs or a carpenter planes" (Holroyd 1997: 43)—words he had used to refer to his self-imposed training as a novel writer. In the *Pall Mall Gazette*, Shaw was mostly confined to reviewing heart-throb fiction and volumes of "biography, musical history, spiritualism, and ghost stories" (Tyson 1991: 6). Many of these works remain completely irrelevant in the history of literature, and their authors—some of whom only published the book Shaw reviewed—long forgotten. This has made it impossible to identify some of them, especially when they are hidden behind some obscure pseudonym.

Occasionally, however, he had the chance to review an exceptional book (the review of one such book, Samuel Butler's *Luck or Cunning*, is included in this volume), and the change in tone and tenor is more than obvious. Not only would Shaw employ a completely different repertoire in his critical style, but something would also rub off on himself: in the case in point, Butler's book constitutes one of the germs of Shaw's lifelong interest in Evolution and Neo-Lamarckism.

During the period Shaw was employed at the *Pall Mall Gazette*, he became outspoken against the evils of capitalism; against how industrial and financial developments had only benefitted a few, while the majority of the population had to live in insalubrious slums and endure appalling working conditions. Not for nothing was he a leading member of the Fabian Society, and one of the most enthralling orators for the cause of Socialism at the time. Had it not been for the committed and controversial editorship of William Thomas (W. T.) Stead in the *Pall Mall Gazette*, however, Shaw would have never been able to join the avant-garde of the 'New Journalism'. To gauge the far-reaching consequences of the many polemic campaigns that Stead launched from his position as editor of the *Pall Mall Gazette*, it suffices to say that the attempt to bring to public attention the dramatic conditions of prostitutes—especially young girls—managed to raise the age of consent for girls from 13 to 16, in a piece of legislation that was popularly known as the "Stead Act" (incidentally, The Criminal Law Amendment Act of 1885 also made "homosexual acts" illegal and was used against Oscar Wilde when he was sent to prison in 1895). With an employer of this sort, Shaw was free to exercise his most acid satire against the establishment without fearing editorial reprisals.

But the evils of capitalism were also endured by reviewers who, like Shaw, had to write their pieces in just a few days after receiving each book. The mass-production of novels and other books accounts for this acceleration in the pace of the reviewer's work. In fact, most of the diary entries that record the books he was given for review suggest that he dispatched volumes at an average rate of one every two or three of days (*The Diaries 1885–1897*). At least, apart from the economic benefits that this job represented, Shaw acquired what was probably his first personal library thanks to the review copies he received.

After three years of enduring more than his share of tenthrate novels, sentimental poetry, and pseudo-science, Shaw left the *Pall Mall Gazette* with a bit of relief and the determination not to have the materials he would review imposed on him ever again. Once his economic situation gradually went from comfortable to wealthy, Shaw had a smaller economic incentive for reviewing books. Despite this, he returned to this type of journalism because of what seems like an inborn drive towards writing, whatever the genre. As Shaw would put it:

> I never felt inclined to write, any more than I ever felt inclined to breathe.... it never occurred to me that my literary sense was exceptional. I gave the whole world credit for it. The fact is, there is nothing miraculous, nothing particularly interesting even, in a natural faculty to the man who has it... No, I never wanted to write. I know now, of course, the value and the scarcity of the literary faculty (though I think it over-rated); but I still don't want it. You cannot want a thing and have it, too. (*Interviews and Recollections* 30–1)

Over the course of the next six decades, Shaw would write reviews for a number of publications. Some of them can be classified as Socialist periodicals that sought to increase their limited circulation by resorting to popular Socialists such as Shaw to attract new readers. Among them one finds the aforementioned *The Christian Socialist*, and others such as

Fabian News, the *Labour Leader*, and *Left News*. In addition to these, Shaw also published his literary criticism in the most prominent periodicals of England, such as *The Star*, *The Daily Chronicle*, *The Saturday Review*, *The Observer*, *The Nation* (later, *The Nation and Athenæum*), and *The New Statesman*—most of which, admittedly, also had a Labour viewpoint and featured well-known Fabians in their managing positions. Thus, one may find some of Shaw's sharpest socioeconomic critique entrenched within his literary criticism, very often laying down the law on Socialism and economic history. For example, in "The Case Against Chesterton," he corrects the author's (West) approach to the evolution of Socialism in Britain:

> Also I would warn Mr West and all whom it may concern not to be misled by the younger generation of British penmen (those under fifty or thereabouts) who believe that their grandfathers all read Mill, and all belonged to a period called Early Victorian, in which the dull dogs had their day. Mill was the inspirer, not, as Mr West implies, of the Socialist reaction of the eighties, but of the rearguard actions fought against it by Benthamite Individualism under such captains as Bradlaugh and Herbert Spencer. Mill's final conversion to Socialism, though claimed for the Fabian side by Mr Sidney Webb, was ignored as completely as Solomon's final conversion to the worship of Ashtaroth.

Whenever he wrote for a publication with a conspicuous political bias, however, Shaw would often take a neutralized—almost scientific—stance that would mar some of his spark as a polemicist. Unsurprisingly, although it is always difficult to tell when Shaw is in earnest, he claims in his review entitled "How Free is the Press" that his "own most polemical writings are to be found in the files of *The Times*, *The Morning Post*, *The Daily Express*, *The World*, and *The Saturday Review*," all of which were controlled by "the classes," by which Shaw meant the ruling plutocratic minorities. These "classes" are the same that Mitchener refers to in *Press Cuttings* when he defines his personal conception of an ideal democracy as "the government of the masses by the classes."

The relationship between Shaw and some of these publications on occasion goes well beyond literary criticism. For example, *The Manchester Guardian*, where Shaw published a review of *Samuel Butler: Author of Erewhon (1835–1902): A Memoir* by Henry Festing Jones, was the only newspaper on the east side of the Atlantic that dared reprint Shaw's letter "Shall Roger Casement Hang?" — an outspoken defense of the Irish nationalist that struck a chord abroad but did not sit well with some at home.

At any rate, it must be conceded that the literary savvy of Bernard Shaw is not to be found in book reviews alone. On occasion, he would not resist the temptation to share his views on a particular aspect of literature in, for example, letters sent to the editor of the *Times Literary Supplement*. Two of these have been included in this volume, and they corroborate the image of Shaw as a tireless worker and reader, for he kept up with the most relevant publications and cultural initiatives of his time. Furthermore, these essays sent *motu proprio* to literary forums illustrate Shaw's vast knowledge of the surrounding circumstances and the critical heritage of the key works in English and foreign literature: from printers to editors, copyediting practices, and translations.

The last major source of Shaw's literary opinions lies in his prefaces. The most relevant passages usually appear in those that have a 'professional' theme, such as the prefaces to *Three Plays for Puritans*, *The Dark Lady of the Sonnets*, and *The Six of Calais*. As is to be expected, these prefaces focus mostly on drama rather than on fiction or poetry.

The later reviews, the letters to periodicals, and the prefaces constitute the other end of the spectrum when contrasted with Shaw's early reviews for the *Pall Mall Gazette*, in the sense that they deal with those authors that Shaw was personally interested in. Thus, it should come as no surprise that we should read a lot about 'Shakespear' (as Shaw spelled it), Ibsen or Dickens in them. Furthermore, as Shaw gained more freedom to choose the subject matter of his literary criticism, he progressively turned to authors that he knew all too well; for example, G. K. Chesterton, H. G. Wells, and Sidney Webb. Even when he was reviewing someone else's work, he would often find an excuse to direct his train of thought towards his illustrious contemporaries, and bring up the latest debate that they had had, frequently through public letters and articles.

The enduring quality of Shaw's literary criticism does not reside—at least not exclusively—in the historical allusions that map the intellectual scene of England at the time, or in the bibliographical records that they contain. Above all else, the witty satire and the astute eye for human nature, together with a style that is full of shocking, extended metaphors and convoluted parallelisms, confer on these reviews a literary quality in their own right. Acid satire livens up many a passage, and Shaw needs no excuse to stick pins into his favorite targets, be they individual or collective:

> My fellow countryman, Lord Northcliffe, whom I do not know personally (otherwise how could I be free to be uncivil to him?) is not, for an Irishman, conspicuously intellectual, though he may pass in England...

Even when he looked back on his younger self in the Preface to *Immaturity*, his first novel, the satirical, ambivalent note on which the preface ends reveals Shaw as a critic that will spare no-one:

> I had the intellectual habit; and my natural combination of critical faculty with literary resource needed only a clear comprehension of life in the light of an intelligible theory: in short, a re-

ligion, to set it in triumphant operation. It was the lack of this last qualification that lamed me in those early days in Victoria Grove, and that set limits to this ungainly first novel of mine, which you will not lose very much by skipping.

The aphoristic style of some passages in these critical pieces is also worth commenting on. For one thing, they synthesize many of Shaw's ideas on literature and the art of writing. Take, for instance, another excerpt from the Preface to *Immaturity*:

> If a writer says what he has to say as accurately and effectively as he can, his style will take care of itself, if he has a style.

This style also fleshes out in a pithy, catchy language that has made Shaw one of the most quoted authors in the history of literature. Here is some advice for dramatists from "How to Make Plays Readable:"

> The safe rule is, Write nothing in a play that you would not write in a novel.

All in all, the expression of shocking ideas through unexpected associations; in short, the perfect combination of humor and literary skill, is what defines the Shavian touch in these reviews. To quote but a single example, again from "The Case Against Chesterton," this is Shaw's approach to Chesterton's alleged anti-Semitism:

> If all the portfolios of the Cabinet were strictly reserved for Jews, and the proceedings of the House of Commons conducted in Yiddish, we have every reason to expect that the country would be governed much more intelligently than it is at present, and with a steady regard to the value of intellectual training, knowledge of languages and literature, and artistic culture, instead of our present implacable and boorish contempt for them.

The same combination is often employed to scrutinize complex literary techniques, with equally uproarious results. See, for example, how he deals with self-proclaimed naturalist novelists who have no first-hand experience of the setting they describe:

> And it must be added, at the risk of giving a violent shock to literary slummers, that every middle-class novelist who professes to arrive at his descriptions of that daily life by the inductive or Zolaistic method, is to that extent a flagrant humbug, although he may, through the ignorance of his readers, be as safe from exposure as an East-end dog-stealer would be if he undertook the fashionable intelligence for a paper circulating exclusively in Bethnal-green.

These are the elements that readers must be on the lookout for when they approach Shaw's literary criticism. They will find many penetrating ideas about literature and, even when that is not the case, they will surely find much to enjoy.

Bernard Shaw and His Times: A Chronology

[*This chronology is common to all five volumes in the Critical Shaw series, and reflects the topics of the series: Politics, Theater, Literature, Music, and Religion. For a comprehensive and detailed chronology of Shaw's life and works, see A. M. Gibbs, A Bernard Shaw Chronology (Basingstoke: Palgrave, 2001).*]

1856 Shaw born in Dublin (26 July).

1859 Charles Darwin publishes *On the Origin of Species by Means of Natural Selection*.

1864 Herbert Spencer publishes *Principles of Biology* (and coins the phrase "survival of the fittest").

1865 The Salvation Army is founded by Methodist preacher William Booth.

1870 The doctrine of papal infallibility is defined as dogma at the First Vatican Council.

1876 Shaw moves from Dublin to London. He begins ghostwriting music reviews for Vandeleur Lee for *The Hornet*.

1879 Shaw begins writing music reviews for *The Saturday Musical Review*, *The Court Journal*, and other publications. He writes his first novel, *Immaturity*, quickly followed by four others: *The Irrational Knot* (1880), *Love Among the Artists* (1881), *Cashel Byron's Profession* (1882), and *An Unsocial Socialist* (1883).

1883 Shaw reads Karl Marx's *Das Kapital* (in a French translation) in the British Museum Reading Room.

1884 The Fabian Society is founded; Shaw joins in the same year. He publishes his first book review in *The Christian Scientist*.

1885 Shaw begins publishing book reviews regularly in *The Pall Mall Gazette*.

1886 Eleanor Marx, daughter of Karl Marx, organizes a reading of Ibsen's *A Doll's House*; Shaw reads the part of Krogstad.

1889 Having written music reviews for over a decade, Shaw becomes a full-time critic for *The Star*, and then (in 1890) *The World*.

1891 Shaw publishes *The Quintessence of Ibsenism* (revised and updated in 1922).

1892 Shaw's first play, *Widowers' Houses*, is performed.

1893 Founding of the Independent Labour Party, a socialist advocacy group.

1894 Shaw resigns from *The World* and henceforth writes only occasional music reviews. *Arms and the Man* is first performed. Shaw becomes acquainted with aspiring theatre critic Reginald Golding Bright.

1895 Shaw becomes full-time drama critic for *The Saturday Review*. He publishes a lengthy review column almost every week for the next two and a half years.

1897 Shaw is elected a member of the Vestry of the Parish of St Pancras (until 1903).

1898 Shaw marries Charlotte Payne-Townshend and resigns as *The Saturday Review* drama critic. He publishes
The Perfect Wagnerite and *Plays: Pleasant and Unpleasant*. One of the "unpleasant" plays, *Mrs Warren's Profession*, is refused a performance licence by the Lord
Chamberlain; the ban will stay in effect until 1924.

1901 *Caesar and Cleopatra* is first performed, with music
written by Shaw. Queen Victoria dies.

1904 J. E. Vedrenne and Harley Granville Barker begin their
management of the Court Theatre (until 1907), with
Shaw as a principal playwright. Eleven Shaw plays are
performed in three seasons.

1905 *Man and Superman* is first performed. Albert Einstein
publishes his theory of relativity.

1906 Founding of the Labour Party. *Major Barbara* and *The
Doctor's Dilemma* are first performed.

1908 *Der tapfere Soldat*, an unauthorized operetta loosely
based on *Arms and the Man*, with music by Oscar
Straus and libretto by Rudolf Bernauer and Leopold
Jacobson, is first performed in Vienna. It is later staged
(1910) in translation as *The Chocolate Soldier*.

1909 *The Shewing-up of Blanco Posnet* is refused a licence by
the Lord Chamberlain. W. B. Yeats and Lady Gregory
stage it at the Abbey Theatre in Dublin. Shaw appears
as a witness before the Joint Select Committee of the
House of Lords and the House of Commons on Stage
Plays (Censorship).

1911 Shaw joins the managing council of the Royal Academy of Dramatic Art. His strong support of RADA's programs will include bequeathing RADA a third of his royalties. Shaw writes an introduction for the Waverley edition of Dickens's *Hard Times*.

1913 *Pygmalion* is first performed.

1914 Beginning of the First World War. Shaw publishes *Common Sense About the War*.

1916 Easter Rising in Dublin against British rule of Ireland.

1917 The Russian Revolution overthrows the imperialist government and installs a communist government under Vladimir Ilyich Lenin. The United States joins the war against Germany. On 17 July Czar Nicholas II and his family are executed.

1918 Representation of the People Act gives the vote to all men over twenty-one, and to women over thirty if they meet certain qualifications (e.g., property owners, university graduates). End of the First World War.

1920 *Heartbreak House* is first performed. Shaw completes *Back to Methuselah*, a five-play cycle on evolutionary themes. League of Nations formed.

1921 The Irish Free State gains independence from Britain. Shaw writes the preface to *Immaturity*.

1922 Joseph Stalin becomes general secretary of the Communist Party Central Committee. Benito Mussolini becomes Italian prime minister.

1923 *Saint Joan* is first performed, with music written by Shaw.

1924 Ramsay MacDonald becomes the first Labour prime minister, in a Labour-Liberal coalition government.

1925 Adolf Hitler publishes *Mein Kampf* [*My Struggle*].

1926 General strike in Great Britain, 4–13 May. Shaw is awarded the 1925 Nobel Prize for Literature.

1928 Representation of the People (Equal Franchise) Act gives the vote to all women over twenty-one. Shaw publishes *The Intelligent Woman's Guide to Socialism and Capitalism*. *The Apple Cart* is first performed.

1929 The Wall Street Crash, 28–29 October, which signalled the beginning of the Great Depression. Shaw speaks as a delegate to the third International Congress of the World League for Sexual Reform. Sir Barry Jackson establishes the Malvern Festival, dedicated to Shaw's plays.

1931 Shaw visits Russia. He celebrates his seventy-fifth birthday on 26 July in Moscow's Concert Hall of Nobles with two thousand guests. He meets Stalin on 29 July.

1932 Unemployment reaches 3.5 million in Great Britain. South Wales and the industrial north experience mass unemployment and poverty. *Too True to Be Good* receives its English première at the Malvern Festival.

1933 Shaw makes his first visit to the United States. He speaks to an audience of thirty-five hundred at the Metropolitan Opera House (11 April). Hitler becomes German chancellor.

1934 *The Six of Calais* is first performed.

1936 Shaw makes his second (and last) visit to the United States. *The Millionairess* is first performed.

1938 *Geneva* is first performed. Shaw rejects a proposal from producer Gabriel Pascal for a musical version of *Pygmalion*.

1939 Beginning of the Second World War.

1941 The United States enters the Second World War.

1943 Charlotte Shaw dies.

1944 Shaw publishes *Everybody's Political What's What?*

1945 End of the Second World War. United Nations formed. The UK Labour Party wins its first majority government. Clement Atlee becomes prime minister. His government implements an extensive nationalization program of British industry and services.

1947 Discovery of the Dead Sea Scrolls in Qumran Caves, West Bank.

1948 World Council of Churches founded in Amsterdam.

1950 Shaw publishes his last book review in *The Observer* (26 March). He dies in Ayot St Lawrence, Hertfordshire (2 November).

A Note on the Text

Sources for the selections of Shaw's literary writings are given in the heading for each selection. Secondary sources on Shaw's literary writings are provided in Sources and Further Reading, where biographies and other fundamental works by Shaw are also listed. Shaw's original spelling and punctuation have been retained, although conflicting editorial practices in the different original texts have been standardized. For example, titles of books, operas, and other works of art are always italicized. All ellipses inserted in the text are editorial, unless otherwise noted. Brief explanatory notes are included in square brackets. In cases where there are multiple references to the same person or event, the note is given only for the first reference.

A final note to readers concerning the arrangement of the table of contents. The reviews have been ordered chronologically within each section, so that the evolution in Shaw's style and in the type of works he reviewed becomes apparent throughout the book. Also, in order to minimize any overlap with any of the other volumes in this *Critical Shaw series*, the "Nonfiction" section has avoided books on politics or religion, for example. A particularly conflicting area was "Drama." In order to prevent any unwanted concomitance with the volume on *Theater*, the "Drama" section herein focuses on questions that, in short, can be analyzed by looking at a printed page, whereas the aforementioned *Shaw on Theater* will delve into areas like drama criticism, performance, acting, and directing.

Part I: Writing, Editing, Publishing, and Censorship

Unlike in the case of drama (*The Quintessence of Ibsenism*) and music ("The Perfect Wagnerite"), Shaw never wrote a compendium of his views on literature and the art of writing in general. It is possible, however, to gain some insight into his literary preferences—and the evolution thereof—by analyzing Shaw's formative years, his favorite readings, the advice he gave to emerging writers, and the reviews of books that deal with aspects of the writing profession: editing, publishing, censorship. It is of particular importance to understand that Shaw was an extremely well-read man who never had much formal education, a paradox that accounts for some of the unconventional opinions expressed in these pieces.

1. "The Author to the Reader," 1887.

[Shaw wrote this opening piece as an introduction to the first edition of the third novel of "his nonage," Love Among the Artists, six years after the novel was finished. The apologetic tone, even if tongue-in-cheek, contrasts sharply with the prevailing tenor of most of the pieces reproduced here. At such an early stage in Shaw's career, both his enthusiasm for originality of plot—the lack of which he criticized in Shakespeare—and his ideal of literature with a purpose are already apparent.]

Dear Sir or Madam:

Will you allow me a word of personal explanation now that I am, for the second time, offering you a novel which is not the outcome of my maturer experience and better sense? If you have read my *Irrational Knot* to the bitter end, you will not accuse me of mock modesty when I admit that it was very long; that it did not introduce you to a single person you could conceivably have been glad to know; and that your knowledge of the world must have forewarned you that no satisfactory ending was possible. You may, it is true, think that a story teller should not let a question of mere possibility stand between his audience and the satisfaction of a happy ending. Yet somehow my conscience stuck at it; for I am not a professional liar: I am even ashamed of the extent to which in my human infirmity I have been an amateur one. No: my stories were meant to be true *ex hypothesi*: the persons were fictitious; but had they been real, they must (or so I thought at the time) have acted as I said. For, if you can believe such a prodigy, I was but an infant of twenty-four when, being at that time, one of the unemployed, I sat down to mend my straitened fortunes by writing *The Irrational Knot*. I had done the same thing once before; and next year, still unemployed, I did it again. That third attempt of mine is about to see the light in this volume. And now a few words of warning to you before you begin it.

1. Though the wisdom of the book is the fruit of a quarter century's experience, yet the earlier years of that period were much preoccupied with questions of bodily growth and nutrition; so that it may be as well to bear in mind that even the youngest of us may be wrong sometimes. 2. *Love among the Artists* is what is called a novel with a purpose; I will not undertake to say at this distant me what the main purpose was; but I remember that I had a notion of illustrating the difference between that enthusiasm for the fine arts which people gather from reading about them, and the genuine artistic faculty which cannot help creating, interpreting, and unaffectedly enjoying music and pictures. 3. This book has no winding-up at the end. Mind: it is not, as in *The Irrational Knot*, a case of the upshot being unsatisfactory! There is absolutely no upshot at all. The parties are married in the middle of the book; and they do not elope with or divorce one another, or do anything unusual or improper. When as much is told concerning them as seemed to me at the time germane to my purpose, the novel breaks off. But, if you prefer something more conclusive, pray do not scruple to add a final chapter of your own invention. 4. If you find yourself displeased with my story, remember that it is not I, but the generous and appreciative publisher of the book, who puts it forward as worth reading. I shall polish it up for you the best way I can, and here and there remove some absurdity out of which I have grown since I wrote it, but I cannot substantially improve it, much less make it what a novel ought to be; for I have given up novel writing these many years, during which I have lost the impudence of the apprentice without gaining the skill of the master.

There is an end to all things, even to stocks of unpublished manuscript. It may be a relief to you to know that when this *Love among the Artists* shall have run its course, you need apprehend no more furbished-up early attempts at fiction from me. I have written but five novels in my life; and of these there will remain then unpublished only the first—a very remarkable work, I assure you, but hardly one which I should be well advised in letting loose whilst my livelihood depends on my credit as a literary workman.

I can recall a certain difficulty, experienced even whilst I was writing the book, in remembering what it was about. Twice I clean forgot the beginning, and had to read back, as I might have read any other man's novel, to learn the story. If I could not remember then, how can I presume on my knowledge of the book now so far as to make promises about it? But I suspect you will find yourself in less sordid company than that into which *The Irrational Knot* plunged you. And I can guarantee you against any plot. You will be candidly dealt with. None of the characters will turn out to be somebody else in the last chapter: no violent accidents or strokes of pure luck will divert events from their normal course: no forger, long lost heir, detective, nor any commonplace of the police court or of the realm of romance shall insult your understanding, or tempt you to read on when you might better be in bed or attending to your business. By this time you should be eager to be at the story. Meanwhile I must not forget that it is only by your exceptional indulgence that I have been suffered to detain you so long about a personal matter; and so I thank you and proceed to business.

29, Fitzroy Square, London, W.

2. "The Book Bills of Narcissus." *The Star*, 12 September 1891, 4:4.

[*Review of Richard Le Gallienne's* The Book-Bills of Narcissus, an Account Rendered. (*Derby: Frank Murray, 1891). Shaw ironically mocks the condescending airs of young writers like Le Galli-*

enne, especially as opposed to many of the committed "riper men"
he cites in the first paragraph. Literature is based on the subject
matter and the technique of the writer, but 'hotheadedness' is also
indispensable.]

Of all the consequences of that deluge of schooling which
has taught everybody to read, and made cheap books remu-
nerative to capitalists, none is more appalling than the ease
with which a clever and imaginative young man may, for a
few shillings, provide himself with an exhaustive second-
hand experience of life. To read this book of [English author
and poet] Mr Le Gallienne's [1866–1947] one would suppose
that he had been through three times as much as Ulysses,
and was old enough and wise enough to be the father of Koheleth, the author of Ecclesiastes. Every page is pervaded by
an assumption of elderly moderation, of gentle tolerance of
the follies of passion, of resigned disillusion, of mellow pa-
ternal kindliness, which will move those who do not know
the truth concerning the author's age to lay down the volume
with a murmured blessing on his kindly voice and on his sil-
ver hair. This is the note of youth nowadays. From our riper
men — our Morrises [English artist, designer, and political activist William Morris, 1834–1896], Ruskins [English art critic
John Ruskin, 1819–1900], Bradlaughs [English politician and
secularist Charles Bradlaugh, 1833–1891], Gladstones [English
statesman William Ewart Gladstone, 1809–1898], Tyndalls
[Irish physicist John Tyndall, 1820–1893], and their contemporaries — we have strenuous words, urgency, combativeness,
readiness to think every halfpennyworth of their convictions
worth fighting for tooth and nail. How superior are our
young men. How calm, how dispassionate, how full of conviction that nothing is worth quarrelling over, and yet how
beautifully indulgent, how infinitely pitiful they are over the
impetuosities and wilfulness of their elders. Later on, of
course, when their knowledge of books is displaced by a

knowledge of life, they become as little children again, and lose this fine philosophic *tout-comprendre-c'est-tout-pardonner* impartiality. But it is wonderfully perfect while it lasts, and keeps

OUR HOTHEADED OLD MEN

duly reproved and checked. As for me, though I am not yet quite old enough to be Mr Le Gallienne's father, I feel a better and soberer man for having read this little book of his.

If an unusually fine literary instinct could make a solid book, Mr Le Gallienne would be at no loss for an enduring reputation. One can see by his style how he appreciates [British poet and essayist] Charles Lamb [1775–1834], [Anglo-Irish novelist Laurence] Sterne [1713–1768], and the most delicate-handed of our modern bookmen. But though the manner is dainty, the matter is too superfine to be real; the author's wisdom is the outcome, not of his mother wit, but of his clergy. Nothing can be prettier than his pleas and persuasions on behalf of Narcissus and George Muncaster; but if I had the heart to ask what these highly praised gentlemen had ever said or thought or done to entitle them to five minutes' attention from any seriously busy man, I fear Mr Le Gallienne, for want of a satisfactory answer, would have to abuse me for being a Philistine. These observations will not injure Mr Le Gallienne (else they had not been made); for his publisher tells me that the whole edition of *Narcissus* was subscribed for before publication. So much can be done by

A GOOD WORKMAN

with his pen, even when he has but little first-hand material to put into his books.

One thing Mr Le Gallienne has taught me. It is that Omar Khayyam must have been a very young man—probably not more than 17 when he wrote his "Fitzgeraldiana." [*Rubaiyat of*

Omar Khayyam of Naishapur, freely translated from the Persian by Edward FitzGerald, 1809–1893] I have even begun to suspect [English poet and playwright Robert] Browning's [1812–1889] "Rabbi Ben Ezra" of being a schoolboy effusion touched up by the poet later in life. Let no one be saddened by the thought that in a year or so more Mr Le Gallienne will gain knowledge otherwise than through his books, and with it temper, bias, one-sidedness, bigotry, and everything that is fatal to the polite negativeness of perfect taste. The change may impair his philosophy; but I think on the whole it will improve his books. No doubt that is only an opinion of mine; but I do not think the readers of *The Star* will undervalue any opinion which appears over the once-familiar signature of

C. DI B. [Corno di Bassetto, Shaw's pen name as a musical critic]

3. "A New Book for Authors and Printers," *The Star*, 1 May 1905.

[Review of a book by Frederick Howard Collins whose full title reads Author and Printer: A Guide for Authors, Editors, Printers, Correctors of the Press, Compositors, and Typists. With full list of abbreviations. An attempt to codify the best typographical practices of the present day *(London: Henry Frowde, 1905). Bernard Shaw's interest in typography and typesetting is well known, especially after he became friends with fellow socialist and artist William Morris (1834–1896) in 1884. Shaw came to appreciate books and printed pages as works of art in their own right, to the extent that he took great care with the general appearance of many editions of his works.]*

Mr [Frederick] Howard Collins [1857–1910] has certainly done this job extraordinarily well—so well, that there is really nothing to be said about it except to recommend his book unconditionally to all authors and printers, journalists and typists, proof-readers and compositors. In the matter of technical treatises authors have been half spoiled and half starved. Dictionaries, encyclopædias and gazetteers have been heaped on them; impertinences about style and grammar come in a constant stream from people who cannot write to people who can; but a codification of typographic usage has hitherto been lacking, except in Mr [English printer Horace Henry] Hart's [1840–1916] little pamphlet [*Rules for Compositors and Readers at the University Press, Oxford*], which was not in the general market. As to the ordinary school textbooks of English composition (some of them actually in use at the universities), and the catchpenny guides to correct punctuation and the like, most of them would set every purchaser ridiculously and disastrously wrong if it were humanly possible to remember—or indeed in any real sense to read—their ignorant and arid lessons. What was wanted was a man with literary faculty enough to write a bearable book, with judgment and common sense enough to hold the balance between usage and logic, with that rather special technical sense which enables a man to see the importance of apparently little and dry tidinesses, with an enlightened appetite for socially useful work, and with means and leisure to devote himself to it. In short, a man in a million. Fortunately, he has been found; and his name is Howard Collins.

The book is well planned technically. It is not a heavy shelf book of reference, useless to nomadic authors. It weighs only fifteen ounces, fits in the jacket pocket, and yet contains over four hundred well packed pages, more legible without spectacles than most dictionaries. In form it is a dictionary and literary encyclopædia, set in double columns. If you write "beleiveable," and it strikes you as not looking all you expected, you turn the word up and find "believable-*not* able" [*sic*]. If you are in a difficulty about punctuation, or do not know how to mark corrections in your proof, you turn up

Proofs or Punctuation, as the case may be, and find as many rules on these subjects as anyone can safely claim authority for. There are blank pages at the end of each letter to supply new references, or make good omissions, if you can find any. The price is five shillings.

It is impossible to give a complete list of all the headings under which the references fall, for Mr Collins has employed that elusive gift of the born indexer, an imaginative divination, often apparently whimsical, of the puzzles presented by the preparation of books for the press, so that he helps you not only in your rational difficulties (which experience soon provides for), but in those addleheadednesses which often paralyze an author without rhyme or reason. Just as [British physician and lexicographer Peter Mark] Roget's [1779–1869] Thesaurus is valuable because Roget was an oddity, so is Mr Collins, too, in that sense, an oddity who knows that the right station for a lifebuoy is not always the most obvious place for falling into the water.

As I began writing for the printer thirty years ago, I have not approached Mr Collins's book in the spirit of a learner; yet the first thing my eye lit on was something I had never noticed before: namely, that I have never in my life spelt M'Gregor according to usage, always using the apostrophe instead of the turned comma, which, it appears, is right in O'Neill. I say "according to usage", because in this, as in many other matters, there is neither right nor wrong. If there were, I could have argued the case out for myself. Usage in printing is like etiquette: it is mostly a matter of usage, not of morals or manners. The thing to be done is not important; but it is highly important that everybody should do it, and be able to depend on everybody else doing it in the same way. In matters where reason enters, Mr Collins does not hesitate to vote with the reasonable minority against the thoughtless majority. Take for example the usage as to whether inverted commas should follow or precede stops. In a sentence in which a quotation occurs there can be no question that it is simply a logical error to place stops belonging to the main sentence within the quotation marks instead of after them. But the contrary usage is so common that I have hardly ever had my copy accurately followed in this respect. Mr Collins prescribes the correct way, following the careful usage of the few and not the thoughtless usage of the many.

I do not praise Mr Collins's rules because they are invariably my own. They are not. Every writer of dramatic dialogue soon finds that usages founded on the art of the essayist and historian defeat his attempts to convey a vivid impression of excited speech: for instance, that a torrent of questions and explanations cannot be represented by the stately series of separate sentences into which an inquiry into the characteristics of [Roman Emperor and philosopher] Marcus Aurelius [AD 121–180 can be broken. Yet even here I find that on the points at issue, Mr Collins qualifies his rule so as to provide for me. Then again, every author with an eye for the appearance of a page of type (if any such there be) must by this time have several artistic quarrels with usages which have grown up during the period of desolating Philistinism which separates [English designer of typefaces William] Caslon [c. 1693–1766] from Morris.

Ever since Morris awakened our artistic conscience to the fact that a book has to be looked at as well as read, and that the most enchanting poem or absorbing story in the world may be made into a disgusting spectacle by vile manufacture and base materials, or, even more effectually, by elaborate and costly snobbishness, certain typographical practices which are rational enough (however unnecessary), have become less and less bearable. For instance, inverted commas and apostrophes are so ruinous to the appearance of a printed page that people with cultivated eyes will finally refuse to buy editions in which *The Merchant of Venice* is printed "The Merchant of Venice"; and don'ts and won'ts and haven'ts and didn'ts (all quite harmless, pretty, and characteristic without the apostrophe) are peppered all over the page. Since Morris's death the finest books produced in England, as far as I know, are the Ashendene Press books of Mr [Charles Harold St John] Hornby [1867–1946], and the Doves Press books of [English bookbinder Thomas James] Cobden Sanderson [1840–1922] and [English printer and engraver] Emery Walker [1851–1933]. But why did the Doves Press begin with a Latin Text to shew the noble type it designed on the lines of [probably French engraver and printer Nicholas Jenson] Jensen [1404–1480]? And why did it go on to the Doves Bible now in progress? No doubt because Latin and Scripture do not require the pepper pot.

Mr Collins leaves all this out of account. He even prints his title page in at least six different types, an outrage for which Morris would have slain him where he stood. But whilst I note the omission I do not blame it: on the contrary, I highly applaud the judgment and resolution with which Mr Collins has resisted the enormous temptation to give a helping hand to pet reforms under the pretext of codifying usage. But he has not made the necessary rule an excuse for countenancing the slipshod abandonment of old usages, which are both handsome and correct. He insists on the use of z instead of s in the termination ize. He points out that £ should follow the pounds figure instead of preceding it. Both these usages are traditional as well as correct.

Yet Mr Collins is human enough to commit one crime. The bloodcurdling vulgarism of programme for program is expressly prescribed by him. I must really send him a telegramme containing an appropriate epigramme on the point.

G.B.S.

4. "How Free is the Press?", *The Nation*, 9 February 1918.

[Review of Anglo-French writer Hilaire Belloc's (1870–1953) The Free Press (London: Allen & Unwin, 1918). Shaw had written an article in The New Age ten years before entitled "The Chesterbelloc: A Lampoon," a term that caught on to refer to the partnership between G. K. Chesterton and Belloc (1870–1953). Shaw had had many problems with censorship by the time he wrote this review — several of his plays having been banned — and he was outspoken against the job of the Lord Chamberlain elsewhere. That is why he takes the opportunity to discuss censorship at large in this review, especially after he had been publicly crucified because of his own opinions about the Great War.]

"To release the truth against whatever odds, even if so doing can no longer help the Commonwealth, is a necessity for the soul," says Mr Belloc. And again, "Those who prefer to sell themselves or be cowed, gain as a rule, not even that ephemeral security for which they betrayed their fellows; meanwhile they leave to us the only permanent form of power, which is the gift of mastery through persuasion."

Now it is more than forty years since my first contribution to the press appeared in print; and I am not sure that this necessity of the soul to which Mr Belloc testifies, thereby echoing Jeremiah (a Jew, I regret to say) who declared that the word was in his heart as a burning fire shut up in his bones, and he was weary with forbearing and could not stay [Jeremiah 20:9], is really a necessity of *the* soul. I must ask whose soul? Certainly not that of your average journalist or of the man who swallows his articles as soothing syrup. The first necessity of such souls when truth is about, as it always is, is camouflage, or, better still, complete cover. I, like Mr Belloc, and those heroes of the free press whom he celebrates in this book: [British man of letters Alfred Richard, editor of *The New Age*]

Mr Orage [1873–1934], the Chestertons [English writer Gilbert Keith Chesterton (1874–1936) and his younger brother Cecil Chesterton (1879–1918)], and himself, have conducted truth raids, and seen all England rush to the cellars every time. It takes a very hardy constitution to stand the truth. Is an evening with [Norwegian dramatist Henrik] Ibsen [1828–1906] as popular as an evening with [Canadian-American actress] Mary Pickford [1892–1979] at the movies? A simple No is hardly emphatic enough. One feels the need of the French *Point!* so useful in similar emergencies to Molière.

Before I forget it—for I am going to wander considerably—let me say that Mr Belloc's pamphlet is true enough within its own express limitations. It serves the press right, the parliament right, and our plutocratic humbugs right. But I think he lets the public off too easily; and as for the free press, by which he means specifically *The New Age*, *The New Witness*, and in general the coterie press, he is a bit of a flatterer. An amiable weakness; but still, a weakness.

The coterie press is no doubt a free press in a sense; and I have often availed myself of its freedom to say things I should not have been allowed to say elsewhere. When I want somebody to throw a stone at the Lord Mayor, or the Lord Chamberlain, or any other panjandrum, I do not offer six-and-eightpence to my solicitor to do it: I offer a shilling to a tramp. The tramp is free to throw the stone: the respectable solicitor is not. Similarly, when the missile is a literary one, I do not send it to *The Times*, I offer it to a coterie editor. He has the tramp's freedom. He is not afraid of the advertisers, because he has no advertisements. He is not afraid of the plutocrats, because he has no rich backers. He is not afraid of the lawyers, because he is not worth powder and shot. He is not afraid of losing his social position, because he is not in smart society, and would rather die than get into it. Sometimes he is not afraid of anything, because he has no sense.

In short, Mr Belloc will say with some impatience, the co-terie editor is free; and I do not alter that fact by explaining why he is free. *Parfaitement, cher Hilaire* (which I may translate as "Who deniges of it, Betsy?"); but does this freedom, this irresponsibility, carry with it any guarantee of liberality or ve-racity? Clearly not: all that it does is, within certain limits, to allow the coterie paper to be liberal and veracious if it likes. But if you come to that, do not Lord [Alfred Charles William Harmsworth, 1st Viscount] Northcliffe's [1865–1922] millions set him free to attack and destroy people who could crush a coterie paper by a libel action or by setting Dora [De-fence of the Realm Act] at it, if Lord Northcliffe liked? Let us not deceive ourselves: we are between the nether mill-stone of the press that is too poor to tell the truth and the upper one of the press that is too rich. Mr Belloc says that the falsehood of the press operates more by suppression of truth than assertion of lies. Well, I am prepared to maintain that every coterie editor in the world suppresses more truth, according to his lights, than Lord Northcliffe. He perceives more. My fellow countryman, Lord Northcliffe, whom I do not know personally (otherwise how could I be free to be uncivil to him?) is not, for an Irishman, conspicuously intel-lectual, though he may pass in England; and it must be plain to everyone that his brother [Harold Sidney Harmsworth, later 1st Viscount Rothermere, 1868–1940] was far more com-pletely and unreservedly sincere in his denunciation of the Germans as police-court murderers for actually killing Eng-lishmen in war, and in his conception of the British Museum as a comfortable place for his armchair and Turkey carpet, than any coterie paper has ever dared to be in any single sen-tence it has published. What happens is not that a certain born liar named Harmsworth publishes a paper to tell his lies in, and that a child of integrity named Belloc or Shaw pub-lishes another to tell the utter truth. It is simply that Belloc and Harmsworth publish papers to say what they sincerely want to have said as far as the police will let them. Their success is according to the number of people who agree with them. Consequently, as Harmsworth's tastes are widespread, his paper catches on; the public rallies to him; he is made a peer; he makes and unmakes ministers and commanders as [Richard Neville, 16th Earl of] Warwick [1428–1471] made and unmade kings; and he establishes his brother, in the middle of an epoch-making war, as chief of a national service [the Air Ministry] on which our fate in the war will probably depend, without having to offer the public the smallest evidence that the said brother is capable of conducting a whelk-stall successfully. Belloc, on the other hand, having very select intellectual tastes, has presently to sell his paper as a coterie paper, and set up as a war prophet in the columns of the sort of paper he denounces as corrupt, in which employment his gains are like the stripes of Autolycus, mighty ones and millions [*The Winter's Tale*, IV, 3].

That both Northcliffe and the coterie editor immediately find themselves entangled in the coils of their own circulation, and obliged, on pain of being unable to meet their engagements, to consult their readers' opinions as well as their own, does not leave the coterie editor with any advantage. I have belonged to too many coteries to have any illusions on this point. My correspondents frequently appeal to me to intervene in some public question on the ground that I am a fearless champion of the truth and have never hesitated to say what I think. I reply always, "Heaven save your innocence! If you only knew all the things I think and dare not say!"

Let us have a look at the general ethical character of Mr Belloc's free press. His favorite example is The New Witness, *ci-devant* The Eye-Witness, founded by himself, and now edited by Mr Gilbert K. Chesterton as *locum tenens* for Mr Cecil Chesterton, who is in arms in defence of his country. Well, The New Witness is easily the wickedest paper in the world as far as my knowledge goes. G. K. C. as Antichrist has achieved a diabolical enormity which goes to the very verge of breaking down through over-acting. His policy is that of [German naval officer, journalist, and politician] Count Reventlow [1869–1943] (with the boot on the other leg, of course); but although Reventlow has a much stronger historical case (for what are the trumpery exploits of the new toy soldiers of the new toy kings of Prussia beside our terrific record of invasion, piracy, plunder, conquest, and arrogant claim to rule the waves as well as make Governor General-ships of all the earth for our younger sons?) he cannot touch Mr Chesterton in skill as a pleader, or ferocity as a crusader. There is no "Vengeance is mine, saith the Lord" [Romans 12:19] nonsense about Mr Chesterton. For him, vengeance is the Napoleon of Notting Hill's. He calls on Kensington and Croydon and Tooting and Balham to wipe out the accursed races of Central Europe; to bind their kings in chains; to cast them into the abyss, as holy Michael cast Lucifer from Heaven. Not one chivalrous word escapes him when the Hun is his theme. We are to curse the Germans when they are up and kick them when they are down. To turn the page from Mr Chesterton preaching hate against the Prussians to [English music critic] Mr Ernest Newman [1868–1959] extolling [German composer and pianist Ludwig van] Beethoven [1770–1827] and [German composer Johann Sebastian] Bach [1685–1750] is to turn from the blasphemies of a stage demon to the judgments of sanity and civilization.

Dare I ask Mr Belloc why Mr Chesterton tolerates Mr New-man? He has almost boasted of his ignorance of and indiffer-ence to music. I have no inside knowledge of the matter; but I strongly suspect that The New Witness is as much in the hands of a moneyed interest as the Cocoa Press or the North-cliffe Press or any of the other journalistic ventures that grind the axes of the rich.

Let me hasten to add that, if my suspicion is well founded, the particular interest which supports Mr Chesterton is as gloriously indifferent to his patriotic views on the war as he himself is to Mr Newman's unpatriotic preference of Handel to [English composer Thomas Augustine] Dr Arne [1710–1778] and of Mozart to [English composer] Sir Henry Bishop [1786–1855]. In fact, I drag the matter in expressly to show that Mr Chesterton, by an extraordinary piece of luck, is really free to say what he likes about everything except music (which he does not want to say anything about); and this he would not be if the money behind the paper were political money or smart society money or commercial money. Therefore the diabolical element in Mr Chesterton's gospel of murderous hate on a basis of our heavenly nature as opposed to the hellish nature of the Prussian, is quite wanton: he is as free to be bravely magnanimous, chivalrous, Christian, fair and reasonable before Europe, and contrite before history and Heaven, as he is to be just the opposite. Otherwise he would chuck *The New Witness* as he chucked The Daily News. What makes his choice frightfully wicked to me is that it is not natural choice but artistic virtuosity. He is not really a devil. He can no more hate the Kaiser than Shakespear could hate Iago or Richard. Mr Belloc is a good hater: the proof is that though he is a humorist, there is not in this little book of his, launched as a torpedo at poor Northcliffe, a single conscious joke. There are two unconscious ones. He speaks of "two dots arranged in a spiral" (let him arrange two dots in a spiral if he can); and he says that a newspaper report is less truthful than the thousand tongues of rumor because it tells the same thing simultaneously to a million people in the same words. And this is not a joke at all, because when all the witnesses tell the story in the same words, the case is sure to be a conspiracy. But Mr Chesterton, in his wildest hymns of hate, will break into a joke on his top note, preferably some outrageous pun. He has actually written during the war a book called The Crimes of England, putting Reventlow's case ten times better than Reventlow could put it himself; and no Sinn Feiner alive can write on the oppression of Ireland as he does. Talk of his handling of the violated treaty of 1839 [the First Treaty of London], the scrap of paper! You should hear him on the Treaty of Limerick [1691]. To put it in the Irish way, his war articles are not devilry: they are pure devilment. To put it in the English way, they are art for art's sake: the political variety of Whistlerism [English writer Reverend Charles Watts Whistler, 1856–1913].

So much for your free press at its freest. As Napoleon made war because he could do it so well, the brothers Chesterton write invective because they do it so well. Betrayed as they are at every step to connoisseurs, Gilbert by his humor, and Cecil by his good humor (his smile becomes sunnier at every epithet), they are taken at their word by readers who are not connoisseurs (if any such can read really artistic writing) and play [Alexandre Dumas's] The Corsican Brothers in the costume of The Christian Brothers. And in the strangest way, having no Northcliffe to forge chains for them, they forge chains for themselves, making rules for their artistic and intellectual games which finally leave them speechless on the most vital issues of the day. Take for example the case of the new Bishop of Hereford. Everybody knows the bishop's views on the Virgin Birth and the Resurrection. Everyone chuckled cynically over the solemn assurance of his ecclesiastical superior that there was no evidence that the postulant held any such views. Granted that "the capitalist press" had to allow its readers to gather the truth between the lines, still, it was bolder than The New Witness, which dared not print any lines to read between. The New Witness may not allude to Evolution, to the Virgin Birth, to the Resurrection, or even to the Garden of Eden, lest it should have to choose between modernism and patent bosh. It has laid on itself the fantastic bond that it must believe what [Italian painter Buonamico] Buffalmacco [first half of the 14th century] believed when he painted the walls of the Campo Santo in Pisa, and must forget what has been learnt since. When we are threatened, and indeed already oppressed, by a tyranny of pseudo-science worse than even the tyranny of pseudo-education, The New Witness must take the Inquisition's view of eugenics and welfare work, and dares not venture into argument because it would have to refer to later authorities than Aristotle and Thomas Aquinas, and thus get ahead of Buffalmacco. It has forbidden itself to talk a word of sense about [British Liberal politician] Mr Herbert Samuel [1870–1963], because Mr Samuel is a Jew, and Buffalmacco must place him with Judas Iscariot in hell. The consequence is that it has to live on Buffalmacco's fat, so to speak, to an extent that may eventually make even the Chestertons unreadable. It is hard enough to keep up the interest of a journal even by the freest play upon the actual events of the current week in every department. But if you must ignore not only the current week, but the last three or four centuries, and dare not hint that the earth may be round, you are committing yourself to a literary *tour de force* which begins by being impossible and must end by being ridiculous.

The New Age, Mr Belloc's other example of the free press, may be compared to the venture of a too clever painter who, finding the Academy and all the regular galleries closed to him, opens a Salon of the Rejected to provide an exhibition for himself. The experiment has been remarkably successful: Mr Orage has secured a free pulpit for himself; and his contributors are often as readable as he. Even when he has to fill up with trash, it is not really worse than the average "middles" of his contemporaries, though it may be less plausible and trade-finished. But outside Mr Orage's own notes the paper has no policy and no character. It is a hotch-potch, stimulating thought in general, but not prompting opinion like *The Nation* or *The New Statesman*, nor reflecting it like

The Spectator. It cannot get things done any more than *Notes and Queries* can: it is probable that politicians pay much more attention to John Bull. Its freedom is the freedom of the explosive which is not confined in a cannon, spending itself incalculably in all directions.

Organized capital and Judaism do not trouble themselves much with *The Freethinker*, the organ of the atheists, or *The War Cry*, the organ of the Salvation Army. Yet the late editor of the *Freethinker* was not the same man in his private correspondence with [English novelist George] Meredith [1828–1909] as in his editorial columns. He knew quite well that the sort of atheist who called the Bethlehem stable The Pig and Whistle, not merely to change the atmosphere of the discussion, but with the quaintly snobbish notion that nothing miraculous could happen in a vulgar public house, was a danger to Secularism; yet he was not free to say so: too many of his subscribers would have suspected him of superstition, if not of downright Christianity, and abandoned him. The leaders of the Salvation Army know as well as old [British Methodist preacher, founder of the Salvation Army] General Booth [1829–1912] did that religion does not stand or fall with belief in the adventure of Jonah and the great fish, nor consist of a race for the prize of Heaven; but they dare not say so: they would be cast out as atheists by "some of our old folk." Those who pay the piper call the tune, unless the piper is a veritable Pied Piper whose tune no one can resist.

And here, I think, is the factor to which Mr Belloc gives too little space in his book. There are no irresistible Pied Pipers; but the skill of the piper counts for what it is worth. No release from the pressure of capitalism can make an editor free if he lacks character and judgment. If he has them, he can make a capitalist paper as free as a coterie paper. When The Times makes a series of *gaffes* culminating in the rejection of the [Henry Petty-Fitzmaurice, 5th Marquess of] Lansdowne letter [1917], it is not because advertizers or proprietors have dictated them, but because the editor, though he may be stuffed with all sorts of excellent qualities, does not know what to put in and what to leave out in his correspondence columns. [English journalist Henry William] Mr Massingham [1860–1924], in the teeth of his proprietors and of all the vested interests, political and commercial, which controlled the daily papers he edited, succeeded in changing the politics and outlook of The Star and The Chronicle from the Whig-ridden Socialist Radicalism of the 'eighties to the Collectivist Progressivism of the 'nineties. Capital has neither a body to be kicked nor a soul to be damned: advertizers are only a mob, without sense enough, as Mr Belloc points out, to use the opportunities offered them by the highly specialized coterie papers. An editor is a man: something much more formidable. Mr Belloc himself has achieved the astounding and hardly sane feat of establishing, with other people's capital, a press organ of the Holy Roman Empire in London in the twentieth century. He is driven to conclude that the able-minded editor with convictions will finally beat the whole field, and destroy the forces that now make his strife so inhumanly hazardous.

My own most polemical writings are to be found in the files of The Times, The Morning Post, The Daily Express, The World, and The Saturday Review. I found out early in my career that a Conservative paper may steal a horse when a Radical paper dare not look over a hedge, and that the rich, though very determined that the poor shall read nothing unconventional, are equally determined not to be preached at themselves. In short, I found that only for the classes would I be allowed, and indeed tacitly required, to write on revolutionary assumptions. I filled their columns with sedition; and they filled my pockets (not very deep ones then) with money. In the press as in other departments the greatest freedom may be found where there is least talk about it.

G. B. S.

5. From the Preface to *Immaturity* (1879), 1921.

[Bernard Shaw wrote a preface to his first novel more than forty years after it was written, when it was first published. In it, he puts forward many of his views on literature and the art of writing—many of which he came to grips with after a long evolution in his own career as a writer. The Preface begins with a brief description of the London Shaw encountered when he migrated there in 1876—a fragment that has been included to give readers an idea of what London was like at the time Shaw had not yet begun his literary career—and of the impecunious situation of his household, which was a significant factor in his turning to reviewing as a source of income.]

The scene of one of [English writer] Mr Arnold Bennett's [1867–1931] novels is laid in a certain *cul de sac* off the Brompton Road, nearly opposite the West Brompton District Post Office. He calls it Alexandra Grove; but its actual name is Victoria Grove. As he describes it, the houses now contrive a double rent to pay, as the gardens have been fitted up with studios, thus quietly modernizing London by the back-to-back housing so vehemently denounced as a relic of barbarism in Leeds. When I arrived there as an Irish emigrant of 20, this intensification of population had not occurred. The houses were semi-detached villas with plenty of air space round them (you could call it garden). On the other side of the back wall were orchards; for the huge Poor Law Infirmary which now occupies this space, with its tower on the Fulham Road, was not yet built. The land between West Brompton and Fulham and Putney, now closely packed with streets and suburban roads, had still plenty of orchard and market garden to give it a countrified air and to make it possible to live there, as I did for years, without feeling that one must flee to the country or wither in the smoke. All the parallel Groves connected the Fulham Road with King's Road, Chelsea, where Cremorne Gardens, an unlaid ghost from the eighteenth century, was desperately fighting off its final exorcism as a rendezvous of the half world. Hence these now blameless thoroughfares were then reputed Bohemian, whilst Victoria Grove, as a blind alley, remained as respectable as Clapham.

I came to London from Dublin in the spring of 1876, and found my mother and my one surviving sister (I had no brothers) established in No. 13 Victoria Grove, trying to turn their musical accomplishments to account: my mother by teaching, my sister by singing. My father, left in Dublin, spared us a pound a week from his slender resources; and by getting into debt and occasionally extracting ourselves by drawing on a maternal inheritance of £4000 over which my mother had a power of appointment, and which therefore could be realized bit by bit as her three children came of age, we managed to keep going somehow.

Impecuniosity was necessarily chronic in the household. And here let me distinguish between this sort of poverty and that which furnishes an element of romance in the early lives of many famous men. I am almost tempted to say that it is the only sort of poverty that counts, short of the privations that make success impossible. We all know the man whose mother brought him up with nineteen brothers and sisters on an income of eighteen shillings a week earned by her own labor. The road from the log cabin to the White House, from the bench in the factory to the Treasury Bench, from the hovel to the mansion in Park Lane, if not exactly a crowded road, always has a few well fed figures at the end of it to tell us all about it. I always assure these gentlemen that they do not know what poverty and failure is. Beginning with as much as they expected or were accustomed to, they have known nothing but promotion. At each step they have had the income of the society in which they moved, and been able to afford its clothes, its food, its habits, its rents and rates. What more has any prince? If you would know what real poverty is, ask the younger son of a younger son of a younger son. To understand his plight you must start at the top without the income of the top, and curse your stars that you were not lucky enough to start at the bottom.

[*After a lengthy exordium on the historical and sociopolitical antecedents of Shaw's social class as a boy and young man (i.e., the Shabby Genteels), he then moves on to paint, in very humorous terms, the inborn traits of character that were common to 'the Shaws'. This includes his father's dipsomania and the social neglect they endured as a result. Despite all this, Bernard Shaw's self-assured personality made him believe in his own, yet unfulfilled potential from a rather early age, although his means were not comparable to his talent. These circumstances, as we shall see, shaped his formative years as a writer — especially as regards the role of literature at large as a weapon of social transformation.*]

When a young man has achieved nothing and is doing nothing, and when he is obviously so poor that he ought to be doing something very energetically, it is rather trying to find him assuming an authority in conversation, and an equality in terms, which only conspicuous success and distinguished ability could make becoming. Yet this is what is done, quite unconsciously, by young persons who have in them the potentiality of such success and ability.

Napoleon could hardly have felt much reverence for his average French generals before the French Revolution, when he was apparently only a by-no-means irreproachable subaltern from Corsica. No such general could possibly have liked him or his manners at that time, though after [the battle of] Austerlitz [December 2, 1805] even first rate generals blushed with gratification at the most condescending word of praise from him. It must have been intolerable in Stratford-on-Avon in 1584 for a local magnate of mature age, knight of the shire and justice of the peace, to be contemplated *de haut en bas* by a dissolute young poacher, and even to amuse him by intellectual inadequacy. I am sure Shakespear was too civil by nature to make any such demonstration consciously; but it is inconceivable that the future author of Lear, who was to die a landowning magnate, and be described in the parish register as a Gent., could have treated [English magistrate and politician] Sir Thomas Lucy [1532–1600] quite as an ordinary country gentleman of mature age expects to be treated by an ordinary poacher in his teens.

The truth is that all men are in a false position in society until they have realized their possibilities, and imposed them on their neighbors. They are tormented by a continual shortcoming in themselves; yet they irritate others by a continual overweening. This discord can be resolved by acknowledged success or failure only: everyone is ill at ease until he has found his natural place, whether it be above or below his birthplace. The overrated inheritor of a position for which he has no capacity, and the underrated nobody who is a born genius, are alike why because they are alike out of place. Besides, this finding of one's place may be made very puzzling by the fact that there is no place in ordinary society for extraordinary individuals. For the worldly wiseman, with common ambitions, the matter is simple enough: money, title, precedence, a seat in parliament, a portfolio in the cabinet, will mean success both to him and his circle. But what about people like St Francis [of Assisi, 1181–1226] and St Clare [of Assisi, 1194–1253]? Of what use to them are the means to live the life of the country house and the west end mansion? They have literally no business in them, and must necessarily cut an unhappy and ridiculous figure there. They have to make a society of Franciscans and Poor Clares for themselves before they can work or live socially. It is true that those who are called saints are not saintly all the time and in everything. In eating and drinking, lodging and sleeping, chatting and playing: in short, in everything but working out their destiny as saints, what is good enough for a ploughman is good enough for a poet, a philosopher, a saint, or a higher mathematician. But [theologian and philosopher Charles] Hodge's [1797–1878] work is not good enough for Newton, nor Falstaff's conversation holy enough for [English poet Percy Bysshe] Shelley [1792–1822]. Christ adapted himself so amiably to the fashionable life of his time in his leisure that he was reproached for being a gluttonous man and a winebibber, and for frequenting frivolous and worthless sets. But he did not work where he feasted, nor flatter the Pharisees, nor ask the Romans to buy him with a sinecure. He knew when he was being entertained, well treated, lionized: not an unpleasant adventure for once in a way; and he did not quarrel with the people who were so nice to him. Besides, to sample society is part of a prophet's business: he must sample the governing class above all, because his inborn knowledge of human nature will not explain the anomalies produced in it by Capitalism and Sacerdotalism. But he can never feel at home in it. The born Communist, before he knows what he is, and understands why, is always awkward and unhappy in plutocratic society and in the poorer societies which ape it to the extent of their little means: in short, wherever spiritual values are assessed like Income Tax. In his nonage he is imposed on by the prestige which the propertied classes have conferred on themselves and inculcated in the schools, and by the comfort and refinement and splendor of their equipment in contrast to the squalor of the proletariat. If he has been brought up to regard himself as one of the propertied classes, and has its whole equipment of false standards of worth, lacking nothing but the indispensable pecuniary equipment without which his education is utterly meaningless, his embarrassment and bewilderment are pitiable, and his isolation often complete; for he is left alone between the poor whom he regards as beneath him and the rich whose standards of expenditure are beyond his means. He is ashamed of his poverty, in continual dread of doing the wrong tiling, resentfully insubordinate and seditious in a social order which he not only accepts but in which he actually claims a privileged part.

As I write, there is a craze for what is called psychoanalysis, or the cure of diseases by explaining to the patient what is the matter with him: an excellent plan if you happen to know what is the matter with him, especially when the explanation is that there is nothing the matter with him. Thus a bee, desperately trying to reach a flower bed through a window pane, concludes that he is the victim of evil spirits or that he is mad, his end being exhaustion, despair, and death. Yet, if he only knew, there is nothing wrong with him: all he has to do is go out as he came in, through open window or door. Your born Communist begins like the bee on the pane. He worries himself and everybody else until he dies of peevishness, or else is led by some propagandist pamphlet, or by his own intellectual impulses (if he has any), to investigate the economic structure of our society.

Immediately everything becomes clear to him. Property is theft: respectability founded on poverty is blasphemy: marriage founded on property is prostitution: it is easier for a camel to go through the eye of a needle than for a rich man to enter the kingdom of heaven. He now knows where he is, and where this society which has so intimidated him is. He is cured of his *mauvaise honte*, and may now be as much at his ease with the princes of this world as Caesar was with the pirates whom he intended to crucify when, as presently happened, the fortune of war made their captive their conqueror.

If he be not a born Communist, but a predatory combative man, eager to do the other fellow down, and happy in a contrast between his prosperity and the indigence of others, happy also in a robust contempt for cowards and weaklings, the very same discovery of the nature of our Capitalism will nerve him to play the Capitalist game for all it and he are worth. But for the most part men drift with the society into which they are born, and make the best of its accidents without changing its morals or understanding its principles.

As it happens, I was a born Communist and Iconoclast (or Quaker) without knowing it; and I never got on easy terms with plutocracy and snobbery until I took to the study of economics, beginning with [American political economist] Henry George [1839–1897] and Karl Marx. In my twentieth year, at Victoria Grove, not being on Caesarian easy terms with the pirates or their retainers, I felt much as Caesar might have done if he had imagined the pirate ship to be the Mayflower, and was still more inclined to mistrust himself than to mistrust the crew, however little respect they might pay him. Not that my opinions were conventional. Read my preface to Back to Methuselah, and you will see me as the complete infidel of that day. I had read much poetry; but only one poet was sacred to me: Shelley. I had read his works piously from end to end, and was in my negations atheist and republican to the backbone. I say in my negations; for I had not reached any affirmative position. When, at a public meeting of the Shelley Society, I scandalized many of the members by saying that I had joined because, like Shelley, I was a Socialist, an atheist, and a vegetarian, I did not know that I could have expressed my position more accurately by simply saying that my conception of God was that insisted on in the first Article of the Church of England, then as now vehemently repudiated by all pious persons, who will have it that God is a substantial gentleman of uncertain and occasionally savage temper, and a spirit only in the sense in which an archbishop is a spirit. I had never thought of reading the Articles of the Church of England; and if I had I should still have used the word atheist as a declaration that I was on the side of [political activist, founder of the National Secular Society Charles] Bradlaugh [1833–1891] and [British secularist and editor George William] Foote [1850–1915] and others who, as avowed Secularists and Atheists, were being persecuted and imprisoned for my opinions.

[Shaw goes on to describe how his upbringing and family life had a major influence on his early atheism. In the omitted pages, Shaw discusses much of his religious creed, and of his conception of the institution of the family, two of the themes he frequently used in his plays. After discussing the incidents that led him to choose London as his destination, Shaw takes up the subject of his becoming a writer. He begins by portraying his years as a critic and reviewer.]

For the first couple of years of my life in London I did nothing decisive. I acted as ghost for a musician who had accepted a berth as musical critic; and as such ghosts must not appear, and I was therefore cut off from the paper and could not correct proofs, my criticisms, mostly very ruthless ones, appeared with such misprints, such mutilations and venal interpolations by other hands, so inextricably mixed up with other criticisms most offensive to my artistic sense, that I have ever since hidden this activity of mine as a guilty secret, lest someone should dig out these old notices and imagine that I was responsible for everything in them and with them. Even now I can hardly bring myself to reveal that the name of the paper was The Hornet, and that it had passed then into the hands of a certain Captain Donald Shaw, who was not related to me, and whom I never met. It died on his hands, and partly, perhaps, at mine.

[Shaw was later employed for some time at the Edison Telephone Company, but he "escaped these trials presently." In the paragraphs below he recounts his beginnings as an aspiring novelist, paying special attention to his influences and sources, as well as to his ideal of style. Many of the traits he comments on as part of his literary style inform his views on literature and his take on the books he reviewed.]

Shaw also explains the circumstances and events that inspired him to create the plot and characters for Immaturity.]

Except for a day or two in 1881, when I earned a few pounds by counting the votes at an election in Leyton, I was an Unemployable, an ablebodied pauper in fact if not in law, until the year 1885, when for the first time I earned enough money directly by my pen to pay my way. My income for that year amounted to £112; and from that time until the war of 1914–18 momentarily threatened us all with bankruptcy, I had no pecuniary anxieties except those produced by the possession of money, not by the lack of it. My penury phase was over.

The telephone episode occurred in 1879; and in that year I had done what every literary adventurer did in those days, and many do still. I had written a novel. My office training had left me with a habit of doing something regularly every day as a fundamental condition of industry as distinguished from idleness. I knew I was making no headway unless I was doing this, and that I should never produce a book in any other fashion. I bought supplies of white paper, demy size, by sixpennorths at a time; folded it in quarto; and condemned myself to fill five pages of it a day, rain or shine, dull or inspired. I had so much of the schoolboy and the clerk still in me that if my five pages ended in the middle of a sentence I did not finish it until next day. On the other hand, if I missed a day, I made up for it by doing a double task on the morrow. On this plan I produced five novels in five years. It was my professional apprenticeship, doggedly suffered with all the diffidence and dissatisfaction of a learner with a very critical master, myself to wit, whom there was no pleasing and no evading, and persevered in to save my self-respect in a condition of impecuniosity which, for two acute moments (I still recall them with a wry face), added broken boots and carefully hidden raggedness to cuffs whose edges were trimmed by the scissors, and a tall hat so limp with age that I had to

wear it back-to-front to enable me to take it off without dou-
bling up the brim.

I had no success as a novelist. I sent the five novels to
all the publishers in London and some in America. None
would venture on them. Fifty or sixty refusals without a single acceptance forced me into a fierce self-sufficiency. I became undiscourageable, acquiring a superhuman insensitive-
ness to praise or blame which has been useful to me at times
since, though at other times it has retarded my business affairs by making me indifferent to the publication and performances of my works, and even impatient of them as an
unwelcome interruption to the labor of writing their successors. Instead of seizing every opportunity of bringing them
before the public, I have often, on plausible but really trivial
pretexts, put off proposals which I should have embraced
with all the normal author's keenness for publicity.

Thus, after five years of novel writing, I was a complete
professional failure. The more I wrote and the better I wrote
the less I pleased the publishers. This first novel of mine [Im-
maturity], though rejected, at least elicited some expressions
of willingness to read any future attempts. [William] Black-
wood [and sons Publishing] actually accepted and then re-
voked. [British editor and publisher] Sir George Macmillan
[1855–1936], then a junior, not only sent me a longish and evidently considered report by the firm's reader, [journalist and
editor, later 1st Viscount Morley of Blackburn] John (afterwards Lord) Morley [1838–1923], but suggested to him that I
might be of some use to him in his capacity as editor of the
Pall Mall Gazette.

All such responses ceased with my second novel; and I had
no means of knowing, and was too young and inexperienced
to guess, that what was the matter was not any lack of literary competence on my part, but the antagonism raised by
my hostility to respectable Victorian thought and society. I
was left without a ray of hope; yet I did not stop writing nov-

els until, having planned my fifth effort on a colossal scale, I found at the end of what were to me only the first two sections of it, that I had no more to say and had better wait until I had educated myself much farther. And when, after an interval of critical journalism, I resumed the writing of fiction, I did so as a playwright and not as a novelist.

Four of the five novels of my nonage, as I call them, at last got into print as described in the preface [to *The Irrational Knot*] already cited. But the first of them never got published at all. Opening the old parcel, as I do now (it is like opening a grave that has been closed for forty-two years), I find a pile of cahiers of twenty pages each, and realize with some dismay that I am face-to-face with a novel containing nearly 200,000 words. The title is Immaturity. The handwriting, which slopes slightly backwards, has all the regularity and legibility of my old cash book. Unfortunately, the mice have eaten so much of two of the cahiers that the ends of the lines are missing. This is awkward; for I have just told myself that I must make no attempt to correct the work of the apprentice with the hand of the master; that such as it is it must remain; that I am too old now to touch it without producing new incongruities more disagreeable than any that are possible between the style of 1879 and the taste of 1921. Yet, if the mice have eaten much, I must play the sedulous ape, like [Scottish novelist Robert Louis] Stevenson [1850–1894], and imitate my own youthful manner like any literary forger.

It may be asked why I should print the thing at all: why not let ill alone? I am quite disposed to do so; but somehow one must not do such things. If Beethoven had destroyed his septet for wind instruments when he had advanced to the ninth symphony and the Mass in D, many people who delight in the septet and cannot make head or tail of symphony or Mass would suffer a wanton deprivation; and though my early style now makes me laugh at its pedantry, yet I have a great respect for the priggish conscientiousness of my first efforts. They prove too that, like [German writer Johann Wolf-gang von] Goethe [1749–1832], I knew all along, and have added more to my power of handling, illustrating, and ad-dressing my material than to the material itself.

Anyhow, I have little doubt that Immaturity will be at least readable by the easygoing bookbuyers who will devour any-thing in the shape of a novel, however ridiculously out of fashion it may be. I know that some readers will like it much better than my later works. There must be a certain quality of youth in it which I could not now recapture, and which may even have charm as well as weakness and absurdity. Having re-read the other four novels for publication and republica-tion at one time or another, I can guarantee the propriety of my early style. It was the last thing in correctness. I have never aimed at style in my life: style is a sort of melody that comes into my sentences by itself. If a writer says what he has to say as accurately and effectively as he can, his style will take care of itself, if he has a style. But I did set up one condi-tion in my early days. I resolved that I would write nothing that should not be intelligible to a foreigner with a dictionary, like the French of [French philosopher] Voltaire [1694–1778]; and I therefore avoided idiom. (Later on I came to seek idiom as being the most highly vitalized form of language). Con-sequently I do not expect to find the English of Immaturity idiomatic. Also, there will be nothing of the voice of the pub-lic speaker in it: the voice that rings through so much of my later work. Not until Immaturity was finished, late in 1879, did I for the first time rise to my feet in a little debating club called The Zetetical Society, to make, in a condition of heart-breaking nervousness, my first assault on an audience.

Perhaps I had better add a word as to the characters in the book. I do so with some reluctance, because it is misleading to mention even the smallest circumstance connecting a fic-titious person with a living one. If Shakespear had happened to mention that he made the Prince of Denmark carry a set of tablets and make notes in them because he had seen [English writer and courtier] Sir Walter Raleigh [c. 1554–1618] doing so, it would by this time be an invincible tradition in English literature that Raleigh was the original of Hamlet. We should have writers following up the clue, as they would call it, to the conclusion that Raleigh was the real author of the play. One day, as I was sitting in the reading room of the British Museum, beginning my fifth and last novel, *An Unsocial Socialist*, I saw a young lady with an attractive and arresting expression, bold, vivid, and very clever, working at one of the desks. On that glimpse of a face I instantly conceived the character and wrote the description of Agatha Wylie. I have never exchanged a word with that lady; never made her acquaintance; saw her again under the same circumstances but very few times; yet if I mention her name, which became well known in literature (she too was writing a novel then, probably, and perhaps had the hero suggested to her by my profile), she will be set down as Agatha Wylie to her dying day, with heaven knows how much more scandalous invention added to account for my supposed intimate knowledge of her character. Before and since, I have used living models as freely as a painter does, and in much the same way: that is, I have sometimes made a fairly faithful portrait founded on intimate personal intercourse, and sometimes, as in Agatha's case, developed what a passing glance suggested to my imagination. In the latter case it has happened sometimes that the incidents I have invented on the spur of such a glance have hit the facts so nearly that I have found myself accused of unpardonable violations of personal privacy. I hardly expect to be believed when I say that I once invented a servant for one of my models and found afterwards that he actually had just such a servant. Between the two extremes of actual portraiture and pure fancy work suggested by a glance or an anecdote, I have copied nature with many degrees of fidelity, combining studies from life in the same book or play with those types and composites and traditional figures of the novel and the stage which are called pure fictions. Many of the characters in this first novel of mine owed something to persons I had met, including members of my family (not to mention myself); but none of them are portraits; and with one exception the models are unknown to the public. That exception was [English painter] Cecil Lawson [1849–1882], whose early death lost us the only landscape painter who ever reminded me of the spacious and fascinating experiments of Rubens in that branch of painting. When I lived at Victoria Grove the Lawsons: father, mother, Malcolm, and two sisters, lived in one of the handsome old houses in Cheyne Walk, Chelsea. Cecil and another brother, being married, boarded out. Malcolm was a musician; and the sisters sang. One, a soprano, dark, quick, plump and bright, sang joyously. The other, a contralto, sang with heartbreaking intensity of expression, which she deepened by dressing esthetically, as it was called then, meaning in the Rossettian [English Pre-Raphaelite poet and painter Dante Gabriel Rossetti, 1828–1882] taste. Miss Lawson produced this effect, not by the ugly extravagances which made the fashionable milliners' version of the esthetic mode ridiculous, but by very simple grey and brown gowns which somehow harmonized with her habitual expression of sadness and even suffering; so that when she sang "Oh, dont deceive me: oh, never leave me," she produced a picture as well as a tone poem. Cecil, who had just acquired a position by the few masterpieces which remain to us, was very much "in the movement" at the old Grosvenor Gallery (now the Aeolian Hall), then new, and passing through the sensational vogue achieved by its revelations of [English artist Sir Edward Coley] Burne Jones [1833–1898] and Whistler.

Malcolm was conducting a Gluck Society, at which I had discovered [German composer Christoph Willibald Ritter von] Gluck [1714–1787] through a recital of Alceste, in which [British composer, poet, and singer Théophile-Jules-Henri]

Theo Marzials [1850–1920], who had a charming baritone voice, sang the part of Hercules. My mother had met Marzials in the course of her musical activities: he introduced her to Malcolm Lawson: she lent him a hand in the chorus of the Gluck Society; and the result was that I found myself invited to visit the Lawsons, who were at home in Cheyne Walk every Sunday evening. I suffered such agonies of shyness that I sometimes walked up and down the Embankment for twenty minutes or more before venturing to knock at the door: indeed I should have funked it altogether, and hurried home asking myself what was the use of torturing myself when it was so easy to run away, if I had not been instinctively aware that I must never let myself off in this manner if I meant ever to do anything in the world. Few men can have suffered more than I did in my youth from simple cowardice or been more horribly ashamed of it. I shirked and hid when the peril, real or imaginary, was of the sort that I had no vital interest in facing; but when such an interest was at stake, I went ahead and suffered accordingly. The worst of it was that when I appeared in the Lawsons' drawingroom I did not appeal to the good nature of the company as a pardonably and even becomingly bashful novice. I had not then tuned the Shavian note to any sort of harmony; and I have no doubt the Lawsons found me discordant, crudely self-assertive, and insufferable. I hope they, and all the others on whom I jarred at this time, forgave me in later years, when it turned out that I really had something to assert after all. The house and its artistic atmosphere were most congenial to me; and I liked all the Lawsons; but I had not mastered the art of society at that time, and could not bear making an inartistic exhibition of myself; so I soon ceased to plague them, and, except for an occasional chance meeting with Malcolm, passed out of their lives after touching them very lightly in passing.

Cecil Lawson was the spoilt child of that household. He pontificated on art in a wayward grumbling incoherent musing fashion of his own. When, following my youthful and very irritating system of contradicting everyone from whom I thought I could learn anything, I suggested that Whistler was something short of the greatest artist of all time, he could not form a sentence to crush me with, but groaned inarticulately for a moment, like a clock about to strike, and then uttered the words Titian Turner Rembrandt Velasquez Whistler. He was goodlooking, not a big man, but trimly built, with just enough crisply curled hair to proclaim the artist without compromising the man. I had seen his work in the public exhibitions (never in private); and, thanks to my boyish prowlings in the Dublin National Gallery (as a boy I wanted to be a painter, never a writer), I knew its value. His untimely death, which occurred soon after my visits, must have broken up the Sunday evenings at Cheyne Walk very badly. I did not venture to intrude after it.

I used him in *Immaturity* as a model for the artist Cyril Scott, an invented name which has since been made famous by a British composer. I chose it because Cyril resembled Cecil metrically, and because I thought Lawson was a Scot (he was, I learn, born in Shropshire). But I must again warn the reader against taking the man in the book as an authentic portrait of the great painter, or inferring that his courtship and marriage or any of the circumstances I have invented for him, represent facts in Lawson's life. I knew nothing whatever about him except what I saw of him during my few visits to Cheyne Walk; and I have learnt nothing since. He set my imagination to work: that was all.

I have now told as much as seems to me necessary of the circumstances and relevant antecedents of my first book. It is the book of a raw youth, still quite out of touch with the country to which he had transported himself; and if I am to be entirely communicative on this subject, I must add that the mere rawness which so soon rubs off was complicated by a deeper strangeness which has made me all my life a sojourner on this planet rather than a native of it. Whether it be that I was born mad or a little too sane, my kingdom was not of this world: I was at home only in the realm of my imagination, and at my ease only with the mighty dead. Therefore I had to become an actor, and create for myself a fantastic personality fit and apt for dealing with men, and adaptable to the various parts I had to play as author, journalist, orator, politician, committee man, man of the world, and so forth. In this I succeeded later on only too well. In my boyhood I saw [British actor] Charles Mathews [1803–1878] act in a farce called Cool as a Cucumber. The hero was a young man just returned from a tour of the world, upon which he had been sent to cure him of an apparently hopeless bashfulness; and the fun lay in the cure having overshot the mark and transformed him into a monster of outrageous impudence. I am not sure that something of the kind did not happen to me; for when my imposture was at last accomplished, and I daily pulled the threads of the puppet who represented me in the public press, the applause that greeted it was not unlike that which Mathews drew in *Cool as a Cucumber*. Certainly the growls of resentful disgust with which my advances were resisted closely resembled those of the unfortunate old gentleman in the farce whose pictures and furniture the young man so coolly rearranged to his own taste. At the time of which I am writing, however, I had not yet learnt to act, nor come to understand that my natural character was impossible on the great stage of London. When I had to come out of the realm of imagination into that of actuality I was still uncomfortable. I was outside society, outside politics, outside sport, outside the Church. If the term had been invented then I should have been called The Complete Outsider. But the epithet would have been appropriate only within the limits of British barbarism. The moment music, painting, literature, or science came into question the positions were reversed: it was I who was the Insider. I had the intellectual habit; and my natural combination of critical faculty with literary resource needed only a clear comprehension of life in the light of an intelligible theory: in short, a religion, to set it in triumphant operation. It was the lack of this last qualification that lamed me in those early days in Victoria Grove, and that set limits to this ungainly first novel of mine, which you will not lose very much by skipping.

Ayot St Lawrence.

Summer, 1921.

Part II: Fiction

As a critic, Shaw had the chance to review the latter novels of the Victorian period as well as the early manifestations of naturalism. This means that his pieces of criticism begin with the great tradition that inspired and influenced him and move on to address the work of authors who—in parallel with what Shaw would later do on the stage—tried to denounce social ills by exposing questions that the public was not used to observing in a work of literature.

The pieces that follow also illustrate Shaw's own ideas on literature and style—much can be inferred from what he attacks, derides, or is simply absent. Two questions stand out: whether literature should be a "mirror held up to nature" and whether it should be a form of "art for art's sake."

1. "A New Novel by Mr Wilkie Collins," *The Pall Mall Gazette*, 18 September 1886.

[*Review of Wilkie Collins's* The Evil Genius (*London: Chatto and Windus, 1886). As usual with Shaw's reviews, he received the book only a week before the review was in print. Two recurrent elements are prominent in this piece. First, a frontal rejection of trite, automated plot—though Shaw is guilty of that sin in his plays on occasion—a criticism that he usually directs towards Victorian writers. And second, a natural tendency to stick pins into Shakespeare whenever the chance arises. Even when Shaw's 'anti-bardolatry' is founded on sound principles, he likes to go out of his way to choose Shakespeare for the object of his invectives.*]

Is it too much to hope that Mr Wilkie Collins [1824–1889] may be remembered as the last really able novelist who shackled and crippled his genius, and worried his admirers almost into giving up reading him, by systematically cumbering his stories with what are called "plots"? The perverse ingenuity with which he devises these Procrustean scaffolds cannot excuse the cruelty with which he stretches or chops the children of his imagination to fit them. The proper framework for a book is its own natural skeleton: if it be born without one, then let it perish as a shapeless abortion: no external apparatus of splints and crutches will make it presentable. Shakspeare has set us a bad example in this matter. He unfortunately suffered himself to be persuaded by custom and prejudice that plots were necessary; and as he was far too great a man to be capable of inventing them, he stole them. His sin soon found him out. The stolen plots forced him to deform his plays by uncharacteristic actions, inconsistencies, anachronisms, digressions, wordy trivialities, impertinent messengers, tedious journeys, and uninteresting letters, to which, after all, nobody attended; for we find the bard, by the mouth of Hamlet, complaining that the clowns made the pit laugh whilst the serious actors were wearying it by "some necessary question of the play." Would we have such clowns now! Shakspeare was not wiser than the whole world. His irritation at having taken a great deal of trouble for nothing was quite natural: but the pit and the clowns were right and he was wrong. The wise readers skip all explanations in novels: the wise playgoer, during the exposition of the drama, sleeps if alone, or, if companioned, discusses Home Rule. It is a mistake to suppose that the public cannot accept a situation without knowing exactly what has led to it. The flâneurs who stop to witness a street fight do not find the spectacle a whit less enjoyable and instructive because they do not happen to know the antecedents of the combatants or the particulars of their feud. The fight's the thing.

Mr Wilkie Collins's plots, unlike Shakspeare's, are honestly come by. He makes them for himself with travail and heavy sorrow, hardly disguising his sense of the respect and gratitude we owe him in return. To so conscientious a workman no honest person will deny respect. But gratitude is out of the question: enough that we try to forgive him! Perhaps Mr Wilkie Collins innocently believes that it is in average human nature to like his cryptograms, his deciphering experts, his lawyers, his letters, his extracts from diaries, his agony-column advertisements, his detectives, his telegrams, and his complicated railway and hotel arrangements. If so, he errs: these things are only tolerable for the sake of the stories they all but strangle. In "The Evil Genius" we have hardly one volume of human life and character to two volumes of plot. We bear with this because we cannot help ourselves, just as we submit to take our milk two-thirds water. Would the milkman but leave us the milk and water in separate jugs, we should willingly pay the same price and throw the water away. Fain would we take in Mr Wilkie Collins's plot and his story in separate covers; but, like the milkman, he insists on mixing them and then denying our analysis.

"The Evil Genius" begins well with an amusing jury discussing a criminal case, and with the most entertaining loves of Mrs Westerfield and James Beljames. The story of the neglected child who escapes from drudgery in a sordid school to happiness in a refined home, and then is driven by her unlucky star to wreck that home, is full of interest. The two scenes which form the dramatic climax of this part of the narrative are especially effective. But the plot soon begins to close in and crush the life out of the book. A marionette lawyer enters; and Mr Wilkie Collins strives desperately to make him seem alive. Characteristics supposed to be inherited from a French ancestry are tacked on to him. His appetite for truffles is enlarged upon. His mechanical plottering is relieved at five-minute intervals by a jerk at the wires, which makes the poor puppet start spasmodically. In vain! there is no life in his gambols: he is only there to advise every one to carry on the plot, and to supply missing links by letters to his wife such as no male creature ever yet did or will write. He is clumsily abetted by a certain Captain Bennydeck (there is but one novelist alive who could have perpetrated such a name), a sanctimonious bore, who makes an infirm bid for the dignity of hero late in the book, and is eventually, like a virtuous but ineffectual politician, kicked upstairs into the odour of philanthropy, and left with an off chance of marrying the disgraced governess. The mother-in-law, Mrs Presty, though she too is used chiefly to engineer the plot, has some independent merits. The child Kitty is delightful: the brightest pages in the book are those which record her doings and sayings. The dialogue, as usual in a Wilkie Collins novel, is sometimes natural and expressive; sometimes a mere string of terse statements, having no purpose except to advance or to explain the plot incubus, and no humanity or interest except as examples of the author's mannerisms. On the whole, novels are like other works of art: uninteresting just so far as they are machine made.

2. "Mr George Moore's New Novel," *The Pall Mall Gazette*, 19 July 1887.

[Review of George Moore's A Mere Accident *(London: Vizetelly and Co., 1887). The subject of Moore's 'licentious' writing is discussed in passing. Above all, Shaw delves on the author's technique of characterization—what makes a character plausible and natural while retaining a sense of individualization. As usual, Shaw likes to make his point by contrast; i.e., by finding fault with Moore's style. In general, we often find Shaw commenting on (denying) the idea that literature should be a mirror held up to nature.]*

It is customary to say of such books as [Irish novelist] Mr George Moore's [1852–1933] that they are not *virginibus puerisque.* Yet the lasses and lads are the very people who read them—if they ever do read them—without being any the worse. Those who have been allowed the run of the library in their childhood know by experience that in young hands [English playwright and novelist Henry Fielding's (1707–1754)] "Tom Jones" is as innocent as [English preacher and writer John Bunyan's (1628–1688)] "The Pilgrim's Progress," and that [French writer, journalist, and critic Théophile Gautier's (1811–1872)] "Mademoiselle de Maupin" is unreadably dull to little bookworms whose choice of literature is still subject to the parental censorship. As to people old enough to insist on choosing for themselves, they are under no compulsion to read Mr Moore's novels; and as his licence is now notorious, and his method not in the least insidious, it is only necessary, each time he publishes a book, to indicate plainly how far he has gone in it. Our readers can then decide for themselves whether the book is to be widely read or not; for Mr Moore's existence as a novelist depends wholly on the general reader and not on the particular reviewer.

The "mere accident" which gives the novel now in question its name is this. A young lady, a clergyman's daughter, about to be happily married, is overtaken on a lonely road by a tramp and outraged. Next day she goes mad, throws herself from a window, and dies. In describing this "realistically," Mr Moore has not done his worst: by making the victim insensible, he has contrived to avoid the most painful moment of his narrative. From his point of view this is perhaps a sacrifice of principle—a flinching from his duty. From the point of view of the British public, it will be welcomed as a commendable reticence that might have been carried further, even to the point of not writing the book. For there is no moral. The incident is described for its own sake. It has no consequences or antecedents to recommend it; and unless Mr Moore wished to bring home to us in a startling way the danger of allowing young ladies to go out without an escort, he must stoop to be classed with the vulgar novelists who depend for their effects on the mere sensation stirred up by any appalling crime or abnormal occurrence. In their school, the taste of the sensationalist author determines the particular crime selected; and Mr Moore's ready preference for a rape is explained by the opportunity it affords him for one of his favourite sham clinical lectures on morbid sexual conditions. Let it be freely admitted that these discourses would, if truly realistic, have a scientific value sufficient to fortify Mr Moore against prudish criticism. But as they are realistic only as symptoms of the condition of Mr Moore's own imagination, which hardly deserves a set of volumes all to itself, they have no more claim on our forbearance than the gratuitously romantic passages in a shilling shocker. The objection, in fact, to Mr Moore, is not that he is realistic, but that he is a romancer who, in order that he may take liberties, persuades himself that he is a pathologist. Now, whilst there are people who like to take liberties, and other people who like to submit to them, they will be taken, and, within the due limits of personal freedom, must not be interfered with; but pray let us have no hypocritical pretence that they are disinterested researchers in psychology or sociology. They are not even an acceptable protest against the evil of obscurantism; for their effect is really to reinforce it. The remedy for obscurantism is responsible scientific instruction, and not licentious fiction.

The workmanship of "A Mere Accident" can be most conveniently considered by calling a truce—a temporary truce—with Mr Moore on the subject of his moral accountability. It has been often urged upon him that "fine writing" is his weak point. He evidently thinks it just the reverse; and he is right. To appeal to the intelligence, and lead it to convictions which become a permanent spring of emotion, is all very well for writers who can do it; but Mr Moore's business is to strike the fancy and rouse the imagination with pictures and rhythms. Accordingly he first "gets up" the needful Sussex scenery as if he were commissioned to write a guide book, and then he describes it thus:

> The country is as flat as a smooth sea. Chanctonbury Ring stands up like a mighty cliff on a northern shore: its crown of trees is grim. The abrupt ascents of Toddington Mount bear away to the left, and tide-like the fields flow up into the great gulf between.

That is not the landscape style of Bunyan, or [English pamphleteer and journalist William] Cobbett [1763–1835], or [English travel writer] George Borrow [1803–1881]; but it is the style of styles to serve Mr Moore's turn; and he sticks to it wisely, and does it well. But when, inspired by [English writer and critic] Mr Walter Pater [1839–1894], he applies the same method to mediæval Latin, and pours out the result in twenty-page doses, the critic, detecting "cram," winks, and—unless he skips—even sleeps. Nor, despite his interest in the doctrine of heredity, is he disposed to admit the term "psychical investigation" as appropriate to a long explanation of the hero's temperament, in which "direct mingling of perfect health with spinal weakness had germinated into a marked yearning for the heroic ages—for the supernatural as contrasted with the meanness of the routine of existence." Pretentious fustian of this kind abounds in the book; but the persons of the story are none the less shrewdly sketched; for Mr Moore, within his range, is no bad observer. It is a range peopled by drunkards and vagabonds, by the "average sensual man," the half educated, the morbidly adolescent, the provincial and ignorant gentry—in short the unfit and inadequate for all noble parts in life. Among them there is not stuff enough to make a successful costermonger. Since they have their place among the many failures of our civilization, they must have their limner and chronicler. Only, one would fain meet some handsome and wholesome fellow-creature among them, if only as a standard to measure the shortcoming of the others. Here is Mr Moore's own description of his hero:

> To the superficial, therefore, John Norton will appear but the incarnation of egotism and priggishness; but those who see deeper will have recognized that he is one who has suffered bitterly, as bitterly as the outcast who lies dead in his rags beneath the light of the policeman's lantern.

A couple of hundred pages or so of pseudo-psychologocial analysis of this gentleman's emotions will reconcile most readers to his sufferings. As to the young lady with "the delicate plenitudes of the bent neck bound with white cambric," in the author's most characteristic style, it need only be said that what there is natural of her is evidently drawn from an Irish model, and that it is not her fault that Mr Moore did not find a better use for her.

3. "Realism, Real and Unreal," *The Pall Mall Gazette*, 29 September 1887.

[Review of W. E. Norris's Major and Minor (London: Richard Bentley and Son, 1887). Once again, Shaw discusses the question of to what extent literature should be a faithful representation of reality—as a result of reviewing a novel that he classifies as "naturalist." This is linked to the debate about which is the most beneficial approach to literature as a society-changing tool: focusing on the 'flowers' or on the 'sewer'. Shaw worked laboriously and somewhat mechanically during his formative years as an aspiring novelist, so it should come as no surprise that he praises the same habit in Norris and Trollope.]

Were [English novelist William Edward] Mr Norris [1847–1925], without further explanation, set down here as a realistic novelist, misunderstanding would inevitably ensue. Mr George Moore might amazedly demand why Mr Norris was classed with him; and it is not impossible that Mr Norris might second him very strongly in the inquiry. The Real has always been a hard bird to catch. Plato did not succeed in getting it under his hat until he had divested it of everything that is real to the realists of noveldom today: these gentlemen are not Platonic realists. They do not seem to have got much further than an opinion that the romance of the drawing-room is less real than the romance of the kitchen, the romance of the kitchen than that of the slum, that of the slum than that of the sewer, and, generally, that reality is always in inverse proportion to self-control, education, health, and decency. For this discouraging view [French naturalist writer Émile] M. Zola [1840–1902] and his "tail"—which seems to grow, by-the-by, faster than he can bite it off—are less to blame than society, in which, quite unquestionably, conditions discreditable to civilization make up the greater part of our national life. Nor is there any form of toleration of evil more contemptible than the "good taste" which pretends not to know this, and strives to boycott those who refuse to join the conspiracy of silence. Whilst the slums exist and the sewers are out of order, it is better to force them on the attention even of the polite classes than to engage in the manufacture of eau-de-cologne for sprinkling purposes, and sedulously ignore, like [the character from Dickens's *Little Dorrit*] Mrs General, everything that is not perfectly proper, placid, and pleasant. But it must not, in the heat of the reaction against Mrs General, be forgotten that the proper, the placid, and the pleasant, even when quantitatively less than the improper, the hysterical, and the noisome, are quite as real. And when the separate question as to which is fitter for the three-volume treatment arises, it is to be considered that no born romancer can help imparting a certain attraction, morbid or healthy, to his subject matter; and that when he treats of the improper, the hysterical, and the noisome, he must, whether he will or no, clothe them with the fascinations of his art. If, for example, he takes a culpable prostitute for his heroine, he makes a heroine of a culpable prostitute; and no mechanical heaping of infamy and disease upon her in the third volume will quite despoil her of that glamour. And as to the prostitute whom it is inhuman to call culpable—the woman who can only save herself and her family from starvation by eking out her miserable wage by prostitution—it is not clear that she can be helped by serving her up as a new sensation for the novel-reading classes. The corruption of society today is caused by evils which can be remedied only by the aspiration of the masses towards better things, and not by the shrinking of the classes from horrors known to them only by clever descriptions. Besides, one cannot help suspecting that those who shrink do not read, and that the rest dreadfully enjoy, the paper sensation. When, on any definite issue, the apathy or selfishness of the classes stands in the way of a needed reform, then have at their consciences by all means, without the very slightest regard for their "delicacy." But to persist in showing the classes repulsive pictures of evils which they are powerless to abolish, without ever striving to show the masses the better conditions which they have the power to make real as soon as they have the will, is shallow policy put forward as an excuse for coarse art.

So much for the present concerning the realistic school to which Mr Norris does not belong. There is a naturalist school to which he does belong; and its founder was [English novelist] Anthony Trollope [1815–1882]. Society has not yet forgiven that excellent novelist for having worked so many hours a day, like a carpenter or tailor, instead of periodically going mad with inspiration and hewing Barchester Towers at one frenzied stroke out of chaos, that being notoriously the only genuine artistic method. Yet, if we except the giants of the craft, he is entitled to rank among English writers as the first sincerely naturalistic novelist of our day. He delivered us from the marvels, senseless accidents, and cat's-cradle plots of old romance, and gave us, to the best of his ability, a faithful picture of the daily life of the upper and middle classes. If any contemptuously exclaim here, "Aha! The upper and middle classes! Why did not the snob give us the daily life of the slum and the gutter, on which all society rests to-day?" the answer is simple and convincing. He, as an honest realist, only told what he knew; and, being a middle-class man, he did not and could not know the daily life of the slum and gutter. And it must be added, at the risk of giving a violent shock to literary slummers, that every middle-class novelist who professes to arrive at his descriptions of that daily life by the inductive or Zolaistic method, is to that extent a flagrant humbug, although he may, through the ignorance of his readers, be as safe from exposure as an East-end dog-stealer would be if he undertook the fashionable intelligence for a paper circulating exclusively in Bethnal-green.

Mr Norris is by no means Anthony Trollope over again, though he exploits the same region, and produces good work rapidly enough to suggest that he, too, must turn out so much manuscript per hour, rain or shine. But, standing on Trollope's shoulders and belonging to a later generation, he is droller and brighter than Trollope; he knows the time of day in the political and social movement better; and he can, on emergency, go deeper into human motive, though it is hardly fair to say that his average profundity is greater. In "Major and Minor" he has taken the world easily. Major and Minor are brothers, who, since one is virtuous and the other rascally, would in an ordinary novel run a heavy risk of being very much underdone and overdone respectively. Mr Norris has done both to a turn, never overstepping the modesty of nature in his treatment of them except for a moment in the third volume, where he has indulged himself with a superfluous blackening of the villain's eye, very much as Dickens, in one of the most ridiculous moments of his immaturity, set the elder Chuzzlewit belabouring Mr Pecksniff with a nobby stick. In the first volume, too, there is a chapter or so of unpleasant suspense for the reader. When the father of the brothers disinherits the elder; settles the estate on the younger; and then relents, it becomes evident to experienced readers that he must die before he carries out his intention of revoking the will. A horrible curiosity as to how Mr Norris is going to polish off this hale old man takes possession of the imagination, and is so demoralizing that one is fain to say, as Macbeth did in a similar mental attitude, that "'twere well it were done quickly." Mr Norris finally does the deed with a chunk of old red sandstone, but contrives to avoid suspicion of plagiarism from a well-known passage in [American writer] Bret Harte [1836–1902]. On the whole, the worst that can be said of "Major and Minor" is that it might have been better in two volumes only, like "My Friend Jim." But it is an amusing and sensible novel: and its realism is perfectly sincere and in no way offensive.

4. "A Novelist Born, but Not Yet Made," The Pall Mall Gazette, 5 December 1887.

[Review of A Modern Magician, *by Joseph Fitzgerald Molloy. (London: Ward and Downey, 1887). Although later in his career Shaw would reject linguistic prescriptivism and "laying down the law" on questions like split infinitives, there seemed to be limits to Shaw's syntactic permissiveness. The fact that the author reviewed is Irish exposes the limitations to accepted linguistic diversity within the English-speaking world at the time, although for the most part Shaw only condemns unnecessarily verbose turns of phrase. It is important to note that Shaw was one of the experts who, as part of the BBC's Pronunciation Committee, sanctioned a particular, standardized spoken style: BBC English.]*

In the days of "The Colleen Bawn" [Irish playwright] Mr Dion Boucicault [1820–1890] used to enchant us by a ballad concerning a gentleman who, without displaying either conspicuous virtue or even ordinary good sense, won all hearts by the irresistible plea that "old Ireland was his country, and his name it was Molloy." It is difficult to avoid a rush to the conclusion that the author of "A Modern Magician" is heir as well as namesake to Mr Boucicault's hero. As a story teller he is the [character in Ben Jonson's *Every Man in his Humour*] Bobadil of fashionable mysticism: as a literary workman he is a pretentious bungler: his syntax is inconceivable, his dialogue impossible, his style a desperately careful expression of desperately slovenly thinking, his notions of practical affairs absurd, and his conception of science and philosophy a superstitious guess: yet he has an indescribable flourish, a dash of half-ridiculous poetry, a pathetic irresponsibility, a captivating gleam of Irish imagination, and, above all, an unsuspicious good-nature, that compel a humane public to read his books rather than mortify him by a neglect which he has done nothing malicious to deserve. And, indeed, the reading is not unpleasant, except to the tender-hearted reviewer, who finds forced upon him at every page the barbarous duty of convicting [Irish writer and critic Joseph] Mr Fitzgerald Molloy [1858–1908] of some solecism which would irretrievably damn a literary workman merely born in England and named Smith or Jackson.

Here is an example of the syntax that has served Mr Molloy in six fairly successful books. "It had been better if you accepted her invitation, because it will be uncertain when I get back." As this occurs in a dialogue, its inaccuracy might be forgiven if it were colloquial. But Mr Molloy scorns the colloquial: his most acute attacks of literary form have prostrated him in mid-dialogue. Thus, his heroine, instead of saying to her husband, "You were right in what you thought about me," declaims, "The conclusions you drew regarding me were just." A detective, after the usual murder in the third volume, wants to say, "We found out who he was by his papers," but cannot get any nearer to it than, "His watch, ring, purse, and papers were found on the body: the latter led to the discovery of his identity." A husband says to his wife, "The law shall enforce you to live with me"; and a young wife conversing familiarly with her aunt says, "He may have wed me because of some passing fancy," as calmly as if such speeches were human. Not until the aunt presently observes that "when two persons don't agree, one always believes the other doesn't understand," can the reader recover some opinion of Mr Molloy's shrewdness.

The above are examples of bungling, which is much more disgraceful to a man of letters than mere blundering. But Mr Molloy blunders too: he speaks of "mutual kinsmanship"; writes "sunk" for "sank"; and repeatedly puts his adjectives at the beginning of the sentence and then makes his nominative an accusative. When he at last induces his grammar to go smoothly, he gets into trouble with the police, sending his hero to Scotland-yard to give notice of his wife's elopement, and subsequently allowing him the privilege of being bailed out as a matter of course on a charge of murder.

Mr Molloy frequently puts off the story teller and assumes the sage. Here are a few samples of his weightier utterances: "Until a foretold event is accomplished it is not a fact." "A king in his palace may be as miserable as a beggar in his hovel." "From whence [sic] have men started, and to where [sic] do they tend?" "Few men and women with sacred fire in their hearts make loyal and loving spouses. Wherefore this should be, God knows." The following is a graceful version of the proverb about leading a horse to the water. "Others may carry grapes to our lips: we alone can taste of them." On the whole, the equine illustration, if the less elegant, is the better, since horses not only may be but customarily are led to the water, whereas it is etiquette for "others" to allow us to help ourselves instead of carrying grapes to our lips. One more example of Mr Molloy's philosophic style. When his hero falls in love, we are told that "the influence of the feminine on the male, exemplified in all the kingdoms of nature, finding utmost expression in humanity, was here perceptible."

It only remains to draw the unexpected conclusion that a man may be a tolerable novelist without knowing how to write. Shocking as some of the above samples of Mr Molloy's workmanship may be to experts, the people whom he calls "the bran-brained crowd" will find "A Modern Magician" quite readable. There are shrewd bits, imaginative bits, naively absurd bits, and yards of outrageous fustian about "earth shaking on her axis convulsed by fear," and "confusion of sounds as of wailing infants strangled at birth"; but there is hardly any of the flat, commonplace, correct padding that kills the ordinary three-volume novel. Mr Molloy has the natural gift in style—a good ear: what he lacks is intellectual training, address, and comprehension of society, as distinguished from familiarity with "at-homes." His imagination, though it has apparently made him the dupe of the shallow imposters whose exposure and disgrace is the chief amusement of the Society for Psychical Research [founded in 1882 to study paranormal events and abilities], has also enabled him to transfigure Wimbledon Common into something like the Wolfschlucht in [the German opera] "Der Freischütz." After all, one must be a born romancer to place an incantation scene on the lines of "Macbeth" and Bulwer Lytton's "Strange Story," at Wimbledon. Even foggy London is represented as a mist peopled with phantoms; and Mr Molloy's grave statement that "few Londoners have ever seen the City by night" would not be absurd if he had added "as I see it in my mind's eye"; which is no doubt what he meant.

Mr Fitzgerald Molloy is a writer born, not made. Will he kindly take the trouble to get made before he again challenges criticism from the literary point of view?

5. From the Introduction to Dickens's *Hard Times*, 1911.

[Shaw wrote this introduction for the Waverley (London) subscription edition. Dickens was, in Shaw's own words, a writer that "must have left his mark on me" because he started reading his novels at a very early age. Dickens's influence is noticeable in Shaw's novels, as well as in the "readable" style of his plays. Shaw champions three particular aspects of Dickens's arts of language in relation to Hard Times: the socialist germ of his social criticism, his dialogues (musical and detailed, if unnaturally bookish), and the use of humor to express ideas.]

John Ruskin once declared *Hard Times* Dickens's best novel. It is worth while asking why Ruskin thought this, because he would have been the first to admit that the habit of placing works of art in competition with one another, and wrangling as to which is the best, is the habit of the sportsman, not of the enlightened judge of art. Let us take it that what Ruskin meant was that *Hard Times* was one of his special favorites among Dickens's books. Was this the caprice of fancy? or is there any rational explanation of the preference? I think there is.

Hard Times is the first fruit of that very interesting occurrence which our religious sects call, sometimes conversion, sometimes being saved, sometimes attaining to conviction of sin. Now the great conversions of the XIX century were not convictions of individual, but of social sin. The first half of the XIX century considered itself the greatest of all the centuries. The second discovered that it was the wickedest of all the centuries. The first half despised and pitied the Middle Ages as barbarous, cruel, superstitious, ignorant. The second half saw no hope for mankind except in the recovery of the faith, the art, the humanity of the Middle Ages. In [British historian and politician Thomas Babington] Macaulay's [1800–1859] *History of England*, the world is so happy, so progressive, so firmly set in the right path, that the author cannot mention even the National Debt without proclaiming that the deeper the country goes into debt, the more it prospers. In Morris's *News from Nowhere* [1890] there is nothing left of all the institutions that Macaulay glorified except an old building, so ugly that it is used only as a manure market, that was once the British House of Parliament. *Hard Times* was written in 1854, just at the turn of the half century; and in it we see Dickens with his eyes newly open and his conscience newly stricken by the discovery of the real state of England. In the book that went immediately before, *Bleak House*, he was still denouncing evils and ridiculing absurdities that were mere symptoms of the anarchy that followed the industrial revolution of the XVIII and XIX centuries, and the conquest of political power by Commercialism in 1832. In *Bleak House*

Dickens knows nothing of the industrial revolution: he imagines that what is wrong is that when a dispute arises over the division of the plunder of the nation, the Court of Chancery, instead of settling the dispute cheaply and promptly, beggars the disputants and pockets both their shares. His description of our party system, with its Coodle, Doodle, Foodle, etc., has never been surpassed for accuracy and for penetration of superficial pretence. But he had not dug down to the bed rock of the imposture. His portrait of the ironmaster who visits Sir Leicester Dedlock, and who is so solidly superior to him, might have been drawn by Macaulay: there is not a touch of Bounderby in it. His horrible and not untruthful portraits of the brickmakers whose abject and battered wives call them "master," and his picture of the now vanished slum between Drury Lane and Catherine Street which he calls Tom All Alone's, suggest (save in the one case of the outcast Jo, who is, like Oliver Twist, a child, and therefore outside the old self-help panacea of Dickens's time) nothing but individual delinquencies, local plague-spots, negligent authorities.

In *Hard Times* you will find all this changed. Coketown, which you can see to-day for yourself in all its grime in the Potteries (the real name of it is Hanley in Staffordshire on the London and North Western Railway), is not, like Tom All Alone's, a patch of slum in a fine city, easily cleared away, as Tom's actually was about fifty years after Dickens called attention to it. Coketown is the whole place; and its rich manufacturers are proud of its dirt, and declare that they like to see the sun blacked out with smoke, because it means that the furnaces are busy and money is being made; whilst its poor factory hands have never known any other sort of town, and are as content with it as a rat is with a hole. Mr Rouncewell, the pillar of society who snubs Sir Leicester with such dignity, has become Mr Bounderby, the self-made humbug. The Chancery suitors who are driving themselves mad by hanging about the Courts in the hope of getting a judgment in their favor instead of trying to earn an honest living, are replaced by factory operatives who toil miserably and incessantly only to see the streams of gold they set flowing slip through their fingers into the pockets of men who revile and oppress them.

Clearly this is not the Dickens who burlesqued the old song of the "Fine Old English Gentleman," and saw in the evils he attacked only the sins and wickednesses and follies of a great civilization. This is Karl Marx, [Scottish philosopher and writer Thomas] Carlyle [1795–1881], Ruskin, Morris, [English socialist poet and philosopher Edward] Carpenter [1844–1929], rising up against civilization itself as against a disease, and declaring that it is not our disorder but our order that is horrible; that it is not our criminals but our magnates that are robbing and murdering us; and that it is not merely Tom All Alone's that must be demolished and abolished, pulled down, rooted up, and made for ever impossible so that nothing shall remain of it but History's record of its infamy, but our entire social system. For that was how men felt, and how some of them spoke, in the early days of the Great Conversion which produced, first, such books as the Latter Day Pamphlets of Carlyle, Dickens's *Hard Times*, and the tracts and sociological novels of the Christian Socialists, and later on the Socialist movement which has now spread all over the world, and which has succeeded in convincing even those who most abhor the name of Socialism that the condition of the civilized world is deplorable, and that the remedy is far beyond the means of individual righteousness. In short, whereas formerly men said to the victim of society who ventured to complain, "Go and reform yourself before you pretend to reform Society," it now has to admit that until Society is reformed, no man can reform himself except in the most insignificantly small ways. He may cease picking your pocket of half crowns; but he cannot cease taking a quarter of a million a year from the community for nothing at one end of the scale, or living under conditions in which health, decency, and gentleness are impossible at the other, if he happens to be born to such a lot.

You must therefore resign yourself, if you are reading Dickens's books in the order in which they were written, to bid adieu now to the light-hearted and only occasionally indignant Dickens of the earlier books, and get such entertainment as you can from him now that the occasional indignation has spread and deepened into a passionate revolt against the whole industrial order of the modern world. Here you will find no more villains and heroes, but only oppressors and victims, oppressing and suffering in spite of themselves, driven by a huge machinery which grinds to pieces the people it should nourish and ennoble, and having for its directors the basest and most foolish of us instead of the noblest and most farsighted.

Many readers find the change disappointing. Others find Dickens worth reading almost for the first time. The increase in strength and intensity is enormous: the power that indicts a nation so terribly is much more impressive than that which ridicules individuals. But it cannot be said that there is an increase of simple pleasure for the reader, though the books are not therefore less attractive. One cannot say that it is pleasanter to look at a battle than at a merry-go-round; but there can be no question which draws the larger crowd.

[Having introduced the evolution of Dickens as a novelist, Shaw analyzes Hard Times *specifically, paying special attention to humor and the language of its characters.]*

[...] *Hard Times* was written to make you uncomfortable; and it will make you uncomfortable (and serve you right) though it will perhaps interest you more, and certainly leave a deeper scar on you, than any two of its forerunners.

At the same time you need not fear to find Dickens losing his good humor and sense of fun and becoming serious in Mr Gradgrind's way. On the contrary, Dickens in this book casts off, and casts off for ever, all restraint on his wild sense of humor. He had always been inclined to break loose: there are passages in the speeches of Mrs Nickleby and Pecksniff which are impossible as well as funny. But now it is no longer a question of passages: here he begins at last to exercise quite recklessly his power of presenting a character to you in the most fantastic and outrageous terms, putting into its mouth from one end of the book to the other hardly one word which could conceivably be uttered by any sane human being, and yet leaving you with an unmistakeable and exactly truthful portrait of a character that you recognize at once as not only real but typical. Nobody ever talked, or ever will talk, as Silas Wegg talks to Boffin and Mr Venus, or as Mr Venus reports Pleasant Riderhood to have talked, or as Rogue Riderhood talks, or as John Chivery talks. They utter rhapsodies of non-sense conceived in an ecstasy of mirth. And this begins in Hard Times. [...]

This disregard of naturalness in speech is extraordinarily entertaining in the comic method; but it must be admitted that it is not only not entertaining, but sometimes hardly bearable when it does not make us laugh. There are two per-sons in Hard Times, Louisa Gradgrind and Cissy Jupe, who are serious throughout. Louisa is a figure of poetic tragedy; and there is no question of naturalness in her case: she speaks from beginning to end as an inspired prophetess, conscious of her own doom and finally bearing to her father the judg-ment of Providence on his blind conceit. If you once consent to overlook her marriage, which is none the less an act of prostitution because she does it to obtain advantages for her brother and not for herself, there is nothing in the solemn po-etry of her deadly speech that jars. But Cissy is nothing if not natural; and though Cissy is as true to nature in her character as Mrs Sparsit, she "speaks like a book" in the most intolerable sense of the words. In her interview with Mr James Harthouse, her unconscious courage and simplicity, and his hopeless defeat by them, are quite natural and right; and the contrast between the humble girl of the people and the smart sarcastic man of the world whom she so completely vanquishes is excellently dramatic; but Dickens has allowed himself to be carried away by the scene into a ridiculous substitution of his own most literary and least colloquial style for any language that could conceivably be credited to Cissy.

> "Mr Harthouse: the only reparation that remains with you is to leave her immediately and finally. I am quite sure that you can mitigate in no other way the wrong and harm you have done. I am quite sure that it is the only compensation you have left it in your power to make. I do not say that it is much, or that it is enough; but it is something, and it is necessary. Therefore, though without any other authority than I have given you, and even without the knowledge of any other person than yourself and myself, I ask you to depart from this place to-night, under an obligation never to return to it."

This is the language of a Lord Chief Justice, not of the dunce of an elementary school in the Potteries.

[The problems posed by the unnatural idiolect of some of Dickens's characters leads to a broader discussion of the faithfulness of the setting Dickens portrays, and of realism in literature in general.]

But this is only a surface failure, just as the extravagances of Mrs Sparsit are only surface extravagances. There is, however, one real failure in the book. Slackbridge, the trade union organizer, is a mere figment of the middle-class imagination. No such man would be listened to by a meeting of English factory hands. Not that such meetings are less susceptible to humbug than meetings of any other class. Not

that trade union organizers, worn out by the terribly weari-
some and trying work of going from place to place repeating
the same commonplaces and trying to "stoke up" meetings to
enthusiasm with them, are less apt than other politicians to
end as windbags, and sometimes to depend on stimulants to
pull them through their work. Not, in short, that the trade
union platform is any less humbug-ridden than the platforms
of our more highly placed political parties. But even at their
worst trade union organizers are not a bit like Slackbridge.
Note, too, that Dickens mentions that there was a chairman
at the meeting (as if that were rather surprising), and that this
chairman makes no attempt to preserve the usual order of
public meeting, but allows speakers to address the assembly
and interrupt one another in an entirely disorderly way. All
this is pure middle-class ignorance. It is much as if a tramp
were to write a description of millionaires smoking large cig-
ars in church, with their wives in low-necked dresses and
diamonds. We cannot say that Dickens did not know the
working classes, because he knew humanity too well to be
ignorant of any class. But this sort of knowledge is as compatible with ignorance of class manners and customs as with
ignorance of foreign languages. Dickens knew certain classes
of working folk very well: domestic servants, village artisans,
and employees of petty tradesmen, for example. But of the
segregated factory populations of our purely industrial towns
he knew no more than an observant professional man can
pick up on a flying visit to Manchester.

It is especially important to notice that Dickens expressly
says in this book that the workers were wrong to organize
themselves in trade unions, thereby endorsing what was perhaps the only practical mistake of the Gradgrind school that
really mattered much. And having thus thoughtlessly
adopted, or at least repeated, this error, long since exploded,
of the philosophic Radical school from which he started, he
turns his back frankly on Democracy, and adopts the ideal-

ized Toryism of Carlyle and Ruskin, in which the aristocracy are the masters and superiors of the people, and also the servants of the people and of God. Here is a significant passage.

"Now perhaps," said Mr Bounderby, "you will let the gentleman know how you would set this muddle (as you are so fond of calling it) to rights."

"I donno, sir. I canna be expecten to't. Tis not me as should be looken to for that, sir. Tis they as is put ower me, and ower aw the rest of us. What do they tak upon themseln, sir, if not to do it?" And to this Dickens sticks for the rest of his life. In *Our Mutual Friend* he appeals again and again to the governing classes, asking them with every device of reproach, invective, sarcasm, and ridicule of which he is master, what they have to say to this or that evil which it is their professed business to amend or avoid. Nowhere does he appeal to the working classes to take their fate into their own hands and try the democratic plan.

Another phrase used by Stephen Blackpool in this remarkable fifth chapter is important. "Nor yet lettin alone will never do it." It is Dickens's express repudiation of *laissez-faire*.

There is nothing more in the book that needs any glossary, except, perhaps, the strange figure of the Victorian "swell," Mr James Harthouse. His pose has gone out of fashion. Here and there you may still see a man—even a youth—with a single eyeglass, an elaborately bored and weary air, and a little stock of cynicisms and indifferentisms contrasting oddly with a mortal anxiety about his clothes. All he needs is a pair of Dundreary [title character in Tom Taylor's play *Our American Cousin*, 1865] whiskers, like the officers in [Anglo-French artist Louis William] Desanges' [1822–1887] military pictures, to be a fair imitation of Mr James Harthouse. But he is not in the fashion: he is an eccentric, as Whistler was an eccentric, as [English writer and caricaturist Henry Maximilian] Max Beerbohm [1872–1956] and the neo-dandies of the *fin de siècle* were eccentrics. It is now the fashion to be strenuous, to be energetic, to hustle as American millionaires are supposed (rather erroneously) to hustle. But the soul of the swell is still unchanged. He has changed his name again and again, become a Masher, a Toff, a Johnny and what not; but fundamentally he remains what he always was, an Idler, and therefore a man bound to find some trick of thought and speech that reduces the world to a thing as empty and purposeless and hopeless as himself. Mr Harthouse reappears, more seriously and kindly taken, as Eugene Wrayburn and Mortimer Lightwood in *Our Mutual Friend*. He reappears as a club in The Finches of the Grove in *Great Expectations*. He will reappear in all his essentials in fact and in fiction until he is at last shamed or coerced into honest industry and becomes not only unintelligible but inconceivable.

Note, finally, that in this book Dickens proclaims that marriages are not made in heaven, and that those which are not confirmed there, should be dissolved.

6. "The Case Against Chesterton," *The New Statesman*, 13 May 1916.

[Review of Julius West's G. K. Chesterton. A Critical Study. *(London: Martin Secker, 1915). This piece, although not a review of a piece of fiction, enables readers to appraise both the reception of Chesterton's work in his own lifetime and Shaw's personal take on Chesterton's literary production. The facts that West was a member of the Fabian society and that he had made comments on Shaw's ideas account for the opening paragraphs on Socialism and economic theory.]*

In Russia the intelligent are a class with a name. In England they are nameless and despised, or, when that is impossible owing to their bumptiousness, mistrusted. Our plan has the advantage that every Englishman passes as possibly intelligent until he opens his mouth or takes up his pen, just as he passes for an intrepid pugilist until someone assaults him. And as in practice nobody ever does assault him, he has only to avoid the pen and confine his remarks to simple meteorological observations and demands for beer to keep up the national character of Britain as the mother of strong silent men, all able to use their fists.

[Russian-born, English historian and translator] Mr Julius West [1891–1918] is of Allied extraction. I have never been able to decide exactly what Mr Gilbert Chesterton's nationality is, except that he is certainly not an Englishman: at least, I take it that an Englishman would not in England seem extraordinary and even unique. When he is not writing he is talking; and he is often doing both: yet he has not compromised himself. And Mr Julius West has written a book about Mr Chesterton, which book I am supposed to be reviewing. It is distinguished from most books of the kind by the circumstance that Mr West has apparently read Mr Chesterton's works, which is contrary to all precedent, and also by a command of our language which is a very agreeable change from our own mere habit of it. His English, like Mr [Polish-born, English novelist, born Józef Teodor Konrad Korzeniowski, Joseph] Conrad's [1857–1924] English, has a quality seldom attained by purely British writers. No doubt this is because English words have to mean something to a foreigner before he can use them at all, whereas to an Englishman they are only noises to express his high spirits or his ill humour as the case may be. Anyhow, Mr West contrives to be very readable on a subject on which most unmitigatedly English writers are mere petulant nuisances.

Once in his book Mr West has failed in tact. To declare that all attempts to parody Mr Chesterton have been failures, and then to dedicate the book containing the declaration to [British writer and literary editor] Mr J[ohn]. C[ollings]. Squire [1884–1958], is excusable only by absence of mind. Also I would warn Mr West and all whom it may concern not to be misled by the younger generation of British penmen (those under fifty or thereabouts) who believe that their grandfathers all read [British political theorist John Stuart] Mill [1806–1873], and all belonged to a period called Early Victorian, in which the dull dogs had their day. Mill was the inspirer, not, as Mr West implies, of the Socialist reaction of the eighties, but of the rearguard actions fought against it by Benthamite Individualism [after British philosopher and jurist Jeremy Bentham, 1748–1832] under such captains as Bradlaugh and [English biologist and political theorist] Herbert Spencer [1820–1903]. Mill's final conversion to Socialism, though claimed for the Fabian side by [English economist] Mr Sidney Webb [1859–1947], was ignored as completely as Solomon's final conversion to the worship of Ashtaroth [1 Kings 11:5]; and the statement lately slipped into currency that the Fabian Society was, like its strongly Individualist and Malthusian [after English cleric and political economist Thomas Robert Malthus, 1766–1834] predecessor the Dialectical Society, founded on Mill, is not merely wide of the mark: it actually hits the back of the target. Mr West has been led by it to say that I hold all Mill's beliefs. There was a time when all the Intelligent held Mill's disbeliefs; and this lasted until his disbeliefs became so general that they were no longer perceptible, like the disbelief in the flatness of the earth. But very few people knew that Mill had any beliefs at all, except perhaps in peasant proprietorship, which was anathema to the Socialists.

Mr West has also heard that I am "an avowed and utter Puritan," and that Mr Chesterton is a Catholic Tory. I do not object to being called a Puritan, because it means only that I do not drive through the town with a painted Monte Carlo countess; and Mr Chesterton probably does not object to have it intimated in the same excessive way that he is neither a Methodist nor a Manchester doctrinaire. But both statements are overdone: they are the literary equivalents of burning down the house to roast the pig. I should roughly class [Scottish theologian] John Knox [c. 1513–1572] among the famous fools of history, and [French theologian John] Calvin [1509–1564] among its famous scoundrels; and the spectacle of Mr Chesterton on his knees every Easter before a creature of like passions (in homœopathic dilution) with himself and much less brains, confessing his sins and receiving absolution, is one which the world has not yet seen; nor does Mr Chesterton's outlook on politics resemble that of Sir Leicester Dedlock. I suggest, therefore, that this use of Puritan and Catholic and Tory as abusive epithets, though exhilarating, is apt to mislead those who are not in the family joke.

[Shaw goes on to define Chesterton by explaining why he defies definition, focusing on the 'drink question' for illustrative purposes, although the choice cannot have been coincidental.]

But it has its uses when applied to Mr Chesterton; for there is no man alive who more needs being driven by mere stress of misunderstanding to a serious definition and determination of his own views and destiny. Being an artist of almost magical dexterity in language and casuistry, he indulges in art for art's sake quite recklessly. Compared to him, poor Whistler, whom he despises, was a bigoted missionary, devoting his whole life to the steadfast propaganda of certain qualities in design and painting. No doubt if Whistler had been [Flemish painter Peter Paul] Rubens [1577–1640], with the Chestertonian power and exuberance of that painter, he might have been as unscrupulous as Rubens with his brush or Chesterton with his pen. But be that as it may, he had a definite faith and stuck to it: you always knew where to have him and what he stood for. Does anyone know where to have Chesterton and what he stands for? In the world of romantic ideals, yes: he is as popular as a film drama, though not so vulgar. But in the world of things as they are, who can depend on him? Take, for example, his attitude towards the public-house. If I confessed to him that I helped to build The Fox and Pelican at Grayshott he would scorn me, because it was a reformed public-house, and is now, I think, a People's Refreshment House. My teetotal friends were horrified at my endowing the accursed thing. The local drunkards were even more disgusted by the substitution of stunning good beer, which made them drunk cheaply and precipitately, for the unreformed stuff which spread the process over a whole evening and went to their livers rather than to their heads. I do not defend my reformed public-house; but still less can I defend Mr Chesterton's still more extravagantly reformed sort: the romantic imaginary public-house, the public-house that never was on sea or land, the public-house that has the sign of The Flying Inn, the public-house in which you may drink draughts of beer and rum that would empty the horn of Odin, and grow more splendid and strong and uproariously poetic with every mouthful, the public-house where you can drink without squandering the money you should take home to your wife and children because there is nothing but paper money to pay, where you do not stagger to the sewer trap to be sick in the face of heaven, where—to mention no more unpleasant things—drink is not drink but a dream, and the worship of Dionysos does not turn into a sick headache. Now I say that there is no such public-house: it is an idealistic mask for the real public-house. I doubt whether Mr Chesterton has ever been in a real public-house: I think he ekes out the taproom stories of Dickens and [English author William Wymark] Jacobs [1863–1943] with memories of one or two reluctant visits to saloon bars in the Strand to avoid hurting the feelings of humble admirers insistent on treating him. I began public life by being trotted about the streets of Dublin by Irish nursemaids whom amorous carmen treated, not forgetting a sip of ginger beer for the childher. I spring from a very large family; and every large family has its percentage of drunkards. I have lived in the house with tipplers. I have tested in my own person the alleged inspiration to be derived from what Mr Chesterton will not let me call alcohol and yet honourably shrinks from calling booze; and I can bear witness to its enchanting reduction of my critical faculty as evidenced by the manuscripts which I read over and tore up next day. I have watched the difference between driving a car before lunch and after, and have learnt to insist on taking the wheel myself if even a spoonful of *vin compris* has formed part of the driver's lunch. And I remain incurably convinced that there is no future for Dutch courage or Dutch inspiration or Dutch poetry: alcohol is useful only in parliaments where the boredom is so intolerable that it cannot be endured without narcotising the critical faculty, and incidentally the conscience, at the bar or at dinner.

I therefore take Mr Chesterton's glorification of the rum bottle and the beer barrel as art for art's sake, pure Anacreontic play-boyishness in a hearty popular disguise; and I shall some day organise a presentation to him of a proof impression of [British book illustrator George] Cruikshank's [1792–1878] Bottle. He may frame it as a frightful example of what comes of being serious; but it will glare at him as a reminder of what comes of cutting one's appetite in two and throwing away the better half of it. I have suffered from both halves myself, having been defeated in an election because the drunkards on the register objected to my being a teetotaler, and the teetotalers objected still more to my refusal to cut off the liquor not only of the drunkards but of everyone else as well. They preferred the success of the publican's candidate to that of a man who refused to vilify publicans, having found very capable colleagues and good friends among them; and I daresay Mr Chesterton hails their choice (not as to my person, but on principle) with three times three.

I dwell on the Drink Question because it illustrates the quarrel which the rising generation is fastening—and fastening successfully—on Mr Chesterton. Mr Julius West begins his book by an evidently sincere announcement that he is going to show that Mr Chesterton is a writer of the highest quality and the deepest importance. And yet, whenever he gets away from Mr Chesterton's literary *tours de force*, he finds himself complaining of inconsistency, reaction, obsolescence, aimlessness, and, when science is concerned, something which he would obviously call stupidity if he did not attribute it (rashly, I think) to ignorance. The only conclusion that comes out of it all is that Mr West has no use for Mr Chesterton except as a literary artist and a rhapsode who occasionally contradicts himself by some inspired utterance which he never follows up, and forgets five minutes afterwards as Morris accused Ruskin of doing habitually.

I do not see what else Mr Chesterton can expect at the hands of intellectually conscientious youth. It is his delight on a shiny night in the season of the year to *épater not le bourgeois*, but the extreme left, the revolutionists, the agnostics, the Dwellers on the Threshold of the millennium. This is a pious and necessary work. I have always protested against the devil having all the good tunes of criticism, irony, ridicule and all the other tonics. I well remember the beneficial effect of the scandalised dismay, the sense of unheard-of outrage, which spread through the solemn ranks of Marxism when I first treated an International Socialist Congress to several columns of descriptive reporting in the capitalist press of just that sidesplitting kind which its absurdities deserved; and I have no objection whatever to Mr Chesterton pitching into the teetotalers, the Protestants, the Agnostics, the Scientists, Christian and anti-Christian, the Jews, the Pacificos, the Eugenicans, the Suffragists, the Socialists, and, when the feeble-minded and the children are in question, into all the tribe of

Mr Honeythunder, with every weapon that can put the fear of God into them and keep it there.

All the same, when things have to be done, and people to be endured and dealt with, the man who gets his way is the positive man and not the negative or derisive one. It is unnecessary to urge that there are feeble-minded people in the world; for the war has just now brought out the fact that there are hardly any other people. But there are people so feeble-minded that unless they are kept in tutelage they cannot live at all. And everybody is feeble-minded in one department or another. Mr Chesterton probably needs the tutelage of a solicitor, a doctor, and a stockbroker; and each of these three tutors of his may be feeble-minded to the last degree about golf, on the merits of which Mr Chesterton is, I fancy, supremely sane. My own gorgeous abilities do not exclude pitiable imbecilities in directions which, in self-defence, I abstain from indicating. [English naval administrator and MP] Samuel Pepys [1633] was an able man; but he was weak as water among the wives of the dockyard artificers, and even in the kitchen. I have known people in both sexes who combined extraordinary talent with a ruinous incapacity for living within their incomes. The French institution of a Council of Prudent Persons to look after people who are unable, on one point or another, to look after themselves, is a very reasonable and necessary one; and both I and Mr Chesterton—clever as we are—would probably be the better for one, though I should not envy the prudent ones their job.

[Shaw now discusses the polemic ideas Chesterton expressed about poverty, the Jews, and women. Shaw claims that Chesterton has deliberately chosen to stick to "old formulas" and join the ranks of the anti-Modernists.]

However, let me come down from what is desirable to what is already recognised as necessary. We have masses of feeble-minded people who can no more be left to themselves without gross cruelty than a newly-blinded soldier from the front can be left to negotiate the Mansion House crossings without a guide. What does Mr Chesterton propose to do with them? Let us take it that he has kicked Mr Honeythunder into the horse-pond. Let us assume that he has snatched from the hands of [English economist and labor historian Martha Beatrice] Mrs Sidney Webb [née Potter, 1858–1943] all those perfectly sane and responsible cases whom, merely because they are poor and she is an interfering woman, she has sequestrated from their ordinary avocations and enslaved in a fiendish craze for subjugating her impecunious fellow creatures (I hope I am not understating the Chestertonian and Wellsian [English writer Herbert George Wells, 1866–1946] view of that unquestionably very active and inquisitive lady). He will still have a residuum on his hands. What will he do with them? That is what Mr Julius West and some others evidently want to know. They surmise that he would call them the Little Sisters and Brothers of Jesus, and pack them into a convent or monastery where the Factory Acts do not run. They even suggest that his soul would be so completely satisfied with the kicking and ducking of Honeythunder and the discomfiting of Mrs Sidney Webb, that he would forget all about the feeble-minded and leave them to be resumed by his two victims the moment his back was turned. But they don't *know*. Why? Because Mr Chesterton has never told them.

Take again the children of the poor. Mr Chesterton is, to his honour, a sound Dickensian, and does not think any child ought to be like Jo in *Bleak House*. Well, the practical alternative, until poverty is abolished, is to spend money enough on Jo to bring him up decently. Who is to have the spending of that money and the responsibility for Jo? Clearly, answers the feeling heart, Jo's mother. Now that may solve the problem for Jo A (pardon the official classification), whose mother is a mother in a thousand, or, to be roughly accurate, one of from

25 to 33 per cent. of our impecunious motherhood. But Jo B has no mother. Jo C has a mother who can be trusted with the money if she is inspected a little. Jo D has a gloriously drunken mother who will not only drink Jo's endowment but force him to add to it as a thief, and force his sister to add to it as a child-prostitute. It is no use shrieking that this is a libel on motherhood. If the thistle of poverty bore nothing but grapes we should not want to uproot it. The objection to poverty is precisely that it inevitably produces such results. What would Mr Chesterton do with Jo C and Jo D? Will he say, like the bold bishop, that he had rather see Jo free (as in *Bleak House*) than inspected or torn from his mother's arms? Not without denying his master, Dickens, who was always himself Honey-thundering at "my lords and gentlemen and right honourables and wrong honourables of every degree" to officiously make Jo their business; to demolish Tom-All-Alone's; to endow and inspect and clean up; and to replace Mrs Pardiggle and Bumble and Gradgrind, not by beer and jollity and the fighting part of knight-errantry and mediae-val religion, but by the sworn enemy and vowed destroyer of the accursed Poor Law: in short, by Mrs Sidney Webb. He no sooner showed how Mrs Pardiggle, fool and snob and self-elected irresponsible uninspected inspector, made the miser-able savages she inspected worse, than he went on to show how the two decent ladies she brought with her made them better. The bond of sympathy between Mr Sidney Webb and myself is that we were both brought up on *Little Dorrit*. No use coming Dickens over us. What would Mr Chesterton do with Jo? His reply would make an excellent subject for an ar-ticle in the *New Witness*, which really ought now to be called the Three Witnesses: meaning, not those whom some Trini-tarian forger foisted on [Christian theologian, Doctor of the Church] St Jerome's [347–420] Vulgate for so many centuries, but St Gilbert, St Cecil, and St Hilary.

Then, as to the Jews. We cannot massacre the Jews without carting them all to Russia, which is hardly feasible. We must put up with the Jews, just as we must put up with the Irish in spite of the alarming consequences of allowing young men to be imported from Dublin to London, as Lord Northcliffe was, and as I was. Considering that it is with the greatest difficulty that Englishmen can be induced to put up with one another, it is too much to expect them to love the Jews; but they must let them live, and there's an end on't. Macaulay showed, years before I was born, that the case trumped up by our Jew-baiters could just as easily be trumped up against men with red hair or any other distinctive mark. That demonstration remains unrefuted and indeed irrefutable. Now, since Macaulay's time it has become apparent to all the world that the Jews are the only people in Britain who combine culture and intellectual activity and susceptibility with common-sense and practical business ability. When you speak of the selfish, greedy, pushing plutocrat who makes money and spends it in getting a great deal more of what a navvy likes, you are never thinking of a Jew. And when you speak of the unpractical dreamer, full of books and pictures and noble ideals, but hopeless when it comes to business, and convinced that politics and economics and mathematics are the dry pursuits of soulless and sexless men and women, you are again not thinking of a Jew. If all the portfolios of the Cabinet were strictly reserved for Jews, and the proceedings of the House of Commons conducted in Yiddish, we have every reason to expect that the country would be governed much more intelligently than it is at present, and with a steady regard to the value of intellectual training, knowledge of languages and literature, and artistic culture, instead of our present implacable and boorish contempt for them. These hard facts—for such they are, to our shame—will not yield to jibes at "the Infant Samuel" and implications that no Christian would have behaved as the Lord Chief Justice did about his Marconi shares. If the German Junkers were to drop their silly and snobbish prejudice against the Jews, and admit them to their imperial councils, as our Junkers have done, I should be seriously alarmed; for our tolerance of the Jews is one of the advantages we have over Germany in the war. Does Mr Chesterton, like [English-born German author] Mr Houston [Stewart] Chamberlain [1855–1927], really think that a Jew, *qua* Jew, is a worse man than himself? Mr West has clearly a right to know.

The Suffragists can afford to forgive Mr Chesterton a good deal in consideration of his having given us the best and finest masculine statement yet made of the worth of women. Why he finished by denying them a vote without at the same time disclaiming one for himself is just one of the matters he ought to explain. The highwayman who robbed Squire Western's sister of her jewels at least gave a reason for it; and curiously enough, it was essentially if not verbally the very reason Mr Chesterton gives for robbing women of their political rights. For my part I cannot work up much enthusiasm for the vote (having one myself); but I think, on Mr Chesterton's own grounds, that it is monstrous that any public authority should sit without the counsel and presence of women, no matter how they are chosen; and until women concentrate their claims on this immovable human truth, and recognize that Votes for Women is by itself only a *reductio ad absurdum* of Votes for Men, they will not corner Mr Chesterton, much less the people who are stupider than he, of whom the number is considerable.

Mr Chesterton, as an anti-Modernist, compromises himself perhaps more vitally than as an anti-Socialist. His notion that he is an anti-Socialist is founded on the erroneous superstition that he was once a Socialist. An early fancy for Socialism no more makes a man a Socialist than an early fancy for the architecture of St Sophia's makes him a Moslem. In the spirit of the schoolmaster who offered [English poet and critic Samuel Taylor] Coleridge [1772–1834] a little essay on method to cure his discursiveness, I recommend my own tracts to Mr Chesterton to cure his delusion that social salvation is attainable by a combination of personal righteousness with private property in the form of a picturesque allotment. When Mr Chesterton combines a knowledge of the law of rent with his regard for the law of God, he will become a Socialist for the first time; and his Socialism will stick.

But anti-Modernism is another matter. The law of rent and the law of value are, unfortunately, still in the technical sphere: they are not in the air: they are known only to those who have cared enough about the intellectual soundness of their politics to make a special study of economics. Diners-out do not talk of [English financier Sir Thomas] Gresham's [1519–1579] law, or [British political economist David] Ricardo's [1772–1823] law, or [English economist William Stanley] Jevons's [1835–1882] law, any more to-day than they did when they dined with Shakespeare at the Mermaid, with [English writer, editor, and lexicographer Samuel] Johnson [1709–1784] at the Literary Club, or with Dickens at Tavistock House. But they do talk about Evolution and Natural Selection (often, alas! confusing them damnably) and about Eugenics, about [English naturalist Charles Robert] Darwin [1809–1882] and [Czech scientist Gregor Johann] Mendel [1822–1824], [French philosopher Henri-Louis] Bergson [1859–1941] and [English author Samuel] Butler [1835–1902], [German physicist Heinrich Rudolf] Hertz [1857–1894] and [Italian inventor Guglielmo] Marconi [1874–1937], aeroplanes and trinitrotoluene. Now it is not conceivable that Mr Chesterton is as ignorant of these matters as Shakespear, Johnson and Dickens. He cannot believe that Marconi is a bookmaker with whom certain politicians had shady dealings; that [English polymath Sir Francis] Galton [1822–1911] was a prurient blackguard who invented the word eugenics as a mask for disgusting improprieties; that Evolution is a silly and blasphemous attempt to discredit the Garden of Eden; that motor-cars are nuisances, aeroplanes toys to which Chinese kites are far superior, and war still an affair of battle-axes mightily wielded by armour-plated athletic giants. Yet Mr Chesterton has written a good many sentences which seem to mean either these things or nothing. I will even go so far as to say that it will serve him right if future professors, specialising in the literature of the Capitalistic Era, explain to their students that they must not rely on traditional dates, as it is clear from internal evidence that though Wells and Bennett and Chesterton are dated as contemporaries, Chesterton must have died before the middle of the nineteenth century, and may perhaps be placed as early as the fifteenth or sixteenth as a master of the School of [French humanist and scholar François] Rabelais [c. 1490–1553]. Wells and Bennett, on the other hand, could not possibly have come earlier than the post-Ibsen. "As against this," we may conceive the future professor lecturing, "it is alleged that one of Chesterton's best books is a monograph on Shaw, who is dated as a contemporary of Wells. But the best authorities are agreed that this extraordinarily enlightened author was one of the pioneers of the twenty-fifth century, and that the allusions to him in the books of the nineteenth and twentieth centuries are later interpolations, the pseudo-Chesterton book being probably by Shaw himself, a hypothesis which fully accounts for its heartfelt eulogy. It has been objected that the writer does not seem to have read Shaw's works; but this is clearly an intentional mystification, very characteristic of the freakish founder of the Shavians."

[Shaw brings his argument to a close by outlining his own personal ideas about Chesterton—the writer and the man—in a rather appreciative and idealistic fashion.]

Not to labour the point further, Mr Chesterton does unquestionably affect to throw back to the grandfathers of Mr Bennett, Mr Wells, and Dr [Caleb Williams] Saleeby [1878–1940] rather than forward to the Democracy of Walt Whitman and Edward Carpenter. Like Morris, he goes back to the Middle Ages, but does not, like Morris, finally admit that we are in the Dark Ages and that the Middle Ages are still far ahead of us, and that our news about them is as yet news from nowhere. [German philosopher Friedrich] Nietzsche's [1844–1900] appeal to him to be a good European does not move him. His Radicalism is not that of [English manufacturer and statesman Richard] Cobden [1804–1865] but of [British Whig statesman] Charles James Fox [1749–1806], including his enthusiasm for the French Revolution, so heavily blown on by Marx and his school.

In the end we are left in doubt whether Chesterton is a man who has swallowed all the formulas, and decided that the older ones are on the whole the least absurd, or a man who has never swallowed any modern formulas at all, though he has smelt plenty of them. The difference is important; for though a Modernist may trust a man who, having read the story of Jonah and the Great Fish side by side with a volume of the Higher Criticism, prefers Jonah as not only more amusing but more probable and less far-fetched, yet he will shrink from the guidance of one who does not know what the Higher Critics have to say. Criticisms by mentally deficient people are sometimes extraordinarily enlightening. For example, Mr Chesterton, who has both delicacy and common-sense in a very high degree, could never have done the work of [Austrian neurologist Sigmund] Freud [1856–1939], who has neither delicacy nor common-sense. When Mr Chesterton broke his arm, I deplored it as an accident; but Freud, if he had heard about it, would have concluded that Mr Chesterton had subconsciously done it on purpose to punish himself for some frightful secret crime. Nobody but a fool would have thought of such a thing; but then wise men are always over-looking things that are visible to fools; and though I once broke my own arm and therefore most vehemently reject the Freudian psychoanalysis of Mr Chesterton's mishap, I pay a serious if disrespectful attention to Freud. For I have never forgotten [Italian painter Giorgio] Vasari's [1511–1574] story of [Italian artist] Michael Angelo [1475–1564] laughing at the stonemason's statue because it had no knees. The stonemason took his statue away; sawed through the legs; inserted a pair of knees; and brought it back to his illustrious critic to ask was it right now? "I should never have thought of that," said Michael. Precisely. When will Mr Chesterton take off his hat to Freud, or, say, to Dr Saleeby (who is very far from being mentally deficient except when the Great Inoculation Swindle is in question) as Michael Angelo took off his hat to the stonemason?

However, in all this I am not conducting my own case: I am holding a brief for Mr Julius West and the Modernists. For my own part I would not have Mr Chesterton other than he is. It is just as important that Mr Chesterton should object to our modern education as that Mr Wells and Mr Bennett should object to our want of it. The knight-errant who turns up everywhere because he has no destination sometimes does more than the man who is too busy to attend to anything or see anybody. And though the knight-errant who seeks for giants and cuts their heads off is out of date, nothing can be more modern than Sir Chesterton of Overroads, who seeks for convictions and turns them inside out. Convictions are prisons, says someone (it sounds like Nietszche), and all that can be said in their defence is that the spirit of man is like steam or petrol vapour: it will not do any work until you put it in a strong prison, even at the risk of its bursting the prison and destroying you. Mr Chesterton's spirit is so extremely explosive that it bursts every strong modern prison; so for the present he uses any old, patched, leaky and elastic gasbag that may be lying ready to his hand on the dustheap of history, and uses it less as a cylinder than as a jester's bladder to belabour painlessly the people he thinks ridiculous and shallow. The result is very entertaining to the bystanders, and often highly suggestive and instructive. The thing is done with a peculiar art which combines the intellectual strategy of Butler: "Be Laodicean: hold your convictions lightly," with an energetic determination to fight for every halfpenny as if it were a million, or, as Shakespear put it, "greatly to find quarrel in a straw." He contrives to be as sympathetic as Hamlet and as rumbustious as Fortinbras at the same time. He neither fights principles nor defends them; but he faces opponents gleefully, and indeed invents them and imposes monstrous opinions and fantastic legends on them for the sake of leading a crusade against them, like Don Quixote with the sheep and the windmills. I love to see quiet Quakers like Mr [Edward] Grubb [1854–1939] and conscientious reasoners like [English economist and social scientist] Mr J[ohn]. A[tkinson]. Hobson [1858–1940] suddenly transmogrified into Judases and Lucifers and Antichrists, and assailed with a thundering charge as of all the hosts of heaven, led by the giant figure of Mr Chesterton, who seems always to leave millions of dead in his ensanguined track as he sweeps on. It is pleasant, too, to hear Mr Grubb and Mr Hobson, neither dismembered nor even dusty, indignantly exclaiming, "What the devil do you mean, Mr Chesterton, by knocking off our hats like that?" This apparent exaggerativeness, however, is not necessarily a defective sense of proportion. An error of a millimetre at the cannon's mouth may mean an error of a mile when the shell explodes; and it is the way of big men to think of the mile rather than of the millimetre, and to swear at the gunner with proportionate vehemence. I must not allow this explanation to reflect on Mr Hobson; for Mr Hobson is generally dead on his target whilst Mr Chesterton, in a magnificent frenzy, is all over the shop. But that is in wartime, when all the imaginative people are in a more or less pathological condition, and will tolerate no aim except at the German target.

I agree very heartily with Mr West as to Mr Chesterton's success in his single essay as a playwright. I shirk the theatre so lazily that I have lost the right to call myself a playgoer; but circumstances led to my seeing *Magic* performed several times, and I enjoyed it more and more every time. Mr Chesterton was born with not only brains enough to see something more in the world than sexual intrigue, but with all the essential tricks of the stage at his fingers' ends; and it was delightful to find that the characters which seem so fantastic and even ragdolly (stage characters are usually wax-dolly) in his romances became credible and solid behind the footlights, just the opposite of what his critics expected. The test is a searching one: an exposure to it of many moving and popular scenes in novels would reveal the fact that they are physically impossible and morally absurd. Mr Chesterton is in the English tradition of Shakespear and Fielding and [Scottish writer Sir Walter] Scott [1771–1832] and Dickens, in which you must grip your character so masterfully that you can play with it in the most extravagant fashion. Until you can present an archbishop wielding a red-hot poker and buttering slides for policemen, and yet becoming more and more essentially archiepiscopal at every roar of laughter, you are not really a master in that tradition. The Duke in *Magic* is much better than Micawber or Mrs Wilfer, neither of whom can bear the footlights because, like piping bullfinches, they have only one tune, whilst the Duke sets everything in the universe to his ridiculous music. That is the Shakespearian touch. Is it grateful to ask for more?

G. B. S.

7. "Old Bachelor Sam Butler," The Observer, 26 March 1950.

[Review of The Essential Sam Butler, *edited by G. D. H. Cole (London: Jonathan Cape, 1950). A few months before his death, Shaw published this book review, which was to be his last. It deals with the personal and the philosophical dimension of Butler's works; an approach that reveals itself as the natural consequence of Shaw's critiquing an author with whom he has much in common in those two spheres.]*

At the beginning of my career, when I was a nobody reviewing books for the old Pall Mall Gazette, now long extinct, I received a book entitled Luck or Cunning, and, on reviewing it at some length, was infuriated when some fool of a subeditor treated the book and its author as of no importance, and cut a great chunk out of it. I learned later on that this truncated article of mine seemed almost epoch making to the author, an old bachelor named Butler living in Clifford's Inn, who, though having won a certain select celebrity by a queer Utopia entitled Erewhon (Nowhere backwards), was carrying on a metabiological crusade against Darwinism which was being ignored by the Press and the biologists of that day to such an extent that he had to publish his polemics at his own expense, always at a loss which made marriage an economic impossibility for him.

As I was then under the same disability myself (I was over forty before I could afford to marry) and completely boycotted as a playwright, I was myself a compulsory bachelor and controversialist *contra mundum.* Moreover, as I was one of the select few who had read Erewhon and swore by it, I was to that extent in Butler's camp.

Exactly when and how I made his acquaintance I do not remember. He was 21 years my senior; and I was married before we met. Among his many oddities, he was a strict monogamist yet by no means a celibate; for he remained faithful to the French lady whom he visited once a fortnight, and was wholly innocent of polygamy.

***

He had never had any literary ambition, though he was a born writer; and this was my own case; for in my boyhood I aspired to be, not a Shakespear, but successively a pirate, an operatic baritone, and above all a Michael Angelo. Butler, too, tried for years to be a painter, just as his fellow student in Heatherley's Art School, [English actor and theater manager Sir Johnston] Forbes Robertson [1853–1937], aspired to be a Titian or a Velasquez, never to be an actor. To this day I have to impress on young would-be authors that the strongest taste for high art does not imply any talent for its practice, and that for a born genius it is as tasteless as water is because it is always in our mouths.

When Butler at last gave up the hope that he could ever be anything more in pictorial art than a mediocre painter aiming at correctness of representation instead of self-expression, he took to composing music in the style of [British composer George Frideric] Handel [1685–1759], collaborating with his friend and biographer [Henry] Festing Jones [1851–1928], a musical barrister of genuine talent who told me that Butler never could manage any tempo more elaborate than two or three crotchets in a bar, and that Beethoven was quite beyond him. So this also was a failure; and Butler, though his simple imitations of Handel might almost pass as uninspired originals, had to become Festing's librettist and supply him with some screamingly funny oratorio texts. He hated his father, Canon Butler, who had "beaten Latin grammar into him line by line," but dared not quarrel with him lest he should be disinherited. He despised his mother because she wheedled confessions from him and then betrayed him to his father and

got him another whipping. He set no store by his sisters because they stood by their father, and did not consider that
Sam got more than he deserved. Canon Butler was a genial
old gaffer out of doors, but at home was tyrant, judge, jury
and executioner all in one. A hydrogen bomb could not have
blasted his reputation more devastatingly after his death than
his undutiful son did with his novel called The Way of All
Flesh. Yet Sam was himself a chip of the old block in controversy. He probably never heard of the priceless precept
of [Welsh social reformer] Robert Owen [1771–1858], "Never
argue: repeat your assertion." Sam certainly repeated his as-
sertions; but he argued endlessly, and always treated his opponents as moral delinquents as well as damned fools.

***

Now all these traits do not suggest a Great Man, nor even an
agreeable one, much less the likeable and considerate friend
my wife and I always found him. Yet Sam was a great man
as great men go. Mr [English economist, historian, and writer
George Douglas Howard] Cole [1889–1958], editor of the book
now under review, holds that as The Way of All Flesh is a
great novel, its author must have been a great man. But some
of its readers think it proves that he was a little man. He
himself put the secret of his greatness into a single sentence
of six words, which he addressed to me as we were crossing
the courtyard of the British Museum together. He said, with
the most intense emphasis, "Darwin banished mind from the
universe." He added, "My grandfather quarrelled with Darwin's grandfather; my father quarrelled with Darwin's father;
I quarrelled with Darwin; and my regret for having no son
is that he cannot quarrel with Darwin's son." As a matter
of fact Darwin had converted Butler for six weeks, because
in those days we clever people who called ourselves Secularists, Freethinkers, Agnostics, Atheists, Positivists, Rational-

ists, or what not, and were classed by the orthodox as Infidels doomed to eternal damnation, were Anti-Clericals snatching at any stick big enough to whack the parsons; and as the biggest stick then was the Natural Selection of Darwin and [British naturalist Alfred Russel] Wallace [1823–1913], carried to absurdity by [German biologist Friedrich Leopold August] Weismann [1834–1914], we all, Butler included, grabbed it and layed on joyously. Butler alone thought it out deeply and quickly enough to grasp the horror of its banishment of mind from the universe.

The ensuing controversies only obscured this fundamental issue. They did not affect me because I had read the [author of the Book of Revelation, John of] Patmos Evangelist's "In the Beginning was the Thought" and come up against the neo-Darwinist shallowness as flatly as [Italian politician Giuseppe] Mazzini [1805–1872] of whom I had never read a word. In my preface to Back to Methuselah I dealt with it, and have neither space nor need to expatiate on it again here. (Darwin, by the way, was no more a Darwinist than I am a Shavian.)

***

I will not pretend to criticise Mr Cole's editing of the selection from Butler's writings of which the book in question consists. To Mr Cole the job is child's play calling for no recommendation from me. That is why I tell my own tale at first hand. However, may I suggest that Butler should be classed in the roll of fame neither as novelist nor biologist but as metabiologist, just as we class [German philosopher Georg Wilhelm Friedrich] Hegel [1770–1831] not as physician but as metaphysician. This perhaps is because I call myself a metabiologist, and was the first, as far as I know, to bring that necessary term into the vocabulary.

I must also warn readers that Butler's guess that the author of the Odyssey was a woman is not an Erewhonian joke, and that it is now impossible to read it again without being at least half convinced that he was as right as Dickens was about George Eliot [Mary Ann Evans, 1819–1880].

Part III: Poetry and Fine Arts

The countless hours Shaw spent at the National Gallery of Ireland in his youth, and the reading room of the British Museum in his early years in London—not to mention the endless reading sessions of his boyhood "with the mighty dead"—made him acquainted with the work of a motley corpus of artists and authors. Even though his artistic education was, in this sense, impressionistic and eclectic, Shaw's "power of accurate observation" made him an insightful critic of all sorts of artistic expressions.

1. "Recent Poetry," *To-Day* (2), August 1884.

[Review of a group of books in verse, namely Amy Levy's A Minor Poet, and other Verse (London: T. Fisher Unwin, 1884), Pakenham Beatty's Marcia. A Tragedy (London: Hamilton, Adams, 1884), Ernest Radford's Measured Steps (London: T. Fisher Unwin, 1884), and Michael Field's Callirhoe: Fair Rosamund (London: Bell & Sons, 1884). The references, intertextual links, and other subtleties that Shaw makes use of to expose the creative powers of these four poets are just as edifying and enjoyable as the books themselves. It would perhaps be fair to note that Shaw wrote little poetry, some of which was just spuriously attributed to him, and that it was all the better for the history of literature that he took up drama in the end. Much of Shaw's knowledge of literature can be ascertained by exploring the connections he establishes with other poets.]

I have often wondered why [English poet and civil servant John] Milton [1608–1674] wrote *Paradise Lost*. Perhaps he could not help it. In that case there is nothing more to be said on the subject. Perhaps he thought that it would gratify his fellow-creatures. If so, I think he was wrong; for the humiliation of the literate but lazy persons who are ashamed of not having read his work, and the fatigue of the more resolute who have read it from a sense of duty, and disliked it, probably outweigh the pleasures of those who have relished it. Perhaps he thought he had something to tell which a few people would be the better for hearing. I am not in a position to deny that he had; although it remains to be considered whether the something might not have been put more briefly. But on the whole I do not think that Milton ever raised that question betwixt himself and his genius, because nothing had really occurred, from the time of Eschylus to that of Spenser, to discredit great poems as things admirable and desirable for their own sakes. Nor do the authors of the four books cited above, although their Muses are frequently low-spirited, seem to have been troubled with doubts any more than Milton was. They must have known, as Milton knew, that the faculty of writing a good poem cannot be acquired, and that the chances are a million to one against its existence in any particular individual. For venturing at these heavy odds they deserve some gratitude, which might perhaps be more practically expressed by leaving Milton out of the question in dealing with their works.

The chief piece in Miss [English poet and fiction writer Amy] Levy's [1861–1889] volume is *Medea;* but that title having been anticipated by Euripides, she has put *A Minor Poet* in the place of honour. A Minor Poet is, presumably, one whose verse falls short, not only of Shakspere's and Shelley's, but of average excellence, just as a short man is not one who fails to attain gigantic stature, but one who is beneath the medium height. In the absence of any means of determining average excellence in an art which eludes analysis, I shall not now commit myself to any distinction between major and minor poets. I have an impression, nevertheless, that the great poets deal honestly with us by giving us their experiences rather than their fancies, and affect us by the irony—tragical or farcical, as may happen—of the contrast between the two. Minor poets, on the contrary, finding their experiences uninteresting because they have not much capacity for experience, give us their fancies exclusively. As the combinations and permutations of experience are inexhaustible, great poets, reproducing their experience, are original and interesting. And as the fancies of any two or two hundred imaginative people are as like as eggs, minor poets, reproducing their fancies, are common-place and dull. Miss Levy's minor poet, for example, has failed to persuade anyone to believe in him. Feeling out of sorts because he is not quite all that he ignorantly wishes to be, he demands whether mortal or divine brain ever devised a Hell more fraught with torment than the world for such as he. Tom Leigh, his friend, described as a philosopher, but evidently a twaddling imposter, replies with "neatest, newest phrases, freshly culled from works of newest culture." These fail to relieve the overcharged heart of the minor poet. He bids farewell to his books, to "lofty Shakspeare with the tattered leaves and fathomless great heart," to Goethe, with "triumphant smile, tragic eyes, and pitiless world-wisdom," and to "one wild singer of to-day, whose song is all aflame with passionate bard's blood lash'd into foam by pain and the world's wrong." As this wild singer is unnamed, [Anglo-Irish poet] Mr Pakenham [Thomas] Beatty [1855–1930], [English poet and critic] Mr Ernest [William] Radford [1857–1919], and the author of *Callirhoe* are all in a position to draw the most flattering conclusions from the passage. Finally, the poet comes to the usual intolerable intimation that "there was a woman once," after which he wisely poisons himself. All this is told in Browningesque blank verse with an intelligence and taste which are in direct contrast to the common-place worthlessness of the subject. Curiously enough, on page 4 of the poem occurs a passage in which the writer comes within an ace of the truth, apparently not yet familiar to her, that we are so strongly affected by our mere fancies that the rudest criticism can hardly convince us that they are stale and uninteresting to others. The mock-tragic note of *A Minor Poet* runs through all the other poems, though it is occasionally made acceptable by description and versification which are throughout superior to the conceptions to which they are applied. Some of the smaller poems in the book deserve nothing but praise; and even when the immaturity of the writer is most evident, she is, for the moment at least, quite sincere. In *Xantippe*, which is good enough to suggest comparisons which it can hardly sustain, occur the following lines:—

Then, as all youthful spirits are, was I.
Wholly incredulous that Nature meant
So little, who had promised me so much.

I hope to find, in some future poem of Miss Levy's, a heroine incredulous that Nature means so much though she
seems—in our Minor Poet stage—to promise so little.

Mr Pakenham Beatty is an old offender in the jurisdiction
of critics of poetry. Fortunate are the poets or patriots whom
he admires; for they are certain of a sonnet, or at least a dedi-
cation, describing them in terms by comparison to which the
Psalmist's praises of Jehovah are tame and qualified. Mazzini, [Italian general and politician Giuseppe] Garibaldi
[1807–1882], and "Orion" [English poet Richard Hengist]
Horne [1802–1884], have passed out of reach of his hyperbole;
but [French poet, novelist, and dramatist] Victor Hugo
[1802–1885], Mr [English writer and critic Algernon Charles]
Swinburne [1837–1909], and several less known gentlemen
who apparently enjoy Mr Beatty's private acquaintanceship,
must find considerable difficulty in fulfilling the expectations
which his references to them are calculated to raise. He has
enthusiasm enough for four poets, and discrimination
enough for rather less than one. He does not take up his subjects by halves. His erotic poems, published in 1879, though
free from coarseness and from the ineptitudes of most first
essays in poetry, breathed infatuation rather than love. Two
years later, in a transport of revolutionary fury, he issued a
collection of poems in which his indignation at the tyranny
of [President, and later Emperor of France] Napoleon III
[1808–1873], revived after a lapse of ten years by the persecution of the Nihilists in Russia under the administration
of [Count Mikhail Tarielovich] Loris Melikoff [1826–1888],
found vent in language of such astonishing rancour, that the
unlucky editor of the Freiheit, then in prison for suggesting
measures for which Mr Beatty positively clamoured, must

have felt the truth of the proverb that one man may steal a horse where another may not look over a hedge. Since then, Mr Beatty's feelings on the state of affairs in Russia, far from having cooled, have led him to write a drama entitled *Marcia,* which issued from the press in June of the present year. Marcia is a Pole, and mistress of the Czar of Russia, whom the poet, possibly from a desire to spare the feelings of his original as far as possible, denominates "The Tyrant" without further particularization. She has gained the privilege of releasing at her discretion one of a batch of her countrymen who are on their way to Siberia. The forethought with which she exercises this dispensing power is apparent from her remark to an old man that the remainder of his life is not worth saving, and that his daughter does not look as if she should live much longer than he. Eventually she releases Michael Stolskoi, a poet, who repays her by an impressive lecture upon the infamy of her behaviour. She falls in love with him; and he, though coy at first, soon returns her affection. The Czar discovers this, and Stolskoi is arrested and tried with three confederates, one of whom an Englishman, has the impudence to boast, with reference to India, that

> The indignant spirit of an Englishman
> Chafes at the fetters on another's limbs,
> And freedom finds a champion of her cause
> Where'er her swords strike or her banners wave.

They are condemned to death. Marcia, however, obtains access to Stolskoi's cell with a pistol and some poison. The lovers drink the poison, and, on the Czar entering to superintend the execution personally, Stolskoi shoots him and expires. The story is not in any way founded on facts. The materialist conspirators of real Russia, plotting against a bigoted despot who is but the figure-head of a corrupt bureaucracy, are misrepresented in Mr Beatty's imagination by pious victims appealing to heaven against a godless autocrat whose malicious disposition has made his people miserable, who gloats over instruments of torture, and who has state criminals hanged with a frayed rope, which breaks, and so prolongs their agony. The scenes between Michael and Marcia are the best in the play, and compel a measure of respect for the author's powers in spite of the commonplace fiction with which he has replaced the tragic truth of Russian history in 1880. Soberer than his *Three Women of the People*, and more mature than his early love poems, "Marcia" is an advance on both.

> I would be with the workers in the van
> For somehow, somewhere, rises godlike Man

says Mr Beatty on the title page of *Three Women of the People*, quoting the late [British poet] Arthur [William Edgar] O'Shaughnessy [1844–1881]. It may be worth while to suggest to him, and to all enthusiasts for liberty and progress, that the claims of collective Socialism to be the somehow and of the ranks of the Democratic Federation to be the somewhere, are worthy of consideration in view of the general paucity of results from the publication of fervid verse.

Mr Ernest Radford is too shrewd, and has too keen a sense of the ridiculous, to disregard common sense and polite taste so outrageously as Mr Beatty, in his wilder moments, has done. He is a critic, and knows how to refine his verse. He is also a humourist, and can, on occasion, help himself across the shallows of inspiration by sportive essays in the vein of the late [English poet] Mr [Charles Stuart] Calverley [1831–1884]. Sometimes, indeed, the humourist gets the better (or the worse) of both critic and poet. Mr Radford is not very industrious, apparently. His *Measured Steps* are short and do not carry him very far: *Fits and Starts*, as he calls his humorous pieces, are more fitful than startling. Out of twenty-seven of the former, ten were published at Cambridge in 1882; and five out of the twenty jocular trifles are also reprints, whilst eight of the new ones are astonishing attempts to impart a sane aspect to the repetitions of the triolet by taking familiar street cries for the recurring lines, and intercalating them with bitter asides. The remainder of the volume consists of translations from [German poet and critic Christian Johann Heinrich] Heine [1797–1856]. The *Measured Steps* are so good as far as they go that it is difficult to account for the feeling of dissatisfaction which some of them leave. In two trivial verselets, *Christmas at Plymouth,* Mr Radford complains that he is "sad and seedy." And his pathos does not at any place suggest deeper tragedy than this. Even at his saddest and seediest, he tacitly refuses to be serious, having apparently no settled convictions, and too much sincerity to excite himself without conviction. The comparative infertility of his Muse may be due to his labour as an art-critic, or to his fastidiousness in selecting poems for publication; but her egotistical disregard of any wider feelings than the vague regrets and undefined aspirations of the sad and seedy Individual is less excusable.

"Michael Field," [pseudonym used by Katharine Harris Bradley (1846–1914) and her niece Edith Emma Cooper (1862–1913)] the author of *Callirhöe* and *Fair Rosamund* is a woman who, following the example of [English novelist and poet] Charlotte Brontë [*sic*; 1816–1855] and George Eliot, pays the other sex the compliment of attempting to pass as a member of it. Why this senseless mystification should be dealt with more tenderly than any other species of fraud probably does not now appear plainly to the generous critic who, in the *Spectator,* announced as a great poet the author who was unprovokedly duping him by a misleading title page. In *Callirhöe,* however, the relations between the heroine and the priest Coresus are such as women invent for themselves with delight, whereas nothing analogous to them is to be found in the work of any virile poet. It has been stated on several hands—and certain expressions in the drama and preface seem to countenance the opinion—that the moral of Callirhöe is that people should be enthusiastic. With all my kindly feeling towards the Californian parson who, whether swearing, praying, or gambling, "done it with a zest," a cultus of pure enthusiasm seems to me so preposterous that I cannot believe that Michael Field really means it; nor is it made attractive by the Mænads of the drama, drunken furies whose tie to the altar of Bacchus is their jealous love of his priest. The scene is Calydon. The classical and the romantic—the respectable and the Bohemian—patience and impulse, are at war there as usual. Coresus, the priest of Bacchus, attempts to convert Callirhöe. His motives being obviously personal, she repels him; and he, irritated by the rebuff, calls upon his god to smite Calydon with a plague. This extraordinarily unreasonable demand being complied with (a circumstance which surely does not place the god of enthusiasm in a favourable light), the oracle is consulted by the citizens. The reply is that Callirhöe has offended the gods, and must either die or find a substitute willing to die for her. Coresus leads her to the sacrificial altar, but stabs himself. The plague is stayed; and Callirhöe, struck by the conduct of Coresus, embraces his faith, and enthusiastically commits suicide. The most remarkable character is her brother Emathion, a champion athlete, but a hopeless cur. He it is who is sent, because of his fleetness of foot, to consult the oracle. At the sacred grove he inspires passion in an old pythoness; and the scene in which the wind rises in the grove until the oracle is delivered, he almost beside himself with terror at the supernatural tempest and with loathing at the proffered caresses of the decrepit priestess, is so brutally grotesque, and at the same time so terrible and pitiful, that it is hard to decide whether it is above criticism or beneath it. Whichever it be, the drama is worth reading for its sake. Squeamish readers will be shocked by the tragi-comic old woman, in whose mouth a single tooth appears like a stalagmite in a vast cavern, and from whose peaky nose hangs "a drop." But squeamish readers will not take kindly to so vigorous and frank a writer as Michael Field, who, if she has not yet the originality of a mature poet, has a large share in the freshness of a young one. *Callirhöe*, however, is admirable only for the sake of such episodes as that cited above, and for a charming scene in which a Faun, like [Italian dancer Maria] Taglioni [1804–1884] in *La Sylphide*, or [Belgian soprano Marie] Cabel [1827–1885] in *Dinorah*, dances to his own shadow. As an organic whole it comes to nothing. Machaon, a physician who takes a common-sense and somewhat sceptical view of the proceedings, and who sees, one would think, enough of the cultus of enthusiasm to prejudice him against it for the rest of his life, becomes its high priest in the last act on grounds which he fails to make clear. A cultus of pure enthusiasm is perhaps not unlikely to lead to a practice of pure inconsistency, or, as the modern American calls it, pure cussedness; but unfortunately for the dramatic effect, Machaon seems the last man in the antique world to give way to cussedness in the presence of an impressive national calamity, and a touching domestic tragedy.

In *Fair Rosamund*, Michael Field reminds us, not for the first time, of Charlotte Bronté [*sic*], by the force of her execution, and by her entire want of sympathy with the evil personages she portrays. The old knight, Sir Topaz, seems to be the result of an attempt to create an interesting character out of a passing fancy without any substantial materials. The atmosphere of *Fair Rosamund* is Gothic, as that of *Callirhöe* is Greek, each play being as fresh after the other as if they were from different hands, although the individuality of the author asserts itself with equal force in both.

L. O. STREETER [*Probably means "Lives on Onsaburgh Street."*]

2. "Poet's Corner," *The Pall Mall Gazette*, 25 June 1887.

[Review of Robert Bird's Law Lyrics, 2nd ed. (Paisley and London: A. Gardner, 1887), James Williams's A Lawyer's Leisure (London: Kegan Paul, Trench, and Co. 1887), William Stewart Ross's "Isaure" and other Poems (London: W. Stewart and Co., 1887), Edwin Drew's Reciting and Reading: Studies of Poems (London: Wyman and Sons, 1887), John Farrell's "How he Died" and other Poems (Sydney: Turner and Henderson, 1887), Laura Ormiston Chant's "Verona" and other Poems (London: David Stott, 1887), Robert Brown's "A Trilogy of the Life to Come," and other Poems (London: D. Nutt, 1887), and D. Paterson's The Sad Story of John Dalrymple (Glasgow: Gillespie Brothers, 1887). Shaw's quick turn of phrase and witty style befitted these poetry reviews that usually had to cover a large batch of books in a relatively short text.]

The modest author of "Law Lyrics" does not disclose his name [actually the work of Scottish poet Robert Bird, 1854–?]. He is a follower of [Scottish Poet] Robert Burns [1759–1796], and finds in the court and in the Temple an inspiration which the great Scotch poet found in the fields of Ayrshire. He rhymes with remarkable spirit and freedom, making his verse ring with such happy echoes as "chancellor" and "answer for," "interlocutor," and "shock you for," "judges go," and "grudges so," &c. Should a blackbird come across the little volume, he will be pleased to find himself described as "the coal black singer of the crocus bill."

[English lawyer and writer] Mr James Williams [1851–1911] puts himself out of court by confessing that his harmless and sometimes graceful lines are the outcome of "A Lawyer's Leisure." Valuable verse is the outcome of a poet's hard work and not of anybody's leisure—even a lawyer's.

"Isaure, and other Poems," are inspired by an imagination so vivid and strenuous, and so unrestrained by common intelligence, that they are really not safe to read suddenly or in large instalments. Here is the cry of the jilted lover in "Mabel":

> More love in my little finger,
> More brain in my topmost hair,
> Than blessed the tout ensemble
> Of Lord Fitzdoodle's heir.
> And I was so near to the winning,
> Till came the auriferous spell,
> And the foot of the mamma sent me spinning
> From the apex of heaven to hell.

This, however, gives no idea of the extraordinary impetuosity of [Scottish author William] Mr Stewart Ross's [1844–1906] versification or his singular choice of words. "Black was the sea and gurly, beneath the rolling stars," almost suggests [English writer and mathematician] Mr Lewis Carroll [pen name of Charles Lutwidge Dodgson, 1832–1898]. The following, from "Leonore: a Lay of Dipsomania," somehow strikes the reader specially:

> "Blue devils and insane," they said;
> And men for me a jacket made
> And built a padded room.
> It holds me not, nor earth nor air,
> For, gods and demons, I am there!
> There! by that open tomb.

[English elocutionist and author] Mr Edwin Drew [n.d.] introduces his little book of poems and sketches with the remark that "here and there, perhaps, you may come across a gleam of intelligence." This is certainly modest; and it must be acknowledged, in justice to Mr Drew, that such gleams do actually occur more than once in his pages. He writes with a consistent purpose, mentioning his name and address frequently for the sake of elocutionists who may desire to seek instruction from him or recite his verses. His skill as a critic may be estimated by his judgment of Macaulay. "Lord Macaulay was a man whom I have always regarded with profound admiration. He expressed some extraordinary opinions on men and manners." "Composers," says Mr Drew again, "occasionally favour me by asking me to write lines for them. When I am asked I never can. If I ever have a thought worth attention it is when I am not thinking." In view of this explanation, it may be said that these studies are evidently the result of hard and persistent thinking on Mr Drew's part. His poems include "The Dumb Countess" and "Blood-tub Bill"; and the opening stanza of the latter is a fair sample of what Mr Drew's muse can do:

> If ever villany proclaimed
> Itself on any face
> It was on his, and virtue seemed
> Without the smallest trace.
> A robber and a murderer
> The horrid Blood-tub Bill,
> Who seemed to walk God's earth that he
> Might work the devil's will.

Take an imaginative bushranger; fire his ambition with a copy of the works of [American poet Francis] Bret Harte [1836–1902]; tone him up [or down, according to your point of view] with a stray volume of Mr Robert Browning; polish him in the school of [Scottish poet and playwright] James Thomson [1700–1748]; and [Australian journalist and poet] Mr John Farrell [1851–1904], of Sydney, will have a rival. He handles his lines with some rough force, occasionally showing both humour and eloquence; but the morality of his tales smacks of that taste for indignation meetings and lynching so strongly developed in our pioneers of civilization. It springs, no doubt, from a hatred of evil; but the love of good which might be expected at the root of it is frequently obscured by an addiction to whisky drinking, summary pistolling, profanity, and horseplay; and it suggests the reflection that where Justice is least popular she finds most bloodhounds to help her when she goes a-hunting. Irrational ethics and somewhat sanguinary sentimentality apart, Mr Farrell's undeniably striking work has considerable interest and merit.

A lady so altruistic, so enthusiastic, so facile in utterance, and so sensitive as [English composer and writer Laura] Mrs Ormiston Chant [1848–1923] naturally writes poems. In doing so she shows her faults and her qualities with a rapt unconsciousness. At her worst, she is excessively sentimental, and sometimes writes very bad verse. At her best she is, to use a phrase of her own, "trembling with music," intensely earnest, and happily and nobly inspired. Some of the shorter poems, such as "Finding Love," are memorable expressions of some of the most deeply felt truths of common experience.

[English lawyer, politician, and author] Mr Robert Brown [Jr., 1844–?] is a learned man and an inveterate rhymester, full of scholarly conceits and glittering fancies; but he is only a poet insofar as all men, like Silas Wegg, drop into poetry occasionally. When he "sat beside the margin of the gently swelling deep ere yet the brightest star of heaven had passed the western steep," he moralized thus:

Q.—What is Eternity? A.—Myself. Q.—What am I?
   A.—Progress. Then
Eternity is but the change upon immortal men.
Perfection is a flight of steps half-hidden by God's throne,
Yet all His myriad creatures forever climb thereon.

Mr Brown ought to know that he cannot preserve the reverence of the reader's imagination while presenting it with such a slippery image as that of a throne on a flight of steps. No man who has ever helped to get a cottage pianoforte upstairs can read such a line in the spirit of the author. In the "Trilogy of the Life to Come" there are some attractive passages; but the reader is too often tripped up by perversely ingenious rhymes, or by such cockneyisms as—

> Our fragile nature, overcome with awe,
> Fell at his feet, and I beheld no more.

"John Dalrymple," having many obvious rhymes, is a good name for the hero of a satiric narrative in as much of the metre and manner of Don Juan as Mr [D.] Paterson [likely to be the pseudonym of an unidentified author] can attain to. Mr Paterson is, it appears, a man of business to whom the depression of trade has given a leisure which he makes elegant by essays in verse. They show some wit; but they are difficult of scansion. For example—

> Look at Russia now! Look at Afghanistan!
> That even got the back up of old Gladstone—

is surely a little infelicitous. Nor in the following couplet does the force of the political criticism quite conceal the imperfection of the rhyme:

> "The Grand Old Man! You mean the Grand Old Ass!"
> His guest retorted. Rennie stared aghast.

3. "Some Small Poetry of 1887," *The Pall Mall Gazette*, 27 December 1887.

[*Review of* V.R. and I., 1837–1887, Jubilee Odes, *by* G. Gravener Shrewsbury *(Harrison and Sons, 1887);* A Song of Love and Liberty, or Fifty Golden Years, *by* G. H. Addy *(Field and Tuer, 1887);* A Song of Jubilee and other Poems, *by Mrs R. S. de Courcy Laffan (Kegan Paul, 1887);* Westminster, Past and Present, *by J. Cave Winscombe (W. H. Allen and Co., 1887);* Somnia Medici *(third series), by John A. Goodchild (Kegan Paul, 1887);* Albynne, a Dramatic Medley, *by Esca (W. H. Beer and Co., 1887);* Minora Carmina, *by C.C.Rhys (Swan Sonnenschein, 1887);* Actæon, *by M. B. Williams (The Author, at 15, Bernard-street, W. C., 1887);* The Modern Faustus, an Agnostic Allegory *(London Literary Society, 1887);* Edward the Black Prince, *by Douglas Sladen (Griffith and Ferran, 1887);* Legends and Records of the Church and the Empire, *by Aubrey de Vere (Kegan Paul and Co., 1887);* The Cid Ballads, *translated by the late James Young Gibson,* 2 *vols. (Kegan Paul and Co., 1887);* The Castle of Knaresburgh, *by Richard Abbay, M.A., F.R.A.S. (Kegan Paul and Co., 1887);* The Poems of Giacomo Leopardi, *translated by Frederick Townsend (New York and London: C. P. Putnam's Sons, 1887);* Somnia, *by G. Gladstone Turner (Longmans and Co., 1887);* Sketches in Song, *by G. Lansing Raymond (New York and London: G. P. Putnam's Sons, 1887);* Lower Merion Lilies and other Poems, *by Margaret B. Harvey (Philadelphia: Lippincott Company, 1887);* Echoes of the Anvil, *by William Wilson (Edinburgh and Glasgow: J. Menzies and Co., 1886);* Three Little Emigrants, *by Sarah Morgan Bryan . Piatt (Elliot Stock, 1887);* Lays of the Seaside, *by Aliph Cheem (Army and Navy Stores, 1887);* Who wrote Shakespeare? "Ay, There's the Rub," *by William Henderson (David Stott, 1887); and* Victorian Hymns: English Sacred Songs of Fifty Years *(Kegan Paul and Co., 1887). As usual with many of the collections of poems that Shaw reviewed in his lifetime, some of the authors have not been identified—many of them having written only the book Shaw examined. Several of the poets wrote pieces to commemorate Queen Victoria's Golden Jubilee, celebrated on June 20–21, 1887. It is interesting to note how superficial Shaw's remarks must be—given the number of books to be reviewed and the space allowed in the magazine—which hints at a type of appraisal that would perhaps direct potential readers to poetry of their liking by virtue of impressionistic remarks on theme, tenor, and verse form, for example.]*

England is famous among nations for her poetry. Here are twenty-two volumes of it. Heigho!

First, seven Jubilee poets, knowing nothing, or thereabouts, of the history of the reign, the geography of the Empire, or the personal characteristics of our Royal family, yet loyally ready, like Mr Wemmick's witnesses (or Mr Poland's) to "swear, in a general way, to anything" courtly on these subjects, Jubilee, Liberty, Hail to Thee, Queen of the Sea, and so on. Also, in bolder, less fastidiously correct rhyme, "From age to age, from clime to clime, Rings out the song that is divine;" and, "As o'er the blue dark heaving main, Our sailors true shall bless thy name." [unidentified author] Mr [John Cave] Winscombe, a Unionist, varies his blank verse by a dashing slap at "the brainless logic of the massive brain" of Mr Gladstone. Dr [John Arthur] Goodchild [1851–?] prefaces his third series of *Somnia Medici* with the remark, founded apparently on [Irish Archbishop and scholar James] Ussher's [1581–1656] chronology, that "there be fifty brother eras in the story of mankind" —

> But of all the fifty brothers in the long historic list
> One shall live beyond the others as the Nineteenth after Christ.

"My mind," says [pseudonym for unidentified author] "Esca," in *Albynne, a Dramatic Medley*, "is all a blank except in one thing; and would that were a blank!" If the one thing is blank verse, then, in all sincerity, would it were! [English poet] C. C. R[hys]'s "trivial verses" are no more than they profess to be; but they jingle prettily, and the Jubilee is kept within the bounds of a single page.

Actæon, by M. B. Williams [unidentified poet], has that in it which gives the critic pause. M. B. Williams, who is evidently in his nonage, has read Shelley's "Alastor" and been hard hit by it; and has unsophisticatedly handed his poem in manuscript to a printer and received it back in the shape of a little book without a publisher's name, bearing heavy marks of the free hand allowed by the author to the compositor. Young gentlemen who do this sort of thing are not lightly to be encouraged; and perhaps Mr Williams has already found out that *Actæon* is an immature effort. But it certainly reads as if the author had material for poetry somewhere about him.

The Modern Faustus, an Agnostic Allegory, is no improvement on the established Faustuses, being so extremely agnostic that no one will be the wiser for reading it. The labour of finding this out is enlivened by some passable verse, and an amusing doggerel lecture on evolution. Less abstract but more readable is [English poet and academic] Mr Douglas B[rooke]. W[heelton]. Sladen's [1856–1947] *Edward the Black Prince*, a successful modern example of the old-fashioned stage "history" in blank verse. [Irish poet and critic] Mr Aubrey [Thomas] de Vere's [1814–1902] *Legends and Records of the Church and the Empire* will, even to those who cannot accept the author's philosophy of history, be acceptable as old stories of saints and martyrs finely told in verse of considerable beauty. Old stories of another sort are to hand in the *Cid Ballads*, translated by the late [Scottish translator] James Young Gibson [1826–1886], with whom the lays of Spanish chivalry were a hobby. His two volumes are capital reading for boys. Fully-grown minds are also, alas! no more able to stand the Cid nowadays than Darwin could stand Shakspeare. Young readers will also enjoy [Reverend] Mr Richard

Abbay's [1844–1924] "Castle of Knaresburgh," a metrical account of the relief of York by Prince Rupert [of the Rhine, 1619–1682], and the battle of Marston Moor. In style it is a frankly slavish imitation of Scott, as "The White Mare of Whitestonecliff," which follows it, is of [English humorous poet Richard Harris, whose pen name was] Ingoldsby Barham [1788–1845].

[Italian poet and essayist Giacomo] Leopardi [1798–1837], who died fifty years ago at the age of thirty-nine, was too weak a man to make the sort of reputation that passes frontiers. He was romantically patriotic; and his own circumstances and those of Italy were unhappy enough to tune his harp to notes of woe. The graceful translation of his poems made by [unidentified American translator] Mr Frederick Townsend of New York will serve English readers who may be curious as to the nature and limits of Leopardi's genius. [English poet] Mr G[eorge]. Gladstone Turner [n.d.] shows some boldness in calling his little volumes of verse by such titles as *Errata*, and *Somnia*; but his confidence shall not be abused here by remarks to the effect that his books are aptly named. The only poem in *Somnia* which seems to have had its impulse from real life is "Society," in which Mr Turner expresses an opinion that if Divorce Court circles do not mend their morals somebody will have to be lynched. [American poet and critic George] Mr Lansing Raymond [1839–1929], an American writer, is more alert than Mr Turner: he looks about him and rhymes on this or that more or less happily and by no means profoundly. From the West, too, hails [American poet] Margaret B[oyle]. Harvey [?–1912], author of "Lower Merion Lilies" and other poems. In them there is the unmistakable music and feeling of genuine poetry, with that pleasant strain of the best side of Puritanism, characteristic of the women poets of America.

[Scottish author] Mr William Wilson [1830–?], professional blacksmith and amateur poet, may safely challenge the whole

Savile Club to knock off occasional verses that ring like his or have as much stuff in them. The illustrations to his volume, by Thomas Wilson, are of considerable merit. Of quite different texture are the "child's world ballads" of [Amercian poet] Sarah M[organ]. B[ryan]. Piatt [1836–1919], of whom the *St James's Gazette* once neatly confessed that it found "that Mrs Piatt's Muse is the Muse of the American girl." Aliph Cheem's [pen name of Captain Walter Yeldham, 1837–?] *Lays of the Seaside* are grown-up-and-not-too-intelligent-child's-world ballads. They are comic enough to set an indulgent messroom in a roar, and to stir up all the latent malice in the critic to whom they are seriously submitted. [Scottish printer and poet] Mr William Henderson [1831–1891], in his *Who Wrote Shakspere?* also seems bent on mild jocularity.

Finally, the subject of the Jubilee is brought back by Messrs Kegan Paul's volume, bound in plain white buckram with gold lettering, entitled *Victorian Hymns*, and containing some of the most sincere expressions of pious mood from [English poet] Matthew Arnold [1822–1888], [English poet] Alfred [Lord] Tennyson [1809–1892], [English novelist and poet] Anne Brontë [1820–1849], [English poet] Christina Rossetti [1830–1894], and [English poet] Adelaide [Anne] Procter [1825–1864], besides the expected selection from [John] Keble [1792–1866], [Horatius] Bonar [1808–1889], [Frederick William] Faber [1814–1863], and other hymn writers. The gems of the collection are Tennyson's "Strong Son of God, immortal Love;" Christina Rossetti's exquisite "I would have gone: God bade me stay" from *Goblin Market*; and Anne Brontë's "My God, O let me call Thee mine," with its touching third verse,

> I cannot say my faith is strong
> I dare not hope my love is great,
> But strength and love to Thee belong,
> O do not leave me desolate!

4. "Some Poets," *The Pall Mall Gazette*, 13 October 1888.

[Review of The Pageant of Life, *by George Barlow (London: Swan Sonnenschein and Co., 1888); A Lay of Two Cities, by Jesharelah (London: Passmore and Alabaster, 1888); Dorica, by E. D. S. (London: Regan Paul and Co., 1888); Southern Songs, by D. C. F. Moodie (Cape Town: J. C. Juta and Co., 1887); Perla, by E. W. Bewley (London: Wyman and Sons, 1888); Darkness and Light, by Noel Vandal (London: Swan Sonnenschein and Co., 1888); Woodland and Dreamland, by Rowe Lingston (London: Griffith, Farran, and Co., 1888); and My Jewels, selected by Rowland Hill (London: Williams and Norgate, 1888). Shaw is careful to separate unoriginal ideas in two categories: the trite, and the traditional—but even the traditional becomes trite if one tries to appropriate it.]*

[English poet and librettist] Mr George Barlow [1847–1913] is to be congratulated on having produced a good fat epic in five books without the strain and travail which drove Carlyle to declare that no man can write a book without making himself ill. If the author of *The Pageant of Life* is not in robust health it is certainly not the fault of his work, which is obviously a collection of occasional poems, parcelled into "books" and supplemented with an epic framework and a preface. Thus Mr Barlow has done for himself what time and tradition are supposed by some to have done for Homer. What he has done for others may be summed up as the provision of a sort of metrical commonplace book for persons who are not commonplace. For example, when once the commonplace idea of Christ's divinity is rejected, it becomes a commonplace to say with Mr Barlow:

> My Christ is the Christ of Shelley and Hugo, not the Christ
> of St Augustine or of Dr Manning; the Christ who in the cen-

turies to come will gain inconceivably more (both as a grand poetic figure and as an object of religious veneration) from the right apprehension of his manhood than he has gained (or shall we not rather say lost?) during the centuries that are past through the mistaken theory of his Godhead; the Christ who was loved by the men and women who were his companions, with honest, warm, human love, and never approached by them in the Christian Church's subsequent attitude of cringing awe and superstition.

Again, when one gets advanced views on the woman question, it becomes a commonplace to sing:

All have praised our lips and tresses,
Golden locks or black:
All have sought our love-caresses
All have held us back.
All have checked our souls' aspiring
All have dreaded this.
This has tired men, never tiring
Of the lips they kiss.
All have dreaded lest the morning
Which should find us free
Would be wild with note of warning
Rung by land and sea!
Not one noble soul has trusted;
Roman, Jew, or Greek.
Many and many a sword had rusted
Had they let us speak!

Here is a stanza from the section entitled "Chant of Positivists":

Man first made God, but now retakes
The sceptre from God's hand,—unmakes
What once with fiery thought he made.

God is a dream of mankind's brain
But man dethrones God; man must reign;
Not God, but man must be obeyed.

This would be quite a coruscation if emitted by an Evangelical grocer: from a Positivist it is a mere platitude. Further on comes a stanza which would be a platitude even from the grocer:

And woman too is left to love:
She brings us dreams of things above
The common daily life she scorns.
Woman makes all things beautiful;
For from the hedge her hand can pull
The blossoming rose, and leave the thorns.

Here is a sample of Mr Barlow's energetic style:

I mass my conscripts drawn from strange far regions;
I range my squadrons on time's boundless plain;
I hurl the force of my imperial legions
Against thee, Death, again and yet again.

It will be seen that Mr Barlow is no ridiculous poetaster. He is, in fact, a man of ideas, a propagandist, up to the latest move in Materialistic pessimism and sentimental optimism. The more benighted section of the community will be roused and refreshed by his numbers. And as Mr Barlow comes to call, not the righteous, but sinners, to repentance, he will probably not mind our venturing to remark that those who know beforehand what his book contains will find nothing new in it.

Jesharelah [pseudonym for unidentified author], author of *A Lay of Two Cities*, writes of the typical Babylon and Jerusalem with a naive piety which contrasts as strongly with Mr Barlow's strenuous freethinking as with the library "culture" of [English scholar and poet Reverend] E[dward]. D[aniel]. S[tone]. [1832–1916], who sings ho! the daffodil and other matters in that strain of vapid quaintness and correct sprightliness which we at once associate with a bookish turn, a university education, and an independent income.

From Cape Town comes the third edition of [South African poet] D[uncan]. C[ampbell]. F[rancis]. Moodie's [1838–1891] *Southern Songs*. No words can express the wild hope with which the reviewer emphasizes the fact that there is a remote colony in which minor poetry runs through three editions. Here is a sample of D. C. E M.'s lighter manner:

> The Zebras bound o'er shaking ground in many a wild
> stampedo;
> The Blesbok too, and sportive Gnu, make noise as much as they
> do.

The serious style is less difficult to manage:

> Lo! where on Erin's land gaunt Famine stalks,
> And thro' each stricken household grimly walks—
> See the poor mother with her ghastly child,
> In her bare home that once with plenty smiled—
> Some chance has blown a morsel near her door.
> She strives to reach it—struggling o'er the floor.
> In vain, alas! the enfeebled limbs decline;
> Death rattles in her throat—she falls supine—
> And the poor child, with Famine's silent stare,
> Falls down and dies where now no men appear.

The following impressive description of a waterfall is from [English poet] Mr Edward White Bewley's [1830–1919] *Perla: a Legend of Tequendama*:

> GRAND TEQUENDAMA FALL. At birth the leap
> It took o'er rock six hundred feet was deep;

> And there it has leaped roaring ever since
> Nor sign of failing years does it evince.

This passage, however, does not do justice to the elasticity of Mr Bewley's metre, which will be better appreciated in such a passage as—

> Some hunters, leaving highlands which afar
> Stretch broadening inland toward the southern star,
> Canoed downriver, lake and strait of Maracaibo;
> Their leader, manly, young, a chief well known as Ibo;
> The whole a party picturesque of bright dark hues
> Well matching those of their mahogany canoes.

Noel Vandal [pseudonym for unidentified poet], in *Darkness and Light*, is reflective and edifying. He turns him home; no system, creed, or land, he fears, can teach the duties of the heart, or well direct the labour of the hand, or to the mind the secret deep impart. [English poet] Rowe [Rose] Lingston [n.d.], author of *Woodland and Dreamland*, has a modest measure of the genuine poetic melody and fancy. The translation called "Magali" is one of the prettiest things in the volume.

[English Anthologist] Mr Rowland [G.] Hill's [n.d.] Jewels will be read and recited for many a year wherever the English language is spoken. This gratifying result will be due to Mr Hill's forethought in getting his poetry done for him by "ghosts." The ghosts of Macaulay, Poe, and Shakspeare, in particular, will feel indebted to him for introducing their works to the public under the title of "his jewels."

5. "Tolstoy on Art," *Daily Chronicle*, 10 September 1898.

[Review of What Is Art?, *by Leo Tolstoy. Translation from the Russian original by Aylmer Maude, embodying the Author's last*

alterations and revisions. (London: The Brotherhood). Shaw's cri-tique of Tolstoy's artistic outlook is based on the same premise that he held against orthodox Marxism; namely, that the tastes of the majority—be it the proletariat or any other class—do not necessar-ily imply a better judgement of art. In addition, the very definition of art is discussed: from art as a voluntary expression of feeling to art as the expression of pleasure in work. It is interesting to note that an aristocrat who defends the working class—as was the case with Tolstoy—has a lot in common with the average member of the Fabian society.]

Like all [Russian novelist and philosopher Count Lev Niko-layevich] Tolstoy's [1828–1910] didactic writings, this book is a most effective boobytrap. It is written with so utter a con-tempt for the objections which the routine critic is sure to allege against it, that many a dilletantist reviewer has already accepted it as a butt set up by Providence to show off his own brilliant marksmanship. It seems so easy to dispose of a naif who moralises on the Trojan war as if it were a historical event!

Yet Tolstoy will be better understood in this volume than in his Christian epistles, because art is at present a more fash-ionable subject than Christianity. Most people have a loose impression that Tolstoy as a Christian represents Evangeli-calism gone mad. As a matter of fact, Tolstoy's position, as explained by himself, is, from the Evangelical point of view, as novel as it is blasphemous. What Evangelicalism calls rev-elation, vouchsafed to man's incapacity by Divine wisdom, Tolstoy declares to be a piece of common sense so obvious as to make its statement in the gospels superfluous. "I will go further," he says. "This truth [resist not evil] appears to me so simple and so clear that I am persuaded I should have found it out by myself, even if Christ and His doctrine had never ex-isted." Blasphemy can go no further than this from the point of view of the Bible-worshipper. Again he says, "I beg you,

in the name of the God of truth whom you adore, not to fly
out at me, nor to begin looking for arguments to oppose me
with, before you have meditated, not on what I am going to
write to you, but on the gospel; and not on the gospel as the
word of God or of Christ, but on the gospel considered as
the neatest, simplest, most comprehensible and most practical doctrine on the way in which men ought to live."

What makes this attitude of Tolstoy's so formidable to
Christians who feel that it condemns their own systematic
resistance to evil, is the fact that he is a man with a long, var-
ied and by no means exclusively pious experience of worldly
life. In vain do we spend hours in a highly superior manner
in proving that Tolstoy's notions are unpractical, visionary:
in short, cranky; we cannot get the sting and the startle out of
his flat challenge as to how much we have done and where we
have landed ourselves by the opposite policy. No doubt the
challenge does not make all of us uneasy. But may not that be
because he sees the world from behind the scenes of politics
and society, whilst most of us are sitting to be gulled in the
pit? For, alas! nothing is plainer to the dupe of all the illusions
of civilisation than the folly of the seer who penetrates them.

If Tolstoy has made himself so very disquieting by criticising the world as a man of the world, he has hardly made
himself more agreeable by criticising art as an artist of the
first rank. Among the minor gods of the amateur he kindles a
devastating fire. Naturally, the very extensive literary output
of delirium tremens in our century receives no quarter from
him: he has no patience with nonsense, especially drunken
nonsense, however laboriously or lusciously it may be
rhymed or alliterated. But he spares nobody wholly, dealing
unmercifully with himself, sweeping away [English poet and
novelist] Mr Rudyard Kipling [1865–1936] with the French
decadents, and heaping derision on [German composer Wilhelm Richard] Wagner [1813–1883]. Clearly, this book of his
will not be valued for its specific criticisms, some of which, if

the truth must be told, represent nothing but the inevitable obsolescence of an old man's taste in art. To justify them, Tolstoy applies a test highly characteristic of the Russian aristocrat. A true work of art, he maintains, will always be recognized by the unsophisticated perception of the peasant folk. Hence, Beethoven's Ninth Symphony, not being popular among the Russian peasantry, is not a true work of art!

Leaving the Ninth Symphony to take care of itself, one cannot help being struck by the fact that Russian revolutionists of noble birth invariably display what appears to us a boundless credulity concerning the virtues of the poor. No English county magnate has any doubt as to which way an English agricultural laborer would choose between Tolstoy's favorite [Polish composer and pianist Frédéric François, born Fryderyk Franciszek] Chopin [1810–1849] nocturne (admitted by him to be true art) and the latest music-hall tune. We know perfectly well that the simplicity of our peasants' lives is forced on them by their poverty, and could be dispelled at any moment by a sufficient legacy. We know that the equality which seems to the rich man to be accepted among laborers (because he himself makes no distinction among them) is an illusion, and that social distinctions are more pitifully cherished by our poor than by any other class until we get down to the residuum which has not self-respect enough even for snobbery. Now, whether it is that the Russian peasantry, being illiterate and outlandish, has never been absorbed by European civilisation as ours has been, or else that the distance between peasant and noble in Russia is so great that the two classes do not know one another, and fill up the void in their knowledge by millennial romancing, certain it is that the Russian nobles [Russian scholar, polymath, and anarchist Prince Pyotr Alexeyevich] Kropotkin [1842–1921] and Tolstoy, who have come into our counsels on the side of the people, seem to assume that the laboring classes have entirely es-

caped the class vices, follies and prejudices of the bour-
geoisie.

If it were not for this unmistakeable error in Tolstoy's pre-
misses, it would be very difficult to dissent from any of his
judgments on works of art without feeling in danger of
merely providing him with an additional example of the corruption of taste which he deplores. But when his objection to
a masterpiece is based solely on the incapacity of a peasant to
enjoy it or understand it, the misgiving vanishes. Everything
that he says in condemnation of modern society is richly
deserved by it; but if it were true that the working classes,
numbering, say, four-fifths of the population, had entirely
escaped the penalties of civilisation, and were in a state so
wholesomely natural and benevolent that Beethoven must
stand condemned by their coldness towards his symphonies,
then his whole case against civilisation must fall to the
ground, since such a majority for good would justify any social system. In England, at least, one cannot help believing
that if Tolstoy were reincarnated as a peasant he would find
that the proletarian morality in which he has so much faith
is nothing but the morality of his own class, modified, mostly
for the worse, by ignorance, drudgery, insufficient food, and
bad sanitary conditions of all kinds. It is true that the absolutely idle class has a peculiar and exasperating nonentity
and futility, and that this class wastes a great deal of money
in false art; but it is not numerically a very large class. The
demand of the professional and mercantile classes is quite
sufficient to maintain a considerable body of art, the defects
of which cannot be ascribed to the idleness of its patrons.

If due allowance be made for those considerations which,
be it remembered, weaken society's defence and not Tolstoy's
attack, this book will be found extraordinarily interesting
and enlightening. We must agree with him when he says, "To
thoughtful and sincere people there can be no doubt that the
art of the upper classes can never be the art of the whole peo-

ple." Only, we must make the same reservation with regard to the art of the lower classes. And we must not forget that there is nothing whatever to choose between the average country gentleman and the gamekeeper in respect of distaste for the Ninth Symphony.

Tolstoy's main point, however, is the establishment of his definition of art. It is, he says, "an activity by means of which one man, having experienced a feeling, intentionally transmits it to others." This is the simple truth: the moment it is uttered, whoever is really conversant with art recognizes in it the voice of the master. None the less is Tolstoy perfectly aware that this is not the usual definition of art, which amateurs delight to hear described as that which produces beauty. Tolstoy's own Christian view of how he should treat the professors of this or any other heresy is clearly laid down in those articles of faith, already quoted above, which conclude his *Plaisirs Cruels.* "To dispute with those who are in error is to waste labor and spoil our exposition of the truth. It provokes us to say things that we do not mean, to formulate paradoxes, to exaggerate our thought, and, leaving on one side the essential part of our doctrine, play off tricks of logic on the slips which have provoked us." Fortunately for the entertainment of the readers of *What is Art?* Tolstoy does not carry out his own precepts in it. Backsliding without the slightest compunction into the character of a first rate fighting man, he challenges all the authorities, great and small, who have committed themselves to the beauty theory, and never quits them till he has left them for dead. There is always something especially exhilarating in the spectacle of a Quaker fighting; and Tolstoy's performance in this kind will not soon be forgotten. Our generation has not seen a heartier bout of literary fisticuffs, or one in which the challenger has been more brilliantly victorious.

Since no man, however indefatigable a reader he may be, can make himself acquainted with all that Europe has to say on any subject of general interest, it seldom happens that any great champion meets the opponent we would most like to see him join issue with. For this reason we hear nothing from Tolstoy of William Morris's definition of art as the expression of pleasure in work. This is not exactly the beauty doctrine: it recognizes, as Tolstoy's definition does, that art is the expression of feeling; but it covers a good deal of art work which, whilst proving the artist's need for expression, does not convince us that the artist wanted to convey his feeling to others. There have been many artists who have taken great pains to express themselves to themselves in works of art, but whose action, as regards the circulation of those works, has very evidently been dictated by love of fame or money rather than by any yearning for emotional intercourse with their fellow creatures. It is, of course, easy to say that the works of such men are not true art; but if they convey feeling to others, sometimes more successfully and keenly than some of the works which fall within Tolstoy's definition, the distinction is clearly not a practical one. The truth is that definitions which are applied on the principle that whatever is not white is black never are quite practical. The only safe plan is to ascertain the opposite extremes of artistic motive, determine which end of the scale between them is the higher and which the lower, and place each work in question in its right position on the scale. There are plenty of passages in this very book of Tolstoy's—itself a work of art according to its own definition—which have quite clearly been written to relieve the craving for expression of the author's own combativeness, or fun, or devotion, or even cleverness, and would probably have been written equally had he been the most sardonic pessimist that ever regarded his fellow creatures as beyond redemption.

Tolstoy's justification in ignoring these obvious objections to the accuracy and universality of his treatise is plain enough. Art is socially important—that is, worth writing a book about—only in so far as it wields that power of propagating feeling which he adopts as his criterion of true art. It is hard to knock this truth into the heads of the English nation. We admit the importance of public opinion, which, in a country without intellectual habits (our own, for example), depends altogether on public feeling. Yet, instead of perceiving the gigantic importance which this gives to the theatre, the concert room, and the bookshop as forcing houses of feeling, we slight them as mere places of amusement, and blunder along upon the assumption that the House of Commons, and the platitudes of a few old-fashioned leader writers, are the chief fountains of English sentiment. Tolstoy knows better than that.

> Look carefully [he says] into the causes of the ignorance of the masses, and you may see that the chief cause does not at all lie in the lack of schools and libraries, as we are accustomed to suppose, but in those superstitions, both ecclesiastical and patriotic, with which the people are saturated, and which are unceasingly generated by all the methods of art. Church superstitions are supported and produced by the poetry of prayers, hymns, painting; by the sculpture of images and of statues; by singing, by organs, by music, by architecture, and even by dramatic art in religious ceremonies. Patriotic superstitions are supported and produced by verses and stories, which are supplied even in schools; by music, by songs, by triumphal processions, by royal meetings, by martial pictures, and by monuments. Were it not for this continual activity in all departments of art, perpetuating the ecclesiastical and patriotic intoxication and embitterment of the people, the masses would long ere this have attained to true enlightenment.

It does not at all detract from the value of Tolstoy's thesis that what he denounces as superstitions may appear to many to be wholesome enthusiasms and fruitful convictions. Still less does it matter that his opinions of individual artists are often those of a rather petulant veteran who neither knows nor wants to know much of works that are too new to please him. The valid point is that our artistic institutions are vital social organs, and that the advance of civilisation tends constantly to make them, especially in the presence of democratic institutions and compulsory schooling, more important than the political and ecclesiastical institutions whose traditional prestige is so much greater. We are too stupid to learn from epigrams; otherwise [Scottish writer and politician Andrew] Fletcher of Saltoun's [1655–1716] offer to let whoever wished make the laws of the nation provided he made its songs, would have saved Tolstoy the trouble of telling us the same thing in twenty chapters. At all events, we cannot now complain of want of instruction. With [English physician and translator] Mr [William] Ashton Ellis's [1853–1919] translation of Wagner's Prose to put on the shelves of our libraries beside the works of Ruskin, and this pregnant and trenchant little volume of Tolstoy's to drive the moral home, we shall have ourselves to thank if we do not take greater care of our art in the future than of any other psychological factor in the destiny of the nation.

6. "Painter and Partners," *The Observer*, 23 December 1945.

[*Review of* The Laurel and the Thorn: A Study of G.F. Watts, *by Ronald George Chapman (London: Faber & Faber, 1945). This piece, as one of the rare instances of a Shaw essays on plastic arts, is very illuminating—especially since Shaw befriended and posed for some of the greatest artists of the time (from Auguste Rodin to Alvin Langdon Coburn). As a succinct, general discussion of the Symbolist and Pre-Raphaelite movements, this essay is also a Shavian "who's who" of contemporary art.*]

[English painter and sculptor George Frederic] Watts [1817–1904] was one of the rarest of painters and sculptors. He was born able to draw and paint anything he wanted to draw and paint, or to model it in any plastic material. The resulting picture or statue was not only recognisably like its original but a revelation of qualities and possibilities in it which were invisible to ordinary mortals. And it was always what he intended it to be.

This last gift, though we are apt to take it as a matter of course, is not at all common. Even so great an artist as [French sculptor François Auguste René] Rodin [1840–1917] once showed me a head he had modelled with fingers on its lips, and asked me whether it suggested anything to me, as he did not know what to call it. I told him that [English essayist Thomas Penson] De Quincey [1785–1859] had written of things that are beyond speech as "the burden of the incommunicable." He liked this, and evidently meant to use it, though whether he ever did I do not know. Our mediocre artists paint the best model they can find and afford, and label her Juliet or Francesca or Deirdre, unless they have a turn for nudes, in which case she is catalogued as Venus.

This purposelessness never occurs in Watts's work. His worst picture, called The Dead Knight, can hardly be called a picture at all: it is an ugly surface with his favourite quotation scrawled on it; but it says what he means and means what he says; and in this it is typical of all his works.

***

What more is there to be said of Michael Angelo and [Italian polymath] Leonardo [Da Vinci, 1452–1519]? Really nothing but the size of their jobs. Nobody gave Watts a Sistine Chapel or a Medici mausoleum or a church to decorate. But as far as his canvases went he could fill them with pictures of men and women, not as they could be seen at any moment in the streets but in their highest and utmost which reveal them as prophets, sibyls, poets. His portraits are precious beyond pearls. His Tennyson I cannot answer for, as I never saw Tennyson; but in the portrait and the gigantic statue in Peterborough we have the poet even if the man never looked quite like that. I knew William Morris and [English artist] Walter Crane [1845–1915] well enough to be very familiar with their appearance; and I knew their minds as far as such knowledge is possible. Watts's portraits of them are great because, though they are not photographic, they are psychographic, and give you the true Morris and the true Crane in their full depth and grace. The only other painter known to me who could do this was [Irish artist] John Butler Yeats [1839–1922], father of the poet, an Irishman who lived neglected in Bedford Park when all the celebrities were having themselves painted by [English painter Sir John Everett] Millais [1829–1896] and [English painter and royal portraitist] Frank Holl [1845–1888].

In Watts's day the grand tradition of Raphael and Michael Angelo, with its cant of chiaroscuro, "marvellous foreshortenings," "morbidezza of Andrea del Sarto" (the first open-air painter), and all the other slogans of the academic exhortations to carry on the work and win the overwhelming prestige of Michael Angelo, had produced so many huge daubs, quite unsaleable, that there was nothing for it but an uncompromising return to pre-Raphaelite visible realism. Watts, instead of being swept away by this movement, took not the smallest notice of it, and made for the shining light along the straight and narrow path, as if it had never ended in another city of destruction. His only tragedy (it was Rodin's also) was that a commercialised Europe had no Sistine Chapels for him to paint.

Such work as his must be seen as a life's work, as it can be now at Compton. Single pictures of his at the Academy exhibitions were outglared by the blazing reds and yellows, reeking from varnishing day, when all the other exhibitors worked up their canvases competitively to concert pitch. Millais, for instance, was colour-drunk. Watts's Hope hung beside Millais's blazing Beefeater is murdered. Such crimes made Burlington House a Chamber of Horrors in those days. Only a pilgrimage to Compton (I spent a year within a mile of it) can add Watts to one's parish temples of the great god, Art.

***

[English author and librarian] Mr [Ronald George] Chapman [1917–?] tells the story of Watts's five spiritual wives and an absurd legal union with an incipient genius, the girl model [English actress Dame] Ellen Terry [1847–1928], when he was a middle-aged, lukewarm gentleman and she an actress with a vocation as irresistible as his own. On the only occasion on which Ellen mentioned it to me, she described how, when she was only Watts's model, she came home one day and informed her mother triumphantly that she was going to have a baby. Watts had kissed her; and she was young enough to believe that babies were the result of kisses. For both of them the marriage was an entirely negligible episode which left no ill feeling. Watts tried legalised union again, very successfully this time, if I may judge by my acquaintance with his widow. Ellen tried four other men, but died an independent single woman.

***

As a polygamist Ellen Terry and her discarded husbands was easily surpassed by Watts, though he went through the legal ceremony only twice, both times with women young enough to be his daughters. A man who makes the creation of works of the highest art his sole and supreme business in life needs before all things a woman to be his servant, his mother, his nurse, his devotee, his housekeeper, and not at all necessarily his bedfellow. Clearly Ellen Terry, herself a genius, could not spend her life in this fashion: what she needed was a husband who would do it all for her; and she was not lucky enough to find one. Watts was extraordinarily lucky. As a child he was not mothered; but he was fathered until he was taken on successively by Lady Holland [Mary Augusta Vassall-Fox, 1812–1889], Lady [Georgiana] Duff Gordon, Mrs [Thomas] Prinsep, Mrs [Julia Margaret, sister of Mrs Prinsep] Cameron, Mrs Russell Barrington, and finally (at 74) by his second legal wife [Mary Fraser Tytler, 1849–1938], an amiable, comely woman with whom anyone could be happy, and capable enough to create and run the Compton pottery, manage the Compton gallery, and take the care of Watts in her stride quite easily. Such polygamy leaves Casanova nowhere. As Watts could paint and sculpt in the grand manner as easily as other men can walk or talk, he must be ranked as one of the most fortunate of mortals and yet the most dependent on women.

***

There was nothing surprising to me in this. Although from fifteen to twenty I took over and did the responsible office work of a man of forty, and did it as well as it needed to be done by anyone who hated it as much as I did, I abandoned it at twenty and threw myself on my mother until after years of failure I began to earn a little money. My management of my income consisted wholly of handing it to her and asking her for a pound when my pockets were empty. At forty I could afford to marry, and had to open a bank account and man-age my copyrights and invest my savings; but as to my daily life, it was the same story: everything else was done for me by my wife and her servants. Only, being a bit of an economist and biologist, I did not take my dependence as a matter of course, like most men; I knew it, and was led by it to my belief that Eve came before Adam, and created him as her hunter and warrior, and finally as the feeder of her imagination and of the aspiration towards godhead of the Life Force in her. Many of her creations are only drones; but the geniuses are fastened on by susceptible women and have everything done for them except their own highest work.

***

This book by Mr Ronald Chapman, THE LAUREL AND THE THORN ([English poet Walter Savage] Landor's [1775–1864] description of his laurel), is almost too well and thoroughly done. His description of Little Holland House throws over completely its reputation as Macaulay's pulpit, and shows that it was Watts's temple. When it was demolished and replaced by the Melbury Road studios its glory departed; for Topsy Morris, the idle singer of an empty day, who would have none of the Watts's grand manner, nor Macaulay's Whiggery, and was not only pre-Raphael, but pre-Shakespear and arch-Chaucerian [from Medieval English writer Geoffrey Chaucer, c. 1343–1400], came along with young Burne-Jones and a retinue of craftsmen who despised academic painting at his back, and decided that the Little Holland House set were high art snobs, and drove Watts out of London to the Isle of Wight, and finally to his end in Limnerslease by the Hog's Back in Compton.

Part IV: Drama

Shaw is perhaps at his best as a drama critic. His comments on all the technical details of any production he reviews (lighting, acting, costumes, etc.) are knowledgeable and critical. But Shaw, both as a drama critic and as a playwright, had a lot to say about drama as a literary genre. He would, for example, have truly insightful ideas about how a play should be punctuated, or about whether it should be cut or adapted. Furthermore, he knew more than any of his contemporaries about the whole process of writing a play—from creating vivid dialogues to writing useful stage directions. This section provides a summary of Shaw's views on what a play should be like before it is put on stage.

1. Letter to the editor of *The Chronicle*, September 2, 1892.

[Shaw, who had arrived in London with his command of the English language as his only asset, always derided the type of linguistic prescriptivism typical of the institutions of higher education that he could not attend. This prescriptivism was, in his opinion, especially pernicious, for it asphyxiated literary creativity.]

Sir,

If you do not immediately suppress the person who takes it upon himself to lay down the law almost every day in your columns on the subject of literary composition, I will give up taking *The Chronicle*. The man is a pedant, an ignoramus, an idiot, a self-advertising duffer. A little while ago, when somebody pointed out to him a case of the misuse of "and which," the creature, utterly missing the point, rushed about denouncing every sentence containing "and which" until some public-spirited subscriber of yours stopped him by a curt exposure which would have shamed any corrigible human being into humble silence for at least a month.

Yet he has already broken out in a fresh place. [Scottish author, scholar, and critic] Mr Andrew Lang [1844–1912], moved by a personal antipathy to "split infinitives" and to sentences ending with the word "such" (for example, Shakespeare's line, "No glory lives behind the back of such") once made a jocular attempt to bounce the public out of using them by declaring that they were bad English. Of course, all competent literary workmen laughed at Mr Lang's little trick; but your fatuous specialist, driven out of his "and which" stronghold, is now beginning to rebuke "second-rate newspapers" for using such phrases as "to suddenly go" and "to boldly say."

I ask you, Sir, to put this man out. Give the porter orders to use such violence as may be necessary if he attempts to return, without, however, interfering with his perfect freedom of choice between "to suddenly go," "to go suddenly," and "suddenly to go." See that he does not come back; that is the main thing. And allow me, as one who has some little right to speak on the subject, to assure your readers that they may, without the slightest misgiving, use adverbed infinitives in any of the three ways given above. All they need consider is which of the three best conveys by its rhythm the feeling they wish to express.

Yours, &c.,

G. Bernard Shaw

2. From the Preface to *Three Plays for Puritans*, 1900.

[When Shaw published his Three Plays for Puritans *(The Devil's Disciple, Caesar and Cleopatra, Captain Brassbound's Conversion), he had already mastered the art of playwriting, even though some of his plays had not been performed publicly because of the censorship. In this preface we get a first glance at Shaw's principles about drama, his own motivation for writing drama, and the position he thought his works occupied in relation to other forms of dramatic art, past and present. It is also interesting because it provides an overview what the life of a critic is like, which helps to understand the circumstances under which many of the reviews included here came into being.]*

WHY FOR PURITANS?

Since I gave my *Plays, Pleasant and Unpleasant,* to the world two years ago, many things have happened to me. I had then just entered on the fourth year of my activity as a critic of the London theatres. They very nearly killed me. I had survived seven years of London's music, four or five years of London's pictures, and about as much of its current literature, wrestling critically with them with all my force and skill. After that, the criticism of the theatre came to me as a huge relief in point of bodily exertion. The difference between the leisure of a Persian cat and the labor of a cockney cab horse is not greater than the difference between the official weekly or fortnightly playgoings of the theatre critic and the restless daily rushing to and fro of the music critic, from the stroke of three in the afternoon, when the concerts begin, to the stroke of twelve at night, when the opera ends. The pictures were nearly as bad. An Alpinist once, noticing the massive soles of my boots, asked me whether I climbed mountains. No, I replied: these boots are for the hard floors of the London galleries. Yet I once dealt with music and pictures together in the spare time of an active young revolutionist, and wrote plays and books and other toilsome things into the bargain. But the theatre struck me down like the veriest weakling. I sank under it like a baby fed on starch. My very bones began to perish, so that I had to get them planed and gouged by accomplished surgeons. I fell from heights and broke my limbs in pieces. The doctors said: This man has not eaten meat for twenty years: he must eat it or die. I said: This man has been going to the London theatres for three years; and the soul of him has become inane and is feeding unnaturally on his body. And I was right. I did not change my diet; but I had myself carried up into a mountain where there was no theatre; and there I began to revive. Too weak to work, I wrote books and plays: hence the second and third plays in this volume. And now I am stronger than I have been at any moment since my feet first carried me as a critic across the fatal threshold of a London playhouse.

Why was this? What is the matter with the theatre, that a strong man can die of it? Well, the answer will make a long story; but it must be told. And, to begin, why have I just called the theatre a playhouse? The well-fed Englishman, though he lives and dies a schoolboy, cannot play. He cannot

even play cricket or football: he has to work at them: that is
why he beats the foreigner who plays at them. To him playing means playing the fool. He can hunt and shoot and travel
and fight: he can, when special holiday festivity is suggested
to him, eat and drink, dice and drab, smoke and lounge. But
play he cannot. The moment you make his theatre a place of
amusement instead of a place of edification, you make it, not
a real playhouse, but a place of excitement for the sportsman
and the sensualist. [...]

*[After describing the current state of the theater in England, he goes
on to discuss why certain plays are more successful than others, and
the ideas that this realization gave him as a playwright.]*

The actor-managers were far more successful, because they
produced plays that at least pleased themselves, whereas the
others, with a false theory of how to please everybody, produced plays that pleased nobody. But their occasional personal successes in voluptuous plays, and, in any case, their
careful concealment of failure, confirmed the prevalent error,
which was only exposed fully when the plays had to stand or
fall openly by their own merits. Even Shakespear was played
with his brains cut out. In 1896, when [English actor-
manager] Sir Henry Irving [1838–1905] was disabled by an accident at a moment when Miss Ellen Terry was too ill to appear,
the theatre had to be closed after a brief attempt to rely on the
attraction of a Shakespearean play performed by the stock
company. This may have been Shakespear's fault: indeed Sir
Henry later on complained that he had lost a princely sum
by Shakespear. But Shakespear's reply to this, if he were able
to make it, would be that the princely sum was spent, not on
his dramatic poetry, but on a gorgeous stage ritualism super-
imposed on reckless mutilations of his text, the whole being
addressed to a public as to which nothing is certain except
that its natural bias is towards reverence for Shakespear and

dislike and distrust of ritualism. No doubt the Lyceum ritual appealed to a far more cultivated sensuousness and imaginativeness than the musical farces in which our stage Abbots of Misrule pontificated (with the same financially disastrous result); but in both there was the same intentional brainlessness, founded on the same theory that the public did not want brains, did not want to think, did not want anything but pleasure at the theatre. Unfortunately, this theory happens to be true of a certain section of the public. This section, being courted by the theatres, went to them and drove the other people out. It then discovered, as any expert could have foreseen, that the theatre cannot compete in mere pleasure-mongering either with the other arts or with matter-of-fact gallantry. Stage pictures are the worst pictures, stage music the worst music, stage scenery the worst scenery within reach of the Londoner. The leading lady or gentleman may be as tempting to the admirer in the pit as the dishes in a cook-shop window are to the penniless tramp on the pavement; but people do not, I presume, go to the theatre to be merely tantalized.

The breakdown on the last point was conclusive. For when the managers tried to put their principle of pleasing everybody into practice, Necessity, ever ironical towards Folly, had driven them to seek a universal pleasure to appeal to. And since many have no ear for music or eye for color, the search for universality inevitably flung the managers back on the instinct of sex as the avenue to all hearts. Of course the appeal was a vapid failure. Speaking for my own sex, I can say that the leading lady was not to everybody's taste: her pretty face often became ugly when she tried to make it expressive; her voice lost its charm (if it ever had any) when she had nothing sincere to say; and the stalls, from racial prejudice, were apt to insist on more Rebecca and less Rowena than the pit cared for. It may seem strange, even monstrous, that a man should feel a constant attachment to the hideous witches in

Macbeth, and yet yawn at the prospect of spending another evening in the contemplation of a beauteous young leading lady with voluptuous contours and longlashed eyes, painted and dressed to perfection in the latest fashions. But that is just what happened to me in the theatre.

I did not find that matters were improved by the lady pretending to be "a woman with a past," violently oversexed, or the play being called a problem play, even when the manager, and sometimes, I suspect, the very author, firmly believed the word problem to be the latest euphemism for what Justice Shallow called a *bona roba*, and certainly would not either of them have staked a farthing on the interest of a genuine problem. In fact these so-called problem plays invariably depended for their dramatic interest on foregone conclusions of the most heartwearying conventionality concerning sexual morality. The authors had no problematic views: all they wanted was to capture some of the fascination of Ibsen. It seemed to them that most of Ibsen's heroines were naughty ladies. And they tried to produce Ibsen plays by making their heroines naughty. But they took great care to make them pretty and expensively dressed. Thus the pseudo-Ibsen play was nothing but the ordinary sensuous ritual of the stage become as frankly pornographic as good manners allowed.

I found that the whole business of stage sensuousness, whether as Lyceum Shakespear, musical farce, or sham Ibsen, finally disgusted me, not because I was Pharisaical, or intolerantly refined, but because I was bored; and boredom is a condition which makes men as susceptible to disgust and irritation as headache makes them to noise and glare. Being a man, I have my share of the masculine silliness and vulgarity on the subject of sex which so astonishes women, to whom sex is a serious matter. I am not an Archbishop, and do not pretend to pass my life on one plane or in one mood, and that the highest: on the contrary, I am, I protest, as accessible to the humors of *The Rogue's Comedy* or *The Rake's Progress* as to the pious decencies of *The Sign of the Cross*. Thus Falstaff, coarser than any of the men in our loosest plays, does not bore me: Doll Tearsheet, more abandoned than any of the women, does not shock me. I think that *Romeo and Juliet* would be a poorer play if it were robbed of the solitary fragment it has preserved for us of the conversation of the husband of Juliet's nurse. No: my disgust was not mere thin-skinned prudery. When my moral sense revolted, as it often did to the very fibres, it was invariably at the nauseous compliances of the theatre with conventional virtue. If I despised the musical farces, it was because they never had the courage of their vices. With all their labored efforts to keep up an understanding of furtive naughtiness between the low comedian on the stage and the drunken undergraduate in the stalls, they insisted all the time on their virtue and patriotism and loyalty as pitifully as a poor girl of the pavement will pretend to be a clergyman's daughter. True, I may have been offended when a manager, catering for me with coarse frankness as a slave dealer caters for a Pasha, invited me to forget the common bond of humanity between me and his company by demanding nothing from them but a gloatably voluptuous appearance. But this extreme is never reached at our better theatres. The shop assistants, the typists, the clerks, who, as I have said, preserve the innocence of the theatre, would not dare to let themselves be pleased by it. Even if they did, they would not get it from the managers, who, when they are brought to the only logical conclusion from their principle of making the theatre a temple of pleasure, indignantly refuse to change the dramatic profession for Mrs Warren's. For that is what all this demand for pleasure at the theatre finally comes to; and the answer to it is, not that people ought not to desire sensuous pleasure (they cannot help it) but that the theatre cannot give it to them, even to the extent permitted by the honor and conscience of the best managers, because a theatre is so far from being a pleasant or even a comfortable place that only by making us forget ourselves can it prevent us from realizing its inconveniences. A play that does not do this for the pleasure-seeker allows him to discover that he has chosen a disagreeable and expensive way of spending the evening. He wants to drink, to smoke, to change the spectacle, to get rid of the middle-aged actor and actress who are boring him, and to see shapely young dancing girls and acrobats doing more amusing things in a more plastic manner. In short, he wants the music hall; and he goes there, leaving the managers astonished at this unexpected but quite inevitable result of the attempt to please him. Whereas, had he been enthralled by the play, even with horror, instead of himself enthralling with the dread of his displeasure the manager, the author and the actors, all had been well. And so we must conclude that the theatre is a place which people can only endure when they forget themselves: that is, when their attention is entirely captured, their interest thoroughly roused, their sympathies raised to the eagerest readiness, and their selfishness utterly annihilated.

[Once the qualities of a good play are clear to him, there remains the problem of what can be safely included in a play without incurring problems such as censorship. The problem is discussed against the backdrop of orthodox morals and social conventions at the time. At the same time, the forthcoming discussion casts some light on why Shaw would normally avoid romance in his plays and, to some extent, in his personal life. The passage becomes all the more interesting when Shaw drops an exclusively dramatic perspective and spreads the argument to other literary genres.]

But can the theatre make a show of lovers' endearments? A thousand times no: perish the thought of such unladylike, ungentlemanlike exhibitions. You can have fights, rescues, conflagrations, trials-at-law, avalanches, murders and executions all directly simulated on the stage if you will. But any such realistic treatment of the incidents of sex is quite out of the question. The singer, the dramatic dancer, the exquisite declaimer of impassioned poesy, the rare artist who, bringing something of the art of all three to the ordinary work of the theatre, can enthral an audience by the expression of dramatic feeling alone, may take love for a theme on the stage; but the prosaic walking gentlemen of our fashionable theatres, realistically simulating the incidents of life, cannot touch it without indecorum.

Can any dilemma be more complete? Love is assumed to be the only theme that touches all your audience infallibly, young and old, rich and poor. And yet love is the one subject that the drawingroom drama dare not present.

Out of this dilemma, which is a very old one, has come the romantic play: that is, the play in which love is carefully kept off the stage, whilst it is alleged as the motive of all the actions presented to the audience. The result is, to me at least, an intolerable perversion of human conduct. There are two classes of stories that seem to me to be not only fundamentally false but sordidly base. One is the pseudo-religious story, in which the hero or heroine does good on strictly commercial grounds, reluctantly exercising a little virtue on earth in consideration of receiving in return an exorbitant payment in heaven: much as if an odalisque were to allow a cadi to whip her for a couple of millions in gold. The other is the romance in which the hero, also rigidly commercial, will do nothing except for the sake of the heroine. Surely this is as depressing as it is unreal. Compare with it the treatment of love, frankly indecent according to our notions, in oriental fiction. In *The Arabian Nights* we have a series of stories, some of them very good ones, in which no sort of decorum is observed. The result is that they are infinitely more instructive and enjoyable than our romances, because love is treated in them as naturally as any other passion. There is no cast iron convention as to its effects; no false association of general depravity of character with its corporealities or of general elevation with its sentimentalities; no pretence that a man or woman cannot be courageous and kind and friendly unless infatuatedly in love with somebody (is no poet manly enough to sing *The Old Maids of England?*): rather, indeed, an insistence on the blinding and narrowing power of lovesickness to make princely heroes unhappy and unfortunate. These tales expose, further, the delusion that the interest of this most capricious, most transient, most easily baffled of all instincts, is inexhaustible, and that the field of the English romancer has been cruelly narrowed by the restrictions under which he is permitted to deal with it. The Arabian storyteller, relieved of all such restrictions, heaps character on character, adventure on adventure, marvel on marvel; whilst the English novelist, like the starving tramp who can think of nothing but his hunger, seems to be unable to escape from the obsession of sex, and will rewrite the very gospels because the originals are not written in the sensuously ecstatic style. At the instance of Martin Luther we long ago gave up imposing celibacy on our priests; but we still impose it on our art, with the very undesirable and unexpected result that no editor, publisher, or manager, will now accept a story or produce a play without "love interest" in it. Take, for a recent example, Mr H. G. Wells's *War of Two Worlds* [sic], a tale of the invasion of the earth by the inhabitants of the planet Mars: a capital story, not to be laid down until finished. Love interest is impossible on its scientific plane: nothing could be more impertinent and irritating. Yet Mr Wells has had to pretend that the hero is in love with a young lady manufactured for the purpose, and to imply that it is on her account alone that he feels concerned about the apparently inevitable destruction of the human race by the Martians. Another example. An American novelist, recently deceased, made a hit some years ago by compiling a Bostonian Utopia [*Looking Back-*

ward, by Edward Bellamy, 1850–1898] from the prospectuses of the little bands of devout Communists who have from time to time, since the days of [French philosopher and socialist Charles] Fourier [1772–1837] and [Welsh social reformer and utopian socialist Robert] Owen [1771–1858], tried to establish millennial colonies outside our commercial civilization. Even in this economic Utopia we find the inevitable love affair. The hero, waking up in a distant future from a miraculous sleep, meets a Boston young lady, provided expressly for him to fall in love with. Women have by that time given up wearing skirts; but she, to spare his delicacy, gets one out of a museum of antiquities to wear in his presence until he is hardened to the customs of the new age. When I came to that touching incident, I became as Paolo and Francesca: "in that book I read no more." I will not multiply examples: if such unendurable follies occur in the sort of story made by working out a meteorological or economic hypothesis, the extent to which it is carried in sentimental romances needs no expatiation.

The worst of it is that since man's intellectual consciousness of himself is derived from the descriptions of him in books, a persistent misrepresentation of humanity in literature gets finally accepted and acted upon. If every mirror reflected our noses twice their natural size, we should live and die in the faith that we were all Punches; and we should scout a true mirror as the work of a fool, madman, or jester. Nay, I believe we should, by Lamarckian adaptation, enlarge our noses to the admired size; for I have noticed that when a certain type of feature appears in painting and is admired as beautiful, it presently becomes common in nature; so that the Beatrices and Francescas in the picture galleries of one generation, to whom minor poets address verses entitled To My Lady, come to life as the parlormaids and waitresses of the next. If the conventions of romance are only insisted on long enough and uniformly enough (a condition guaranteed by the uniformity of human folly and vanity), then, for the huge School Board-taught masses who read romance and nothing else, these conventions will become the laws of personal honor. [...]

[All this left an indelible mark on Shaw, who ended up despising his obligations as a drama critic.]

Is it clear now, why the theatre was insufferable to me; why it left its black mark on my bones as it has left its black mark on the character of the nation; why I call the Puritans to rescue it again as they rescued it before when its foolish pursuit of pleasure sunk it in "profaneness and immorality"? I have, I think, always been a Puritan in my attitude towards Art. I am as fond of fine music and handsome building as Milton was, or [English military and political leader Oliver] Cromwell [1599–1658], or Bunyan; but if I found that they were becoming the instruments of a systematic idolatry of sensuousness, I would hold it good statesmanship to blow every cathedral in the world to pieces with dynamite, organ and all, without the least heed to the screams of the art critics and cultured voluptuaries. And when I see that the nineteenth century has crowned the idolatry of Art with the deification of Love, so that every poet is supposed to have pierced to the holy of holies when he has announced that Love is the Supreme, or the Enough, or the All, I feel that Art was safer in the hands of the most fanatical of Cromwell's major generals than it will be if ever it gets into mine. The pleasures of the senses I can sympathize with and share; but the substitution of sensuous ecstasy for intellectual activity and honesty is the very devil. It has already brought us to Flogging Bills in Parliament, and, by reaction, to androgynous heroes on the stage; and if the infection spreads until the democratic attitude becomes thoroughly Romanticist, the country will become unbearable for all realists, Philistine or Platonic. When

it comes to that, the brute force of the strong-minded Bis-
marckian man of action, impatient of humbug, will combine
with the subtlety and spiritual energy of the man of thought
whom shams cannot illude or interest. That combination will
be on one side; and Romanticism will be on the other. In
which event, so much the worse for Romanticism, which will
come down even if it has to drag Democracy down with it.
For all institutions have in the long run to live by the nature
of things, and not by imagination.

ON DIABOLONIAN ETHICS

*[The first part of this section focuses on the philosophical, discursive
nature of Shaw's playwriting, a quality that fleshes out, perhaps
most notably, in the—self-aggrandizing for some—prefaces to his
plays.]*

There is a foolish opinion prevalent that an author should
allow his works to speak for themselves, and that he who
appends and prefixes explanations to them is likely to be as
bad an artist as the painter cited by Cervantes, who wrote
under his picture *This is a Cock*, lest there should be any mistake about it. The pat retort to this thoughtless comparison
is that the painter invariably does so label his picture. What
is a Royal Academy catalogue but a series of statements that
This is *The Vale of Rest*, This is *The School of Athens*, This is
Chill October, This is *The Prince of Wales*, and so on? The reason most dramatists do not publish their plays with prefaces
is that they cannot write them, the business of intellectually conscious philosopher and skilled critic being no part of
the playwright's craft. Naturally, making a virtue of their incapacity, they either repudiate prefaces as shameful, or else,
with a modest air, request some popular critic to supply one,
as much as to say, Were I to tell the truth about myself I must
needs seem vainglorious: were I to tell less than the truth I

should do myself an injustice and deceive my readers. As to the critic thus called in from the outside, what can he do but imply that his friend's transcendent ability as a dramatist is surpassed only by his beautiful nature as a man? Now what I say is, why should I get another man to praise me when I can praise myself? I have no disabilities to plead: produce me your best critic, and I will criticize his head off. As to philosophy, I taught my critics the little they know in my *Quintessence of Ibsenism*; and now they turn their guns—the guns I loaded for them—on me, and proclaim that I write as if mankind had intellect without will, or heart, as they call it. Ingrates: who was it that directed your attention to the distinction between Will and Intellect? Not [German philosopher Arthur] Schopenhauer [1788–1860], I think, but Shaw.

Again, they tell me that So-and-So, who does not write prefaces, is no charlatan. Well, I am. I first caught the ear of the British public on a cart in Hyde Park, to the blaring of brass bands, and this not at all as a reluctant sacrifice of my instinct of privacy to political necessity, but because, like all dramatists and mimes of genuine vocation, I am a natural-born mountebank. I am well aware that the ordinary British citizen requires a profession of shame from all mountebanks by way of homage to the sanctity of the ignoble private life to which he is condemned by his incapacity for public life. Thus Shakespear, after proclaiming that Not marble nor the gilded monuments of Princes should outlive his powerful rhyme, would apologize, in the approved taste, for making himself a motley to the view; and the British citizen has ever since quoted the apology and ignored the fanfare. When an actress writes her memoirs, she impresses on you in every chapter how cruelly it tried her feelings to exhibit her person to the public gaze; but she does not forget to decorate the book with a dozen portraits of herself. I really cannot respond to this demand for mock-modesty. I am ashamed neither of my work nor of the way it is done. I like explaining its merits to the huge majority who dont know good work from bad. It does them good; and it does me good, curing me of nervousness, laziness, and snobbishness. I write prefaces as [English poet, critic, and playwright John] Dryden [1631–1700] did, and treatises as Wagner, because *I can*; and I would give half a dozen of Shakespear's plays for one of the prefaces he ought to have written. I leave the delicacies of retirement to those who are gentlemen first and literary workmen afterwards. The cart and trumpet for me.

[Shaw goes on to explain on what grounds one may conceivably see his plays as novel, original stories, despite the traditional stage tricks and plot twists he employs. The point is illustrated with reference to The Devil's Disciple. In addition, he explains why the label "for puritans" can be applied to this play; specifically, he develops the notion of "Diabolonian Puritanism," which is the type of Puritanism that Shaw portrays.]

BETTER THAN SHAKESPEAR?

[This now classic section summarizes the critical opinions of Shaw's on Shakespearean drama. On the one hand, Shaw despises "bardolatry" (a term he coined) as much as, on the other, he cannot understand why "bardolaters" would cut and adapt Shakespeare's plays. He attempts to veer clear of any such extremes, and comes to the conclusion that Shakespeare is a superb dramatist because of the poetic nature and musicality of his lines (his "word-music"), despite the unoriginal plots and characters or the lack of an ethical message. The opening lines, omitted here, discuss Shaw's Caesar and Cleopatra, and provide the link to Shakespeare's own Caesar and his dramaturgy at large.]

It will be said that these remarks can bear no other construction than an offer of my Cæsar to the public as an improvement on Shakespear's. And in fact, that is their precise purport. But here let me give a friendly warning to those scribes

who have so often exclaimed against my criticisms of Shakespear as blasphemies against a hitherto unquestioned Perfection and Infallibility. Such criticisms are no more new than
the creed of my Diabolonian Puritan or my revival of the
humors of *Cool as a Cucumber*. Too much surprise at them
betrays an acquaintance with Shakespear criticism so limited
as not to include even the prefaces of Dr Johnson and the utterances of Napoleon. I have merely repeated in the dialect
of my own time and in the light of its philosophy what they
said in the dialect and light of theirs. Do not be misled by
the Shakespear fanciers who, ever since his own time, have
delighted in his plays just as they might have delighted in a
particular breed of pigeons if they had never learnt to read.
His genuine critics, from [English playwright, critic, and poet]
Ben Jonson [1572–1637] to [British editor, journalist, and pub-
lisher] Mr Frank Harris [1855–1931], have always kept as far on
this side idolatry as I.

As to our ordinary uncritical citizens, they have been
slowly trudging forward these three centuries to the point
which Shakespear reached at a bound in Elizabeth's time. To-
day most of them have arrived there or thereabouts, with the
result that his plays are at last beginning to be performed
as he wrote them; and the long line of disgraceful farces,
melodramas, and stage pageants which actor-managers, from
[English actors, playwrights, and theater managers David]
Garrick [1717–1779] and [Theophilus] Cibber [1703–1758] to
our own contemporaries, have hacked out of his plays as
peasants have hacked huts out of the Coliseum, are beginning to vanish from the stage. It is a significant fact that the
mutilators of Shakespear, who never could be persuaded that
Shakespear knew his business better than they, have ever
been the most fanatical of his worshippers. The late [Amer-
ican critic and theater manager John] Augustin Daly
[1838–1899] thought no price too extravagant for an addition
to his collection of Shakespear relics; but in arranging Shake-

spear's plays for the stage, he proceeded on the assumption that Shakespear was a botcher and he an artist. I am far too good a Shakespearean ever to forgive [English actor-manager] Sir Henry Irving [1838–1905] for producing a version of *King Lear* so mutilated that the numerous critics who had never read the play could not follow the story of Gloster. Both these idolaters of the Bard must have thought Mr Forbes Robertson mad because he restored Fortinbras to the stage and played as much of *Hamlet* as there was time for instead of as little. And the instant success of the experiment probably altered their minds no further than to make them think the public mad. [English actor-manager] Mr [Frank Robert] Benson [1858–1939] actually gives the play complete at two sittings, causing the aforesaid numerous critics to remark with naïve surprise that Polonius is a complete and interesting character. It was the age of gross ignorance of Shakespear and incapacity for his works that produced the indiscriminate eulogies with which we are familiar. It was the revival of genuine criticism of those works that coincided with the movement for giving genuine instead of spurious and silly representations of his plays. So much for Bardolatry!

It does not follow, however, that the right to criticize Shakespear involves the power of writing better plays. And in fact—do not be surprised at my modesty—I do not profess to write better plays. The writing of practicable stage plays does not present an infinite scope to human talent; and the dramatists who magnify its difficulties are humbugs. The summit of their art has been attained again and again. No man will ever write a better tragedy than *Lear*, a better comedy than *Le Festin de Pierre* or *Peer Gynt*, a better opera than *Don Giovanni*, a better music drama than *The Niblung's Ring*, or, for the matter of that, better fashionable plays and melodramas than are now being turned out by writers whom nobody dreams of mocking with the word immortal. It is the philosophy, the outlook on life, that changes, not the craft of the playwright. A generation that is thoroughly moralized and patriotized, that conceives virtuous indignation as spiritually nutritious, that murders the murderer and robs the thief, that grovels before all sorts of ideals, social, military, ecclesiastical, royal and divine, may be, from my point of view, steeped in error; but it need not want for as good plays as the hand of man can produce. Only, those plays will be neither written nor relished by men in whose philosophy guilt and innocence, and consequently revenge and idolatry, have no meaning. Such men must rewrite all the old plays in terms of their own philosophy; and that is why, as [Scottish barrister and folklorist] Mr [John Stuart] Stuart-Glennie [1841–1910] has pointed out, there can be no new drama without a new philosophy. To which I may add that there can be no Shakespear or Goethe without one either, nor two Shakespears in one philosophic epoch, since, as I have said, the first great comer in that epoch reaps the whole harvest and reduces those who come after to the rank of mere gleaners, or, worse than that, fools who go laboriously through all the motions of the reaper and binder in an empty field. What is the use of writing plays or painting frescoes if you have nothing more to say or shew than was said and shewn by Shakespear, Michael Angelo, and Raphael? If these had not seen things differently, for better or worse, from the dramatic poets of the Townley mysteries, or from Giotto, they could not have produced their works: no, not though their skill of pen and hand had been double what it was. After them there was no need (and *need* alone nerves men to face the persecution in the teeth of which new art is brought to birth) to redo the already done, until in due time, when their philosophy wore itself out, a new race of nineteenth century poets and critics, from [English poet George Gordon] Byron [1788–1824] to William Morris, began, first to speak coldly of Shakespear and Raphael, and then to rediscover, in the medieval art which these Renascence masters had superseded, certain forgotten elements which were germinating again for the new harvest. What is more, they began to discover that the technical skill of the masters was by no means superlative. Indeed, I defy anyone to prove that the great epoch makers in fine art have owed their position to their technical skill. It is true that when we search for examples of a prodigious command of language and of graphic line, we can think of nobody better than Shakespear and Michael Angelo. But both of them laid their arts waste for centuries by leading later artists to seek greatness in copying their technique. The technique was acquired, refined on, and surpassed over and over again; but the supremacy of the two great exemplars remained undisputed. As a matter of easily observable fact, every generation produces men of extraordinary special faculty, artistic, mathematical and linguistic, who for lack of new ideas, or indeed of any ideas worth mentioning, achieve no distinction outside music halls and class rooms, although they can do things easily that the great epoch makers did clumsily or not at all. The contempt of the academic pedant for the original artist is often founded on a genuine superiority of technical knowledge and aptitude: he is sometimes a better anatomical draughtsman than Raphael, a better hand at triple counterpoint than Beethoven, a better versifier than Byron. Nay, this is true not merely of pedants, but of men who have produced works of art of some note. If technical facility were the secret of greatness in art, Mr Swinburne would be greater than Browning and Byron rolled into one, Stevenson greater than Scott or Dickens, [German composer Felix] Mendelssohn [1809–1847] than Wagner, [Irish painter and illustrator Daniel] Maclise [1806–1870] than [English painter Ford] Madox Brown [1821–1893]. Besides, new ideas make their technique as water makes its channel; and the technician without ideas is as useless as the canal constructor without water, though he may do very skilfully what the Mississippi does very rudely. To clinch the argument, you have only to observe that the epoch maker himself has generally begun working professionally before his new ideas have mastered him sufficiently to insist on constant expression by his art. In such cases you are compelled to admit that if he had by chance died earlier, his greatness would have remained unachieved, although his technical qualifications would have been well enough established. The early imitative works of great men are usually conspicuously inferior to the best works of their forerunners. Imagine Wagner dying after composing *Rienzi*, or Shelley after *Zastrozzi*! Would any competent critic then have rated Wagner's technical aptitude as high as [Italian composer Gioachino Antonio] Rossini's [1792–1868], [Italian composer Gaspare] Spontini's [1774–1851], or [German composer Giacomo] Meyerbeer's [1791–1864]; or Shelley's as high as Moore's? Turn the problem another way: does anyone suppose that if Shakespear had conceived Goethe's or Ibsen's ideas, he would have expressed them any worse than Goethe or Ibsen? Human faculty being what it is, is it likely that in our time any advance, except in external conditions, will take place in the arts of expression sufficient to enable an author, without making himself ridiculous, to undertake to say what he has to say better than Homer or Shakespear? But the humblest author, and much more a rather arrogant one like myself, may profess to have something to say by this time that neither Homer nor Shakespear said. And the playgoer may reasonably ask to have historical events and persons presented to him in the light of his own time, even though Homer and Shakespear have already shewn them in the light of their time. For example, Homer presented Achilles and Ajax as heroes to the world in the *Iliads*. In due time came Shakespear, who said, virtually: I really cannot accept this selfish hound and this brawny brute as great men merely because Homer flattered them in playing to the Greek gallery. Consequently we have, in *Troilus and Cressida*, the verdict of Shakespear's epoch (our own) on the pair. This did not in the least involve any pretence on Shakespear's part to be a greater poet than Homer.

When Shakespear in turn came to deal with Henry V and Julius Cæsar, he did so according to his own essentially knightly conception of a great statesman-commander. But in the XIX century comes the German historian [Theodor] Mommsen [1817–1903], who also takes Cæsar for his hero, and explains the immense difference in scope between the perfect knight [Gaul chieftain] Vercingetorix [c. 82 BC–46 BC] and his great conqueror Julius Cæsar. In this country, Carlyle, with his vein of peasant inspiration, apprehended the sort of greatness that places the true hero of history so far beyond the mere *preux chevalier*, whose fanatical personal honor, gallantry and self-sacrifice, are founded on a passion for death born of inability to bear the weight of a life that will not grant ideal conditions to the liver. This one ray of perception became Carlyle's whole stock-in-trade; and it sufficed to make a literary master of him. In due time, when Mommsen is an old man, and Carlyle dead, come I, and dramatize the by-this-time familiar distinction in *Arms and the Man*, with its comedic conflict between the knightly Bulgarian and the Mommsenite Swiss captain. Whereupon a great many playgoers who have not yet read Shakespear, much less Mommsen and Carlyle, raise a shriek of concern for their knightly ideal as if nobody had ever questioned its sufficiency since the middle ages. Let them thank me for educating them so far. And let them allow me to set forth Cæsar in the same modern light, taking the same liberty with Shakespear as he with Homer, and with no thought of pretending to express the Mommsenite view of Cæsar any better than Shakespear expressed a view which was not even Plutarchian [after Greek historian, who later acquired Roman citizenship, Lucius Plutarch, c. AD 46–AD 120], and must, I fear, be referred to the tradition in stage conquerors established by Marlowe's

Tamerlane as much as to even the chivalrous conception of heroism dramatized in *Henry V*.

[The final paragraph ends on a personal note about how Shaw's own plays relate to the technical and literary techniques described above, and about what posterity might make of his work and every other author's.]

For my own part, I can avouch that such powers of invention, humor and stage ingenuity as I have been able to exercise in *Plays, Pleasant and Unpleasant*, and in these *Three Plays for Puritans*, availed me not at all until I saw the old facts in a new light. Technically, I do not find myself able to proceed otherwise than as former playwrights have done. True, my plays have the latest mechanical improvements: the action is not carried on by impossible soliloquys and asides; and my people get on and off the stage without requiring four doors to a room which in real life would have only one. But my stories are the old stories; my characters are the familiar harlequin and columbine, clown and pantaloon (note the harlequin's leap in the third act of *Cæsar and Cleopatra*); my stage tricks and suspenses and thrills and jests are the ones in vogue when I was a boy, by which time my grandfather was tired of them. To the young people who make their acquaintance for the first time in my plays, they may be as novel as Cyrano's nose to those who have never seen Punch; whilst to older playgoers the unexpectedness of my attempt to substitute natural history for conventional ethics and romantic logic may so transfigure the eternal stage puppets and their inevitable dilemmas as to make their identification impossible for the moment. If so, so much the better for me: I shall perhaps enjoy a few years of immortality. But the whirligig of time will soon bring my audiences to my own point of view; and then the next Shakespear that comes along will turn these petty tentatives of mine into masterpieces final

for their epoch. By that time my twentieth century characteristics will pass unnoticed as a matter of course, whilst the
eighteenth century artificiality that marks the work of every
literary Irishman of my generation will seem antiquated and
silly. It is a dangerous thing to be hailed at once, as a few rash
admirers have hailed me, as above all things original: what
the world calls originality is only an unaccustomed method
of tickling it. Meyerbeer seemed prodigiously original to the
Parisians when he first burst on them. Today, he is only the
crow who followed Beethoven's plough. I am a crow who
have followed many ploughs. No doubt I seem prodigiously
clever to those who have never hopped, hungry and curious,
across the fields of philosophy, politics and art. Karl Marx
said of Stuart Mill that his eminence was due to the flatness
of the surrounding country. In these days of Board Schools,
universal reading, cheap newspapers, and the inevitable ensuing demand for notabilities of all sorts, literary, military,
political and fashionable, to write paragraphs about, that sort
of eminence is within the reach of very moderate ability. Reputations are cheap nowadays. Even were they dear, it would
still be impossible for any public-spirited citizen of the world
to hope that his reputation might endure; for this would be
to hope that the flood of general enlightenment may never
rise above his miserable high-watermark. I hate to think that
Shakespear has lasted 300 years, though he got no further
than Koheleth the Preacher, who died many centuries before
him; or that Plato, more than 2000 years old, is still ahead of
our voters. We must hurry on: we must get rid of reputations:
they are weeds in the soil of ignorance. Cultivate that soil,
and they will flower more beautifully, but only as annuals. If
this preface will at all help to get rid of mine, the writing of it
will have been well worth the pains.

SURREY, 1900.

3. "How to Make Plays Readable," *The Author's Year Book and Guide for 1904*, edited by W. E. Price (New York, 1904).

[Shaw is perhaps the dramatist whose plays are closer to the readable quality of novels, thanks in no small part to his detailed stage directions. This "readability" helped to make his plays widely published—thus making them all the more successful in performance. Shaw revitalized, some would say initiated, the tradition of printing plays for publication in England. His ideas on how a play should be written—not only with the stage in mind—are perhaps best summarized in this piece.]

Five years ago every publisher who was approached with a view to publishing a play at once said, "No use: people won't read plays in England." This was unfortunate, because the economic conditions of theatrical enterprise had by that time made it impossible to ask a manager (except with a deliberate view to his ruin) to produce any but very widely popular plays; and if neither the managers nor the publishers will touch the higher stratum of dramatic art, what is to become of the unfortunate authors whose gifts lie in that stratum? Must they relapse into novel writing, or depend on the fact that though the production of really philosophic plays at the commercial theatres is an economic impossibility in the present state of popular culture, yet the thing may actually occur from time to time, either as a pure error of judgment on the manager's part, or in one of those emergencies created by the failure of the supply of popular plays, when, having to choose between an experiment in high art or the closing of his theatre, the manager accepts what is to him the less of the two evils? I have dissuaded managers from committing these acts of desperation with plays of my own often enough to convince me that a capable dramatic author can get any sort of play, however excellent (or the reverse), produced at one time or another, provided he is ready to take advantage of the manager's infatuation, his artistic enthusiasm, his ambition to be regarded as an intellectual connoisseur, or his occasional destitution in the matter of new plays. But as no honorable author will take up dramatic work seriously on the chance of being enabled, by accident at some uncertain date, to add to the losses of a cornered or too appreciative manager, immediate acceptance and success at the commercial theatres may be left out of the question by the writer of plays which are "above the head of the public"; that is, the sort of head represented by the greatest common measure of, say, 75,000 metropolitan playgoers.

On the other hand, 2,000 purchasers or so, at six shillings, less threepence in the shilling, will pay for the publication of a volume of plays, and leave, perhaps, £100 for the author, which sum, eked out with a little journalism, will at least save him from the starvation threatened by the unmarketable nature of his genius. The play, once published, will probably get performed by the Stage Society or by [impresario and critic Jacob Thomas (J. T.)] Mr Grein [1862–1935], and thus procure for the author some practical experience of the stage, and give him a good advertisement into the bargain, leading possibly to a commercial commission for a popular play "as you [the populace] like it," as soon as he has learnt to write one.

A striking contemporary instance of this process is [German dramatist and novelist Gerhart] Hauptmann [1862–1946], who came to the front as a dramatist through single performances of his plays in Germany by dramatic clubs like the Stage Society, and by their publication. I myself have published ten plays. Seven of them may be classed commercially as unacted. But of these seven, five have been performed at London theatres with the same ceremonies of first-night celebration, press notices, and—what is far more important—the same experience of the stage gained by the author at rehearsal as if they had been built by [English actor and dramatist] Mr [Arthur Wing] Pinero [1855–1934], [English dramatist] Mr [Henry Arthur] Jones [1851–1929], or [English actor and dramatist] Mr Cecil Raleigh [1856–1914] to run a thousand nights. Through that experience and advertisement I was enabled to write and find a manager for a melodrama which brought me in from America alone more money than I could have earned at journalism in the time it took me to write all my ten plays. My two unperformed plays are in that condition for special reasons which do not affect the argument. I chronicle these matters as business facts for our business paper, not as "green-room gossip."

Of course, if I had foolishly and snobbishly stood sneering at Ibsen, at the Independent Theatre, at the New Century Theatre, at the experiments of [English theater manager Charles] Charrington [1854–1926], Grein, [British actor Herbert] Waring [1846–1909], [British actress and director] Miss [Florence] Farr [1860–1917], [English actress and suffragette] Miss [Elizabeth] Robins [1862–1952], and the other pioneers, instead of seizing the opportunity to help dramatic literature and train myself as a practical playwright at the same time, all this would not have happened to me. But the fact that it did happen, not only to me, but to others in proportion to their activity as uncommercial playwrights, seems to me to prove that it is quite worth any young author's while to peg away at the super-popular drama with a reasonable certainty of gaining sufficient stage experience and newspaper renown to ensure him a place among the commercially successful dramatists, if he chooses afterwards to turn his apprenticeship to account by writing what the managers and the public want.

But since this road to fame lies partly through the publication of plays, of what use is it to point it out if the publishers say, "No use: in England people don't read plays"? Well, of course they don't; but pray, whose fault is that? I suggest that it is the fault of the playwrights who deliberately make their plays unreadable by flinging repulsive stage technicalities in the face of the public, and omitting from their descriptions even that simplest common decency of literature, the definite article. I wonder how many readers Charles Dickens would have had, or deserved to have, if he had written in this manner—

> Sykes lights pipe—calls dog—loads pistol with newspaper—takes bludgeon from R. above fireplace and strikes *Nancy. Nancy: Oh, Lord, Bill* (Dies. Sykes wipes brow—shudders—takes hat from chair o.P.—sees ghost, not visible to audience—and exit L.U.E.).

This sort of thing, in which literary people trying their hand at the drama for the first time revel as ludicrously as amateur actors revel in flagrant false hair, misfitting tunics, and tin spears, is not a whit less dishonoring to literature and insulting to the public than an edition of Shakespear would be if it were cut down in this fashion:

> *Sc. 2. Change to carpenter's scene and set room in the Tower behind.*
> *Richard on prompt to centre.*
> RICHARD. Now is winter of our discont't
> Made glorious summer by sun of York;
> And all clouds th. lowered, &c.,
> In deep bosom of ocean buried.

If the reader's imagination may be quenched, his taste offended, and his good sense revolted merely to save the author's time in describing the action of a piece, why should not the same thing be done in handling the dialogue?

But there is another party to be considered besides the author and the reader. There is the actor (who is nowadays the manager also), an exceptionally susceptible, imaginative, fastidious person, easily put out by the slightest incongruity, easily possessed by the slightest suggestion. His work is so pe-

culiar and important; its delicacy depends so much on the extent to which a play can be made real to him and the technical
conditions reduced to unnoticed matters of habit; above all,
it is so necessary to his self-respect that the obligation he is
under to make himself a means to the author's end should
not be made an excuse for disregarding his dignity as a man,
that an author can hardly be too careful to cherish the actor's
illusion and respect his right to be approached as a professional man and not merely ordered to do this or that without
knowing why. Imagine, then, the effect of handing an actor
a part, or an actor-manager a play, drawn up exactly like a
specification for a gas-fitter! How can any man or woman
of letters be so foolishly inconsiderate as to suppose that an
actor-manager, at the moment when he is full of curiosity and
hope as to the opportunity of striking the public imagination
offered him by a writer whom he can only judge according to
his or her power of imaginative and vivid description, really
likes to receive a silly amateur attempt to imitate a flyman's
scene plot and a prompter's memorandum of positions and
list of "props"? When I read the prompt copies that are not
only sent in to managers for acceptance, but actually to the
printers for the delectation of the unprofessional public, I often wonder how many managers or readers would ever get as
far as the second page in Hamlet if it were presented to them
in so loathly a fashion.

Let me give an example of a stage direction of my own
which has been rebuked as a silly joke by people who do
not understand the real relations of author and actor. It runs
thus: "*So-and-So's complexion fades into stone-grey; and all movement and expression desert his eyes,*" This is the sort of stage
direction an actor really wants. Of course, he can no more actually change his complexion to stone-grey than Mr Forbes-
Robertson can actually die after saying, "The rest is silence."
But he can produce the impression suggested by the direction perfectly. *How* he produces it is his business, not mine.

This distinction is important, because, if I wrote such a stage direction as "*turns his back to the audience and furtively dabs vaseline on his eyelashes*," instead of "*his eyes glisten with tears*," I should be guilty of an outrage on both actor and reader. Yet we find almost all our inexperienced dramatic authors taking the greatest pains to commit just such outrages. The fact is, the actor and the reader want exactly the same thing, vivid strokes of description, not stage manager's memoranda of impertinent instructions in the art of acting from literary people who cannot act. It is true that most authors consider themselves born actors, and that most actors consider themselves born authors; but these weaknesses should be confessed under seal of rehearsal, not proclaimed to a derisive world. To do the actor justice, he tries not to carry the stage about with him wherever he goes, whereas the would-be playwright never lets you escape from it, even in print. If the reader attempts to forget that what he is reading is fiction, he promptly has a pin stuck into him by the statement that such and such a piece of furniture is R. or L., or "near the front of the stage," or that the masterpiece of painting on the easel, which the villain or adventuress will presently slash with a knife, is "turned away from the audience." It is just as if a novelist were to write, "A keen pang shot through the mother's heart; for she saw at a glance that her child had not many chapters to live," or "When we left Grimwood, he had just dealt the coward's blow that stretched young Alton Dale a corpse three lines from the foot of the first page of signature C." A dramatist's business is to make the reader forget the stage and the actor forget the audience, not to remind them of both at every turn, like an incompetent "extra gentleman" who turns the wrong side of his banner towards the footlights. Every such reminder is a betrayal in art and a solecism in manners. Why should novices advertise their inexperience by sedulously committing them on every page, and even clinging to the "exits" and "exeunts" which survive from the time when dramatists like [George] Chapman [c. 1559–1634] wrote all their stage directions in Latin, perhaps to avoid spoiling the illusion by them, perhaps only to show off their scholarship?

The safe rule is, Write nothing in a play that you would not write in a novel; and remember that everything that the actor or the scene-painter *shows* to the audience must be described—not technically specified, but imaginatively, vividly, humorously, in a word, artistically described—to the reader by the author. In describing the scene, take just as much trouble to transport your reader there in imagination as you would in a narrative. Your imaginary persons must not call "off the stage"; you must not tell the public that "part of the stage is removed to represent the entrance to a cellar." It will often strain your ingenuity to describe a scene so that a stage-manager can set it from the printed description, yet not a word is let slip that could remind the reader of the footlights. But it can be done: and the reward for the trouble is that people can read your plays—even actor-managers, who suffer just as much from the deadening, disillusioning, vulgarizing effect of the old-fashioned stage direction as other people do.

4. "On Cutting Shakespear," *Fortnightly Review,* August 1919.

[Even though Shaw despised "bardolatry" as a chauvinistic hobby that was based on no artistic consideration, he would always praise Shakespeare's "word-music." This musical quality of Shakespeare's language, which heightens the effect of tragic and comic passages alike, is the main reason why Shaw always advocated for a punctiliously faithful rendering of the original text against the fashion of cutting the passages that sound unintelligible to certain audiences.]

[Scottish critic and writer] Mr William Archer [1856–1924] has quoted me in support of the practice of performing selections from Shakespear's plays instead of the plays in their entirety as he left them.

Everything that Mr Archer says is very true and very sensible. Unfortunately, the results in practice are the productions of [English actor-manager Colley] Cibber [1671–1757], [English actor, playwright, and theater manager David] Garrick [1717–1779], [English actor-manager Sir Henry] Irving [1838–1905], [English actor and theater manager Sir Herbert Beerbohm] Tree [1852–1917], [American critic, manager, and playwright John] Augustin Daly [1838–1899], Sir Frank Benson, and the commercial managers generally, which may be highly entertaining productions, but are somehow not Shakespear, whereas [English actor-manager, critic, and playwright] Mr [Harley] Granville-Barker's [1877–1946] resolutely unreasonable shewing-up of Shakespear's faults and follies to the uttermost comma was at once felt to be a restoration of Shakespear to the stage.

The moment you admit that the producer's business is to improve Shakespear by cutting out everything that he himself would not have written, and everything that he thinks the audience will either not like or not understand, and everything that does not make prosaic sense, you are launched on a slope on which there is no stopping until you reach the abyss where Irving's Lear lies forgotten. The reason stares us in the face. The producer's disapprovals, and consequently his cuts, are the symptoms of the differences between Shakespear and himself; and his assumption that all these differences are differences of superiority on his part and inferiority on Shakespear's, must end in the cutting down or raising up of Shakespear to his level. Tree thought a third-rate ballet more interesting than the colloquy of Cassio with Iago on the subject of temperance. No doubt many people agreed with him. It was certainly more expensive. Irving, when he was producing *Cymbeline*, cut out of his own part the lines:

"'Tis her breathing that
Perfumes the chamber thus. The flame o' the taper
Bows towards her, and would underpeep her lids
To see the unclosed lights, now canopied
Under those windows, white and azure, laced
With blue of heaven's own tinct."

He was genuinely astonished when he was told that he must not do it, as the lines were the most famous for their beauty of all the purple patches in Shakespear. A glance at the passage will shew how very "sensible" his cut was. Mr Archer wants to cut, "O single-soled jest, solely singular for the singleness," because it is "absolutely meaningless." But think of all the other lines that must go with it on the same ground! The gayer side of Shakespear's poetic ecstasy expressed itself in word-dances of jingling nonsense which are, from the point of view of the grave Scots commentator who demands a meaning and a moral from every text, mere delirium and echolalia. But what would Shakespear be without them? "The spring time, the only merry ring time, when birds do sing hey ding a ding ding" is certainly not good sense nor even accurate ornithological observation! Who ever heard a bird sing "hey ding a ding ding" or anything even remotely resembling it? Out with it, then; and away, too, with such absurdities as Beatrice's obviously untrue statement that a star danced at her birth, which must revolt all the obstetricians and astronomers in the audience. As to Othello's fustian about the Propontick and the Hellespont, is this senseless hullabaloo of sonorous vowels and precipitate consonants to be retained when people have trains to catch? Mr Archer is credulous in imagining that in these orchestral passages the wit has evaporated and the meaning become inscrutable. There never was any meaning or wit in them in his sense any more than there is wit or meaning in the crash of Wagner's cymbals or the gallop of his trombones in the Valkyries' ride.

The producer who has a head for syllogisms cuts such passages out. The producer who has an ear for music, like Mr
Granville-Barker, breaks his heart in trying to get them adequately executed.

Then take my own celebrated criticisms of Shakespear,
written when the Bard, like all the other dramatists, was stag-
gering under the terrible impact of Ibsen. Can men whose intellectual standards have been screwed up to Goethe's *Faust*,
Wagner's *Ring*, and "deep revolving" Ibsen's soul histories, be
expected to sit and listen to such penny-reading twaddle as
The Seven Ages of Man, or even Hamlet's soliloquy on suicide?
Out with the lot of them, then: let us cut the cackle and come
to the 'osses.

I might pile Pelion on Ossa with illustrations of the passages that might very well be cut out of Shake-spear's plays
on Mr Archer's grounds and on mine and on Garrick's, Irving's, etc., etc., etc. It is clear that you need only a sufficiently
large and critical committee of producers instead of a single
producer to cut out the entire play, a conclusion which most
managers reach without the assistance of a committee. It is
equally clear that to avoid this reduction to common sense
the only workable plan is Mr Barker's plan, which makes
Shakespear, and not the producer, the ultimate authority.
That Shakespear is a bore and even an absurdity to people
who cannot listen to blank verse and enjoy it as musicians
listen to an opera (Shakespear's methods are extremely like
[Italian composer Giuseppe] Verdi's [1813–1901]); that [English
actor] Mr George [Edward Wade] Robey [1869–1954], hero-
ically trying to find jokes crude enough for an audience of
rustic Tommies, would shrink from Touchstone's story about
the beef and the mustard; that we who think it funny to
call a man's head his nut remain joyless when Shakespear
calls it his costard (not knowing that a costard is an apple);
that Benedick cannot amuse or fascinate the young ladies
who have adored [English actor] Robert [Bilcliffe] Loraine

[1876–1935] and Granville-Barker as Jack Tanner; that William's puns are as dead as [English humorist] Tom Hood's [1835–1874] or [British librettist and author Henry Brougham] Farnie's [1836–1889]; that Elizabethan English is a half-dead language and Euphuist English unintelligible and intolerable: all these undeniable facts are reasons for not performing Shakespear's plays at all, but not reasons for breaking them up and trying to jerry-build modern plays with them, as the Romans broke up the Coliseum to build hovels. Businesslike and economical as that procedure seems (for why waste good material?), experience remorselessly proves that Shakespear making a fool of himself is more interesting than the judicious producer correcting him. The people who really want Shakespear want all of him, and not merely Mr Archer's or anyone else's favorite bits; and this not in the least because they enjoy every word of it, but because they want to be sure of hearing the words they do enjoy, and because the effect of the judiciously selected passages, not to mention injudiciously selected passages, is not the same as that of the whole play, just as the effect of the currants picked out of a bun is not the same as that of the whole bun, indigestible as it may be to people who do not like buns.

There are plenty of modern instances to go upon. I have seen *Peer Gynt* most judiciously and practically cut by [French actor and director Aurélien Marie Lugné] Lugné-Poë [1869–1940], and *The Wild Duck* cut to the bone by Mr Archer. I have seen Wagner at full length at Bayreuth and Munich, and cut most sensibly at Covent Garden. I have actually seen *Il Trovatore*, most swift and concise of operas, cut by [English conductor and impresario] Sir Thomas Beecham [1879–1961]. My own plays, notoriously too long, have been cut with masterly skill by American managers. Mr Henry Arthur Jones made a capital acting version of *A Doll's House*, entitled *Breaking a Butterfly*. I do not allege that the result has always been disastrous failure, though it has sometimes gone that far. A hash makes a better meal than an empty plate. But I do aver without qualification that the mutilation has always been an offence, and the effect different and worse both in degree and in kind from the effect of a remorselessly faithful performance. Wagner's remark when he heard Rossini's *Barber of Seville* performed for once in its integrity in Turin applies to all the works of the great masters. You get something from such a performance that the selections never give you. And I suggest that this is not wholly a mystery. It occurs only when the work is produced under the direction of a manager who understands its value and can find in every passage the charm or the function which induced the author to write it, and who can dictate or suggest the method of execution that brings out that charm or discharges that function. Without this sense and this skill the manager will cut, cut, cut, every time he comes to a difficulty; and he will put the interest of the refreshment bars and the saving of electric light and the observance of the conventional hours of beginning the performance before his duty to the author, maintaining all the time that the manager who cuts most is the author's best friend.

In short, there are a thousand more sensible reasons for cutting not only Shakespear's plays, but all plays, all symphonies, all operas, all epics, and all pictures which are too large for the dining-room. And there is absolutely no reason on earth for not cutting them except the design of the author, who was probably too conceited to be a good judge of his own work.

The sane conclusion is therefore that cutting must be dogmatically ruled out, because, as [ancient Chinese poet and philosopher] Lao-Tse [5th–4th century BCE] said, "of the making of reforms there is no end." The simple thing to do with a Shakespear play is to perform it. The alternative is to let it alone. If Shakespear made a mess of it, it is not likely that Smith or Robinson will succeed where he failed.

5. "Shakespear: A Standard Text," *The Times Literary Supplement*, March 18, 1921.

[*Shaw—in his zeal for finding an accurate way of representing the sounds of speech, which later led to the creation of his own Shavian alphabet—begins his argument by pointing out the limitations of the Roman alphabet to convey subtle nuances in pronunciation. The development of his own alphabet is connected with several other interests of his, such as phonetics, shorthand, musical notation, typesetting, and diction. Shaw then moves on to demonstrate the implications that these questions have for the standardization of an authoritative Shakespear text, and for the general representation of the modulations of speech in drama.*]

Sir,—May I, as a publishing playwright, point out to [English actor, theatrical manager and playwright] Mr William Poel [1852–1934] (who knows it already) that it is at present impossible to write or print a play fully or exactly in ordinary script or type? And it never will be possible until we establish in popular use a fixed and complete notation, such as musicians possess. No such notation exists in a shape intelligible to the general reader. Therefore the first flat fact to be faced is that the printers of the Shakespear Folio and the Quartos could not indicate how the Elizabethan actor spoke his lines, whether they were trying to do so or not. No doubt, when the Elizabethan punctuation of plays is more than usually crazy, as where, for instance, an unaccountable colon appears where there should be no stop at all, it may not be a mere misprint: the compositor may have set up some mark made in his copy by somebody in the theatre for some purpose. It does not follow that it was a stop written by Shakespear for publication. If we found one of Shakespear's handkerchiefs with a knot on it, we might reasonably conjecture that he had knotted it to remind him of something he was afraid of forgetting; but what sane producer of *Othello* would tie a

189

knot in Desdemona's fatal handkerchief on the ground that all Elizabethan handkerchiefs were worn knotted? All actors and all producers and all prompters make marks on their parts and copies to indicate emphasis, strokes of stage business, signals, calls, and the like; but except in the matter of underscoring words, which is common practice, they each make different marks according to private codes of their own. Dots, strokes, crosses, angles indicating the position of the arms, crude footprints mapping the position of the feet, make memoranda perfectly intelligible to the actor who scrawls them, and inscrutable to anyone else. Every producer who knows his business, and does not merely fudge along at rehearsal from entry to entry by trial and error, sprinkles his copy of the play with a homemade shorthand which nobody but he can decipher, Even the prompter, whose copy should serve for his successors as well as himself, distractedly black-leads it until it is often difficult to make out the text, and impossible to understand the directions.

Now imagine manuscript copies treated in this way and then handed to a printer to set up, or to a scrivener to make fair copy for the printer. How is the scrivener to tell whether these dots and dashes and scriggles and crosses and clock-hands and queries and notes of admiration are meant for stops or not? It is easy to say that he can use his common sense; but neither scriveners nor compositors are highly educated enough to understand everything they copy or set up: setting up Shakespear must often be very like setting up Einstein or Homer in the original. Thus what looks like a colon, and is set up as such in the Quarto, may mean, "emphasize the next [or previous] word," or "pause significantly," or "don't forget to pronounce the h," or merely the Elizabethan equivalent to "curtain warning" or "check your floats and take your ambers out of your number one batten." To cherish it as Shakespear's punctuation, or pretend to greater authenticity for it than for the colons of [English dramatist and poet

Nicholas] Rowe [1674–1718] or Dr Johnson or [English poet Alexander] Pope [1688–1744] or Malone or the [Shakespeare scholars Mary Victoria (1809–1898) and Charles (1787–1877)] Cowden Clarkes or Q, or any modern editor, is next door to Baconian [from English philosopher, statesman, and author Francis Bacon] cipher hunting.

Let me recapitulate the process by which the plays got into print. First, Shakespear wrote a play. It may be presumed that he punctuated it; but this is by no means certain. I have on my desk a typed play by a clever young writer whose dialogue is very vivacious, and is that of an educated man accustomed to converse with educated people. It bristles with mad hyphens *à tort et à travers*; but there is not a stop in it from beginning to end except the full stops at the ends of the speeches; and I suspect that these were put in by the typist. [Irish author, playwright, and poet] Oscar Wilde [1854–1900] sent the MS of *An Ideal Husband* to the Haymarket Theatre without taking the trouble to note the entrances and exits of the persons on the stage. There is no degree of carelessness that is not credible to men who know that they will be present to explain matters when serious work begins. But let us assume that Shakespear punctuated his script. From it the scrivener copied out the parts for the actors, and made a legible prompt copy. That the scrivener respected Shakespear's stops and "followed copy" exactly is against even modern experience; and in the XVI–XVII *fin de siècle*, when scriveners were proud of their clergy and tenacious of their technical authority, the scrivener would punctuate as he thought Shakespear (whom he would despise as an amateur) ought to have punctuated, and not as he did or did not punctuate. The copies so produced were then marked at rehearsal in all sorts of ways by all sorts of people for all sorts of theatrical purposes. Thus marked, they were fair-copied again by a scrivener—possibly the same, possibly another—for the printer. Now, as all authors know, the printer who does not consider that punctuation is his special business, and that authors know nothing about it (they mostly know very little), has not yet been born. Besides, the printer of that period would have the tradition that his page should look well, and that the letterpress should not be disfigured, as in modern books, by wide spaces between sentences and words and letters, or by awkward-looking stops. And so we get two opinionated scriveners, a whole company of actors and stage officials, and a tradition-ridden compositor, between Shakespear's holograph and the printed page. Such a process applied to an imperfect and inexact notation, as to the use of which authors and even grammarians are so little agreed that it cannot be used in legal documents, leaves the punctuation of the Quartos and the Folio practically void of authority. Even if it could be proved that Shakespear corrected the proofs of the best Quarto texts, I should still defy any modern editor to follow them stop for stop without publicly washing his hands of all responsibility for them.

This does not mean that there is not a case, and a very strong case, for making facsimiles of the earliest printed texts. A glance through any of the facsimiles already published will discover points at which changes made by modern editors are changes for the worse. But when the utmost has been said that can be said for the readings of the Quartos and the Folio, no middle course is open to a modern editor between a photographic reproduction and a text doctored precisely as the conventional editions have been doctored. If the editor be Mr Granville-Barker, so much the better: he will test the questionable passages on the stage, and retain readings that a mere man of letters would tamper with. If the editor be Mr William Poel, he will print the text in the way that best suggests his divination of its proper delivery. He will run the words together in rapid passages, and bring out keywords in ways undreamt of by [English actor John] Heming [1556–1630] and [English actor Henry] Condell [1576–1627]. Such editions

would be much more valuable and interesting than superfluous repetitions of existing editions made in the study; but
they would not be a whit more "standard" or authentic.

Besides, they would introduce more controversial new
readings than any merely literary editor dare venture. For example, take the following ranting and redundant utterance of
Macbeth:

> Hang out your banners on the outer walls.
> The cry is still they come.

[Anglo-Irish actor] Barry Sullivan [1821–1891] cured both
the rant and the redundancy very simply. He entered at the
back of the stage throwing an order over his shoulder to his
subalterns, and then came down to the footlights to discuss
the military situation. Thus we got the reading:

> Hang out your banners. On the outer walls
> the cry is still they come.

This, tested on the stage as Mr Granville-Barker would test
it, is a convincing improvement. But the authority for it is
not the text as it has come down to us, but Barry Sullivan's
conjecture submitted to Mr Barker's test. And Barry Sullivan went further than that. Instead of saying, as Hamlet, "I
am but mad north-north-west: when the wind is southerly, I
know a hawk from a handsaw," he said, "I know a hawk from
a heron. Pshaw!" This may read strainedly; but when acted
with appropriate business it is so effective that Mr Barker's
stage test would favor its adoption. Such readings, however,
would compel Mr Barker to interpolate scores of stage directions for which there would be no authority but his own
artistic instinct.

As to Mr Poel, there is no living enthusiast more firmly
convinced than he that he knows the mind of Shakespear;
and this conviction has nerved him to do yeoman's service to

his master. It would nerve him equally to feats that Dr Johnson would have funked. The liberties he would take with the
text to square it with his own original and vivid conception
of character, theatrical technique, and Elizabethan political
history and social structure would rouse a cry of controversy.
On that very account a Poel Shakespear should be published,
even if it were to consist of only a few specimen plays; and a
Granville-Barker Shakespear should rival it. But neither edition could be called a standard edition except by the courtesy
which allows every theatre to call itself the Theatre Royal.
And the question which of the two famous Shakespearean
producers were the more unscrupulous would never be
settled.

Now may I be allowed a suggestion of my own? Why not
try to make a record of our language as it is spoken today on
the stage classically? We have in Forbes-Robertson an actor
whose speech is unchallengeable in every English-speaking
land, not only in Oxford and the West End of London, but
in countries where the dialect of Oxford and the West End is
received with shouts of derisive laughter. It does not matter
how Forbes-Robertson pronounces this or that vowel: his
speech will carry any Englishman anywhere. It is unquestionably proper for a king, for a chief justice, for an archbishop, or
for a private gentleman; having acquired it, no one has anything more to learn to qualify himself as a speaker for the
most dignified employment. Well, why not begin with an edition of *Hamlet* in which this Robertsonian speech shall be
recorded by phonetic spelling? I am aware that this cannot
be done completely except by using [Scottish phonetician
Alexander Melville] Bell's [1819–1905] Visible Speech, which
nobody but [his son,] Mr [inventor and engineer Alexander]
Graham Bell [1847–1922] and perhaps a few others can read;
but by ekeing out the ordinary alphabet with a few letters
turned upside down, and coming to a clearly stated understanding as to the meaning of those which remain right side

up, it is quite possible to make a very useful record, supplemented by the existing phonographic records of which Sir Johnston [Forbes-Robertson] can specify the defects exactly. Such a phonetic edition of *Hamlet* could be fairly described as a standard *Hamlet*, valid for its day. The Academic Committee of the Royal Society of Literature could justify its existence by undertaking this work.

As to the text, by all means let Mr Poel's points, and Mr Granville-Barker's points, be considered in making it. Both gentlemen might very well be co-opted to the editing committee. But I implore Mr Poel to dismiss from his mind the notion that there are two punctuations: a grammatical and an oral. The two are the same. Dr Johnson's punctuation of Shakepear's plays, far better on the whole than that of the Quartos or the Folio, is highly suggestive of the stage delivery of [English actor, playwright, manager, and producer David] Garrick's [1717–1779] day. The authorized version of the Bible, punctuated by preachers for preachers, is as oral as it is grammatical. What people call grammatical or literary punctuation is simply unskilled punctuation: the work of writers who pepper a page with commas, and disfigure it with dashes, leaving the printer to supply the semicolons, which he does with a conviction that it is wrong to have two in the same sentence, and that colons are of the nature of sacred music. My own punctuation, which is as definite as the multiplication table, is founded on the best Bible usage (the Bible is not consistently stopped throughout) and on the distinctions I find it necessary and possible to make; and it is both grammatical and oral.

But I must repeat that the notation at my disposal cannot convey the play as it should really exist: that is, in its oral delivery. I have to write melodies without bars, without indications of pitch, pace, or timbre, and without modulation, leaving the actor or producer to divine the proper treatment of what is essentially word-music. I turn over a score by [German composer] Richard Strauss [1864–1949], and envy him his bar divisions, his assurance that his trombone passages will not be played on the triangle, his power of giving directions without making his music unreadable. What would we not give for a copy of Lear marked by Shakespear "somewhat broader," "always quieter and quieter," "amiably," or, less translatably, "mit grossem Schwung und Begeisterung," "mit Steigerung," much less Meyerbeer's "con esplosione," or Verdi's *fffff* or *pppppp*, or *cantando* or *parlando*, or any of the things that I say at rehearsal, and that in my absence must be left to the intuitions of some kindred spirit?

It will be seen now, I hope, that this discussion about the punctuation of the Shakespear Quartos raises the much more serious question of making the great invention of reading and writing really effective and educational. It is at present a wretched makeshift. Children are taught to read at great expense; and they cannot open their mouths without proving that the sound of their noble native speech has never been conveyed to them. They see on paper the words of their poets, and repeat them in the voices of their slums. Men whose noses were rubbed ruthlessly into books and copybooks every day for nine years at elementary schools are unemployable as butlers or West End shop assistants because they cannot form a grammatical sentence nor utter a sound that is admissible in cultivated society. Others, cultivated in country houses, and educated at Eton and Oxford, have their speech represented by Oxford's greatest phonetic experts as follows:

> Tell mii not in mɔnfl nambəz
> Laif iz bat ən emti driim
> Fɔ də sowl iz ded dhət slambəz
> aend thingz aa not whot dhei sijm.

To turn this into coster's cockney, all that is necessary is to change "tell" into "t'yoll," "laif" into "lawf," "aa" into "aw," and "dhei" into "dhy." Ask Forbes-Robertson to declaim the verse, and you will hear something quite different from either: to wit, the English language in the only form that has a right to call itself standard. But this English will be dead presently, unless we take the trouble and cultivate the artistic conscience to provide it with a notation. At most, I suppose, we shall continue to dispute whether "labour" or "labor" is the correct spelling, in crude ignorance of the fact that both inaccuracies are merely confessions of our inability to write the obscure vowel that is the commonest sound in our language. As to enabling me to hand down my plays as [English composer] Sir Edward Elgar [1857–1934] can hand down his Falstaff, I see no chance of that in literature. Perhaps the phonograph may be able to do something for me before I die; otherwise, like Shakespear, I shall take the secret of their performance to the grave with me, and with it almost all their artistic value, leaving posterity (if it troubles itself about them) to gnaw the cold bones of their intellectual skeletons.

Yours truly,
G. Bernard Shaw

6. "On Clive Bell's Article," *The New Republic*, February 22, 1922.

[Clive Bell had written an article in which he accused Shaw of not being an artist, but simply "a didactic," and where he also criticizes Shaw's adaptation of evolutionary theory. This is Shaw's response, where he delves on the intellectual basis of his dramaturgy, as opposed to Bell's emphasis on the senses. It is to be expected, at any rate, that Clive Bell, a formalist critic who informed the aesthetics of the Bloomsbury group, should criticize Shaw's 'didacticism' and social focus.]

As will be seen in the above article, my friend [English critic] Clive Bell [1881–1964] is a fathead and a voluptuary. This is a very comfortable sort of person to be, and very friendly and easy and pleasant to talk to. Bell is a brainy man out of train-ing. So much the better for his friends; for men in training are irritable, dangerous, and apt to hit harder than they know. No fear of that from Clive. The layer of fat on his brain makes him incapable of following up his own meaning; but it makes him good company.

A man out of condition muscularly not only dislikes row-ing or boxing, but cannot conceive anyone liking them. A man out of condition mentally not only dislikes hard think-ing, but cannot conceive anyone enjoying it. To Falstaff, [French boxer Georges] Carpentier [1894–1975] is an object of pity. To Clive, Einstein is the most miserable of mortals. So am I.

He is mistaken as to both of us. Intellect is a passion: and its activity and satisfaction, which can be maintained from seven years old to 107 if you can manage to live so long, are keenly pleasurable if the brain is strong enough for the exercise. [French mathematician and philosopher René] Descartes [1596–1650] must have got far more pleasure out of life than Casanova. Hamlet had more fun than [character in one of Abbé Prévost's novels] Des Grieux, who tried to live on his love for Manon Lescaut, relieved by cheating at cards. Clive tells us how he poisons the clear night air of London with his cheroots after an evening of wine, woman, and song; and he is contemptuously certain that he has enjoyed him-self far more than a handful of old gentlemen in a society of chemists, mathematicians, biologists, or what not, discussing the latest thing in quantums of energy, or electrons, or hor-mones. It is the interest of the tobacconist, the restaurateur, the theatrical manager, the wine merchant and distiller, to suggest that delusion to him. And what a silly delusion it is! No pleasure of the first order is compatible with tobacco and alcohol, which are useful only for killing time and drowning care. For real pleasure men keep their senses and wits clear: they do not deliberately dull and muddle themselves. I have not the smallest doubt that when the human mind is as fully developed as the human reproductive processes now are, men will, like the ancients in *Back to Methuselah*, experience a sustained ecstasy of thought that will make our sexual ecstasies seem child's play.

Clive is troubled—you know it when he cries Who cares?—because a rose grows out of manure. This comes of taking hold of things by the wrong end. Why not rejoice because manure grows into a rose? The most valuable lesson in *Back to Methuselah* is that things are conditioned not by their origins but by their ends. What makes the Ancient wise is not the life he has lived and done with but the life that is before him. Clive says why not live in the present? Because we don't, and won't, and can't. Because there is no such thing as the present: there is only the gate that we are always reaching and never passing through: the gate that leads from the past into the future. Clive, meaning to insist on static sensation, slips inevitably into talking of "*the significance* of all that comes to one through the senses." What then becomes of his figment of sense without significance? "Whatever is precious and beautiful in life," he says, "is precious and beautiful irrespective of beginning and end." Bosh! The only sensations intense enough to be called precious or beautiful are the sensations of irresistible movement to an all-important end: the only perceptions that deserve such epithets are perceptions of some artistic expression of such sensation or prefigured ideal of its possibilities. The pain with which a child cuts its teeth, though felt, is not suffered because the child feels it as Clive pretends to feel his pleasures: that is, it cannot anticipate the next moment of it or remember the last; and so, fretful as it may seem, it does not suffer at all. If Clive ever gets his pleasures down to the point at which he also does not anticipate the future or remember the past, he will not enjoy it in the least. In short, his imaginary present and its all sufficing delight is unconsidered tosh.

The reason Clive enjoys his suppers is that he first works hard enough to need relaxation—at least I presume and hope he does. If he did not he would be miserable, and would probably have to take to drugs to enable him to bear his pleasant evenings at the Russian Ballet. Even now he cannot get through them without the aid of cheroots. I never eat supper; I never smoke; I drink water; and I can sit out *Petrouchka* and enjoy the starlight in Piccadilly all the same. But clearly, if I could be persuaded that *Petrouchka*, instead of being a relaxation, is as creative as the Piccadilly starlight is recreative, I should enjoy it a thousand times more. So would anybody.

No, my Clive: in vain do you sing

> Sun, stand thou still upon Gibeon,
> And thou, Moon, in the valley of Ajalon.

They will not stop for you. [Russian ballerina Lydia] Lopokova [1892–1981] will dance, as you say; but when you stretch your arms to her and cry

> Verweile doch, du bist so schön

you cannot stop, either of you, any more than Paolo and Francesca could stop in the whirlwind. You delight in the music of Mozart; but does it ever stop? It ends; but your delight ends with it. You are a destinate creature, and must hurry along helter-skelter; so what is the use of waving your cheroots at us and assuring us that you are motionless and meaningless? There is nothing in the world more ridiculous than a man running at full speed, and shouting to everyone that he is in no hurry, and does not care two straws where he is going to.

7. "On Printed Plays," *The Times Literary Supplement*, May 17, 1923.

[Shaw revisits the idea that dramatic language is written to be spoken and, as such, it must be intelligible to the audience—regardless of how poetic it may seem on the printed page. It is worthy of note that intelligibility on the stage for Shaw does not necessarily entail simple language, or monosyllabic words. On the whole, the balance between "the score and the libretto" is one of the most difficult skills that a playwright must master.]

Sir,—Your excellent article on The Printed Play last week left out one point of instruction to would-be playwrights (including probably 95 per cent of your readers) which the writer will forgive me for supplying.

In preparing a play for publication, the author's business is to make it intelligible to a reader. In preparing it for performance he has to make it intelligible to a spectator and listener. The last quality is the one in which a writer who has always worked for publication alone is likely to fail in direct proportion to his inveterate practice and his virtuosity. For example, [American writer] Henry James [1843–1916] wished to succeed as a playwright. Not long ago the Stage Society performed an early attempt of his. It was quite successful, and helped to make the reputation of [British actor] Mr Nicholas Hannen [1881–1972] as a comedian. The same society tried one of James's fully matured at-tempts. In spite of a representation by [actress] Miss Ellen O'Malley [?–1961] of the heroine which was as charming and delicate as even the fastidious James could have desired, it was a hopeless failure. Why?

The explanation is simple enough. There is a literary language which is perfectly intelligible to the eye, yet utterly unintelligible to the ear even when it is easily speakable by the mouth. Of that English James was master in the library and slave on the stage. At the last-mentioned performance I experimented on my friends between the acts by repeating some of the most exquisite sentences from the dialogue. I spoke fairly and distinctly, but not one of my victims could understand me or even identify the words I was uttering.

I cannot give any rule for securing audible intelligibility. It is not missed through long words or literary mannerisms or artificiality of style, nor secured by simplicity. Most of the dialogues that have proved effective on the English stage have been written either in the style of Shakespear, which is often Euphuistic in its artificiality, or in that of Dr Johnson, which is, as [Anglo-Irish novelist, playwright, and poet Oliver] Goldsmith [1728–1774] said, a style natural only in a whale. [English playwright] Ben Jonson's [1572–1637] *Volpone* is detestably unreadable; yet, when spoken on the stage it is a model of vivid dialogue. The Jamesian passages with which I experimented did not contain any word of more than two syllables: word for word they were as simple as *The Pilgrim's Progress*. But they "came across" as gibberish. Speech does not differ from literature in its materials. "This my band will rather the multitudinous seas incarnadine" is such a polysyllabic monstrosity as was never spoken anywhere but on the stage; but it is magnificently effective and perfectly intelligible in the theatre. James could have paraphrased it charmingly in words of one syllable and left the audience drearily wondering what on earth Macbeth was saying.

It is significant that many successful writers for the stage have never written for anything else. Others have excelled as public speakers or in conversation. There is, of course, a born genius for dialogue which needs no training. Moliere, Goldsmith, Chesterton, [Irish dramatist and theater manager Isabella Augusta] Lady Gregory [1852–1932] are the first highly literary examples that occur to me. But the disastrous plays of James and the stage failures of novelists obviously much more richly endowed by Nature and culture than many of the

successful playwrights with whom they have tried to compete, suggest that they might have succeeded if only they had
understood that as the pen and the *viva vox* are different instruments, their parts must be scored accordingly.

Possibly this hint may be of use to some of our novelists.
The scarcity of effective playwrights amid a multitude of popular novelists is ridiculous and unnatural.

Yours truly,
G. Bernard Shaw

Part V: Nonfiction — Biography, Philosophy, Science, and Folklore

Shaw's long—if intermittent—career as a reviewer, made him acquainted with the most disparate authors and books, especially in the early stages. The eclectic corpus of reviews he wrote include some on works he would have never read, were it not for his professional duties. These are mostly books that were very popular at the time but had very little to do with literature: treatises on the occult, for example. They reveal the reading habits of a period and constitute a perfect touchstone for Shaw to sharpen his critical abilities. On other occasions, he reviewed works that—not being literary in a strict sense—either deal with the life and works of a major author or describe theories that were influential in Shaw's view of literature.

1. "Folk Lore, English and Scotch," *The Pall Mall Gazette*, 25 August 1885.

[Review of 'Twixt Ben Nevis and Glencoe, *by the Rev. Alexander Stewart (Edinburgh: William Paterson, 1885) and* The Gentleman's Magazine Library*—English Traditions and Foreign Customs. Edited by George Laurence Gomme (London: Elliot Stock, 1885). Shaw was a self-made intellectual as well as a spiritual man who reconciled creationism (at least, the teleology thereof) with evolution in neo-Lamarckian terms. But ghost stories and supernatural trivia were perhaps too much for his nonexistent gullibility. The range of stylistic techniques—from subtle irony to comic argumentation—illuminate Shaw's take on these topics.]*

"TWIXT BEN NEVIS AND GLENCOE"

The banished Duke in *As You Like It*, who found sermons in stones, has probably often been envied on Saturday afternoons by ecclesiastics at a loss for the morrow's discourse. He also found books in the running brooks, but on this point, and probably on the other too, he is equalled by [Scottish scholar and antiquary] Dr Alexander Stewart [1829–1901], who finds articles in streams, storms, rats, mice, birds, and fishes; and strings them into books well padded with anecdotes which, to turn his favourite phrase, he makes no apology for quoting at full length. Such books are not fair game for the reviewer: they are addressed to children of all ages who are willing to shut their eyes and open their mouths. In this attitude the grown-up children will presently be gratified by some startling flattery. "Unrivalled as a soldier, and almost faultless as a man," says the author, "you will have some difficulty, if you try, in finding any one entitled for an instant, and on any claims whatever, to stand with the slightest pretensions to equality of stature besides the, perhaps, greatest man of his age—[Scottish nobleman and poet] James Gra-

ham, Earl and Marquis of Montrose [1612–1650]." The reader,
thus liberally blarneyed, may modestly disclaim the military
skill attributed to him; but he cannot be insensible to the
assurance that he is "almost faultless as a man," though the
compliment must fall somewhat flat on lady readers, who will
possibly contend that Dr Stewart has made a slip and that
the superlative soldier and excellent man referred to is none
other than Montrose. In some instances the author's appreci-
ation of the details of a subject overbalances his judgment of
it as a whole. For example, in discoursing on rats, he opines
that "the scene in 'Hamlet' would lose much of its grim humour and effectiveness if it were not for the rat behind the
arras." This almost reminds one of Mr Wopsle's dresser, who
maintained that the secret of all great actors of *Hamlet* was
that they never permitted their tights to be seen in profile.
Again, when Dr Stewart saw an old woman cure a bad case of
colic by administering water in which a redhot flat-iron had
been plunged, he seems to have believed that the charm lay
in the flat-iron, and that a pint of water warmed in the usual
way in a kettle would have been of no avail. Dr Stewart, in
fact, has the faults of his qualities. His love of legend stretches
his credulity, just as his love of animals impairs his grasp of
Shakspearean tragedy. His admiration of the great poets is
frank hero-worship; and he esteems himself fortunate in having seen an aerolite exactly corresponding to the meteoric
phenomenon described by Homer in the famous passage in
the fourth book of the Iliad, which tells of the descent of Pal-
las from Olympus to the plains of Troy. Pope translated it as a
comet, and [Scottish scholar] Professor [John Stuart] Blackie
[1809–1895] more cautiously calls it a meteor star; but Dr Stewart has identified the genuine article as what the Highlanders
call a *drèag*. He proposes that it shall henceforth be called
"a Minervalite," and engages to call it so himself "in all time
coming." The name is not a handsome or very convenient
one, but it may be forgiven to an amiable and chatty natural-

ist, who, by acting as a sort of scientific and literary ragpicker, has managed to provide us with a miscellany free from sensationalism, and yet full of interest for the snapper-up of unconsidered trifles.

"THE GENTLEMAN'S MAGAZINE LIBRARY"

The Psychical Society will find plenty of ghost stories in [English archeologist and anthropologist] Mr G[eorge]. Laurence Gomme's selection of such of these notes and anecdotes as relate to English traditional lore and the customs of foreign countries and peoples. The classification is not always as happy as the selection. "Ghosts" seems hardly the proper heading for the following:—"At the Council of Trent, the Legate Crescentio, having long laboured at his despatches, rose from his chair and thought he saw an ugly dog advance and run under the table. In haste he called for his servants, but no dog could be found. The Legate took to his bed and died of fright." Notwithstanding the respect due to the memory of Crescentio, Mr Gomme might, without impropriety, have put this case under the heading "Delirium Tremens." The story of the mysterious red man who haunted Napoleon is a genuine—that is, not a true—ghost story. "Who the red man really was has never been known; but that such a person obtained an interview with Napoleon seems to have been placed beyond a doubt." This modest comment is in the finest manner of the ghost-storyteller, whose audience would doubtless be disappointed beyond measure if the red man were reduced to fact as prosaically as the once equally mysterious black man who ordered Mozart's requiem. The accounts of the bite of the tarantula are masterpieces of flagrant mendacity; and it is greatly to be feared that Stephen Storage, who in 1753 obliged the *Gentleman's Magazine* with a "distinct detail" of how he had been "instrumental" (the instrument was his violin) "at the cure of a poor plowman that

was bit by that insect," is now wishing that he had restrained
his invention within reasonable bounds. During the eighteenth century tourists were evidently not only permitted to
tell lies, but encouraged to do so. *The Gentleman's Magazine*
must have acted as a powerful stimulus to the imagination of
the travelled. This was hardly needed; for more than a century before the magazine was started we find so simple and
frank a soldier as Othello confessing before the council at
Venice that he had beguiled his father-in-law with tales of
men whose heads beneath their shoulders grew.

Mr Gomme, like Dr Stewart, has furnished his book with
an index, which will be of great service to persons in search
of information on all sorts of subjects. The general reader,
turning over the pages, will learn many things that are not of
the slightest importance to him, but which he may, nevertheless, wish to know because other people occasionally write or
speak of them.

2. "A Science of Ghosts," *The Pall Mall Gazette*, 24 November, 1886.

[Review of Phantasms of the Living, *by Edmund Gurney, Frederic W. H. Myers, and Frank Podmore (London: Trilbner and Co.,
1886). Shaw displays his most effective and cogent arguments to expose the naivety of these accounts—not without a tad of humor.]*

This formidable array of ghost stories, collected, arranged,
and commented on by Messrs [English scientist Edmund]
Gurney [1847–1888], [English poet, philologist, and founder
of the Society for Psychical Research Frederic William
Henry] Myers [1843–1901], and [English writer Frank] Podmore
[1855–1910], somehow reminds one of those "several manuscript confessions upon which Mr Wemmick set particular
value as being, to use his own words, 'every one of 'em lies,
sir.'" It is useless to mince matters in dealing with ghost sto-

ries—the existence of a liar is more probable than the existence of a ghost. "One of the advantages of personal inquiry," says Mr Myers, in his introduction, "is the security gained by it as to the *bona fides* of the witnesses concerned. They have practically placed themselves on their honour; nor need we doubt that the experiences have been, as a rule, recounted in all sincerity." It is unpleasant but necessary to rejoin that the custom of accepting as conclusive the solemn statements of persons of good repute concerning events that are known to be natural does not hold when marvels are in question. There is a point at which it is easier to impute deliberate falsehood to a Washington or a [French knight Pierre Terrail, seigneur de] Bayard [1473–1524] than to believe them. The most intelligent man may be misled by hallucination: the wisest may suddenly go mad: the best may sin against strict veracity. Such aberrations are more probable than the appearance of a man miles away from where he lies dying. As to ordinary witnesses, the great majority are so ignorantly convinced that seeing is believing, so little aware that the evidence of their senses requires highly skilled interpretation before it can exert weight in the balance of science, that they are the last persons who can be depended upon to give a trustworthy account of what has actually passed in their presence. In saying, therefore, that it yet remains to be seen whether the toughest contents of these two well filled volumes are true, no accusation of intentional falsehood against the deponents is implied. That some of them have said the thing that is not is extremely likely; that they knew they were doing so does not necessarily or even probably follow.

These considerations have hitherto frightened away from "psychical research" almost all who were adequately qualified for it. Indeed, as the very love of the marvellous which makes the subject irresistibly attractive to certain temperaments indicates a lack of the scientific spirit in which it should be studied, adequately qualified men would perhaps not often

be found working at it even if there were nothing to frighten
them away. On other accounts, too, the work cannot be very
pleasant. Invitations to the public to tell ghost stories at once
bring the investigator into contact with a host of witnesses of
whom the most eager, the most communicative, and the most
officious are obscurely epileptic or hysterical persons, incorri-
gibly conceited and mendacious. Even when the investigator
has become expert enough to decide very easily in nine cases
out of ten whether his informants are intellectually honest
or not, still the tenth case is likely to depend on the credit
of a witness who is imaginative and obviously strongly ad-
dicted to the miraculous, but whose intelligence and sincerity make it difficult to reject his story, which is likely to be
the best told of the ten. In the face of all these difficulties, the
three authors have acquitted themselves admirably. Mr Myers's introduction and Mr Gurney's commentary confirm the
impression, which no guest of the Psychical Society has ever
failed to receive, that they are extremely superior men. "How
poor, how fragmentary," exclaims Mr Myers, "were Aristotle's fancies compared with our conception, thus gained, of
cosmic unity! our vibrant message from Sirius and Orion
by the heraldry of the kindred flame! ...The insentient has
awoke, we know not how, into sentiency; the sentient into
the fuller consciousness of human minds." Fine as all this is,
Mr Myers, unexhausted, goes on to talk about the microcosm
and the macrocosm in a way that really does one good to
read. Mr Gurney follows with more sobriety, but not less ability; and Mr Podmore, like a subtle essence, so pervades the
whole that, to quote the preface, "his name could not possibly have been omitted from the title-page."

The main contention of the book, foreshadowed by the
title, is startlingly contrary to all received ideas of the supernatural. Every Englishman believes that he is entitled to a
ghost after death to compensate him for the loss of his body,
and to enable him to haunt anybody that may have murdered

or otherwise ill-used him in the days when he was solid. But our authors contend that a dead man can have no ghost. It is during life that we have the power of "appearing" to our friends; and a plain necessity for fresh legislation arises from the fact that although no privacy can hide us from them if we really make up our minds to haunt them, they have no defence or legal remedy against such incorporeal trespass, except the power of exerting their will so as to detain and converse with our ghosts—a process which gives our bodily selves a bad headache. As to those whose wills are weak, we can simply frighten them out of their wits when we please. We can not only make them see things, we can make them feel, taste, and smell them; write down what we are thinking of; and in fact induce sensations in them as a current in one telegraph wire induces a current in another. Fortunately we can only do this while we are alive and ought to be more usefully employed. Macbeth's strong opinion that when "the brains were out the man would die, and there an end" was well founded; and his vision of Banquo but an hallucination.

For innumerable instances of the exercise of these weird powers, reference must be made to the volumes themselves. Their thousand pages of marvels will save the nervous, the lonely, and the sleepless from tedium during the long winter nights. Those who have no nerves will find interest in cases like that of Miss Drasey, who, we are told, in a footnote to page 110, vol.i., "fainted away, and nearly dropped some dishes she had in her hands." This way of putting it hardly does justice to the uncommon presence of mind of a lady who remembered, even in a swoon, what was due to her fragile charge.

It would be unfair to conclude a notice of Messrs Myers, Gurney, and Podmore's work without an acknowledgment of public indebtedness to them for useful and arduous work diligently and ably done. Human nature being frail, the critical eye cannot be prevented from twinkling occasionally as it travels over their pages; but the reader must not infer therefrom any intention to disparage a valuable and interesting contribution to the elucidation of a branch of science which scientific men have hitherto carefully let alone.

3. "Darwin Denounced," *The Pall Mall Gazette*, 31 May, 1887.

[Review of Samuel Butler's Luck, or Cunning? *(London: Trubner and Co., 1887). Shaw was very interested in the theory of evolution and the philosophical implications it posed for humankind. He was also one of the first to understand that science was replacing religion, for it was another cult where people had to take explanations on faith: as Shaw put it in the Preface to Saint Joan (1923): "why the men who believe in electrons should regard themselves as less credulous than the men who believed in angels is not apparent to me."]*

We are such an inveterately idolatrous people that it would perhaps be well for us if we could go back frankly to the cultus of the graven image, and leave our great men unworshipped. It would take the conceit out of them and do the graven images no harm. Better to adore in silence the brazen effigy in Parliament-square, as do the Primrose Leaguers, than to falsify and pervert, and exaggerate, and gloze, and special-plead in defence of our favourite geniuses, or in impeachment of those of our neighbours. We are overburdened with gods and sects: our Walhalla is as disorderly as the Church of the Holy Sepulchre, in which Moslem soldiers keep the Christian worshippers from coming to blows with one another, would be without the soldiers. We are Gladstonians, Wagnerians, Pasteurians [French microbiologist Louis Pasteur, 1822–1895], Burne-Jonesians, Browningites, Marxites, Darwinians, or else we belong to the simply heathen majority.

In *Luck, or Cunning?* we read of "greater nonsense than it would be prudent even for him [Darwin] to write"; of the years that it will take "to get evolution out of the mess in which Mr Darwin left it"; of a work [Lamarck's *Philosophie Zoologique*] which, though weighted with "defects, shortcomings, and mistakes," is yet "an incomparably sounder work than the 'Origin of Species'"; of how Mr Darwin first grossly misrepresented [French naturalist Georges-Louis Leclerc, Comte de] Buffon [1707–1788] and then told him to go away; of a suave but "singularly fraudulent passage" as to [Scottish publisher and geologist] Robert Chambers [1802–1871]; all capped by two declarations at which [Canadian science writer] Mr [Charles] Grant Allen [1848–1899] will hardly refrain from rending his clothes. "For myself," says Mr Butler, "I know not which most to wonder at—the meanness of the writer himself, or the greatness of the service that, in spite of that meanness, he unquestionably rendered." And, again, "I know no more pitiable figure in either literature or science." After this, it is not surprising to learn that Mr Butler has been "very angrily attacked," and that he has, "as a matter of business," made himself "as unpleasant as he could in his rejoinders."

The usual etiquette of scientific controversy is to shake hands fulsomely with your adversary for at least fifteen minutes, and then seize the first opportunity of hitting him below the belt, taking care to wrangle over his complaint of unfair treatment with the utmost acrimony and ill humour. Mr Butler omits the handshaking, and falls to fairly intended blows at once, choosing to be frankly unamiable rather than hypocritically considerate. The question at issue is—granted the survival of the fittest, were the survivors made fit by mere luck, or did they fit themselves by cunning? Mr Butler is for cunning; and he will have it that Darwin was all for luck. The quarrel is a pretty one; for if you decide in favour of cunning, the Darwinian will reply that it was a great piece of luck

in the survivor to have that cunning; whereas, if you back
luck, the [French naturalist Jean-Baptiste Lamarck, 1744–1829]
Lamarck-Butlerian will urge that the survivor must have had
the cunning to turn his luck to account. Now, evidently the
essence of pure luck is that it brings more than average good
fortune without the exercise of more than average ability.
Luck is luck only in so far as it is independent of cunning.
Otherwise luck and cunning are convertible terms, in which
case the dispute is about words, not about ideas. This is not
Mr Butler's view. He admits pure luck as a factor in evolution,
but denies its sufficiency as an explanation of all the phenom-
ena, and insists that organisms that have the luck to be cunning make further luck for themselves by the deliberate exercise of that cunning, and so introduce design into the universe—not design as we used to conceive it, all-foreseeing
from the first, but "a piecemeal, *solvitur ambulando* design,"
which, as it becomes more self-conscious and intelligent,
tends to supplant natural selection by functional modification. Darwin, says Mr Butler, sought to eliminate design and
functional modification wholly from evolution. Lamarck
thought functional modification more important than natural selection. Ergo, Lamarck was a greater philosopher, if
not a greater naturalist, than Darwin; and the incense we
burn at the shrine of Darwin is stolen from the temple of
Lamarck. The controversy is one of those in which the last
word is everything.

It is not expedient to discuss here the main point raised
by Mr Butler, particularly as he is evidently quite capable of
writing another book on the scientific attainments of the *Pall
Mall Gazette*, if provoked by contradiction. Let it suffice to
acknowledge his skilful terseness and exactness of expression, his frank disdain of affected suavity or imperturbability,
his apparently but not really paradoxical humour, his racy
epigrams, and the geniality of his protest against "a purely au-
tomatic conception of the universe as of something that will

work if a penny be dropped into the box." Ordinarily, a man who should write a book to complain that previous works of his had been overlooked, slighted, or borrowed from without acknowledgment, would be coughed down, or even, when he went on to denounce Darwin as mean and Goethe as a writer of "dull diseased trash" hooted down. The fact that Mr Butler has succeeded in doing this, and yet securing not only a hearing, but considerable attention and interest, is a conclusive proof of the exceptional ability with which he has stated his case.

4. "Nietzsche in English," *Saturday Review*, 11 April, 1896.

[Review of Nietzsche contra Wagner, &c. Vol. 1. *of the Collected Works of Friedrich Nietzsche. Trans. Thomas Common (London: Henry, 1896). Although the extent of Nietzsche's influence on Shaw is often downplayed—or exaggerated—the connections are too many to be coincidental, both in style and in ideas. In addition, one just need look at the volumes by or about Nietzsche that Shaw kept at his residence in Ayot St Lawrence (http://www.nationaltrustcollections.org.uk/) to appraise his interest in the German philosopher. Furthermore, this piece is interesting in itself because of Shaw's introduction on the question of what is philosophy.]*

It is with a most opportune consideration for my Easter holiday that Messrs Henry & Co. have just issued the first volume of their translation of the works of Friedrich Nietzsche. And such a volume, too! containing everything that he wrote just before he reached the point at which Germany made up its mind that he was mad, and shut him up, both figuratively and actually. Whilst I am still at large I may as well explain that Nietzsche is a philosopher—that is to say, something unintelligible to an Englishman. To make my readers realize

what a philosopher is, I can only say that *I* am a philosopher.
If you ask incredulously, "How, then, are your articles so interesting?" I reply that there is nothing so interesting as philosophy, provided its materials are not spurious. For instance,
take my own materials—humanity and the fine arts. Any stu-
dious, timorously ambitious bookworm can run away from
the world with a few shelvesful of history, essays, descriptions, and criticisms, and, having pieced an illusory humanity
and art out of the effects produced by his library on his imagination, build some silly systematization of his worthless ideas
over the abyss of his own nescience. Such a philosopher is
as dull and dry as you please: it is he who brings his profession into disrepute, especially when he talks much about art,
and so persuades people to read him. Without having looked
at more than fifty pictures in his life, or made up his mind
on the smallest point about one of the fifty, he will auda-
ciously take it upon himself to explain the development of
painting from [Greek painter] Zeuxis [5th century BCE] and
[Greek painter] Apelles [of Kos, *c.* 330 BCE] to Raphael and
Michael Angelo. As to the way he will go on about music,
of which he always has an awe-stricken conceit, it spoils my
temper to think of it, especially when one remembers that
musical composition is taught (a monstrous pretension) in
this country by people who read scores, and never by any
chance listen to performances. Now, the right way to go to
work—strange as it may appear—is to look at pictures until you have acquired the power of seeing them. If you look
at several thousand good pictures every year, and form some
sort of practical judgment about every one of them—were it
only that it is not worth troubling over—then at the end of
five years or so you will, if you have a wise eye, be able to see
what is actually in a picture, and not what you think is in it.
Similarly, if you listen critically to music every day for a number of years, you will, if you have a wise ear, acquire the power
of hearing music. And so on with all the arts. When we come

to humanity it is still the same: only by intercourse with men and women can we learn anything about it. This involves an active life, not a contemplative one; for unless you do something in the world, you can have no real business to transact with men; and unless you love and are loved, you can have no intimate relations with them. And you must transact business, wirepull politics, discuss religion, give and receive hate, love and friendship with all sorts of people before you can acquire the sense of humanity. If you are to acquire the sense sufficiently to be a philosopher, you must do all these things unconditionally. You must not say that you will be a gentleman and limit your intercourse to this class or that class; or that you will be a virtuous person and generalize about the affections from a single instance—unless, indeed, you have the rare happiness to stumble at first upon an all-enlightening instance. You must have no convictions, because, as Nietzsche puts it, "convictions are prisons." Thus, I blush to add, you cannot be a philosopher and a good man, though you may be a philosopher and a great one. You will say, perhaps, that if this be so, there should be no philosophers; and perhaps you are right; but though I make you this handsome concession, I do not defer to you to the extent of ceasing to exist. After all, if you insist on the hangman, whose pursuits are far from elevating, you may very well tolerate the philosopher, even if philosophy involves philandering; or, to put it another way, if, in spite of your hangman, you tolerate murder within the sphere of war, it may be necessary to tolerate comparatively venial irregularities within the sphere of philosophy. It is the price of progress; and, after all, it is the philosopher, and not you, who will burn for it.

These are shocking sentiments, I know; but I assure you you will think them mere Sunday School commonplaces when you have read a little of Nietzsche. Nietzsche is worse than shocking, he is simply awful: his epigrams are written with phosphorus on brimstone. The only excuse for reading

them is that before long you must be prepared either to talk
about Nietzsche or else retire from society, especially from
aristocratically minded society (not the same thing, by the
way, as aristocratic society), since Nietzsche is the champion
of privilege, of power, and of inequality. Famous as Nietzsche
has become—he has had a great *succès de scandale* to advertise his penetrating wit—I never heard of him until a few
years ago, when, on the occasion of my contributing to the
literature of philosophy a minute treatise entitled *The Quintessence of Ibsenism*, I was asked whether I had not been inspired by a book called *Out at the other side of Good and Evil*, by
Nietzsche. The title seemed to me promising; and in fact Nietzsche's criticism of morality and idealism is essentially that
demonstrated in my book as at the bottom of Ibsen's plays.
His pungency; his power of putting the merest platitudes of
his position in rousing, startling paradoxes; his way of getting
underneath moral precepts which are so unquestionable to
us that common decency seems to compel unhesitating as-
sent to them, and upsetting them with a scornful laugh: all
this is easy to a witty man who has once well learnt Schopenhauer's lesson, that the intellect by itself is a mere dead piece
of brain machinery, and our ethical and moral systems merely
the pierced cards you stick into it when you want it to play a
certain tune. So far I am on common ground with Nietzsche.
But not for a moment will I suffer any one to compare me
to him as a critic. Never was there a deafer, blinder, socially
and politically inepter academician. He has fancies concerning different periods of history, idealizing the Romans and
the Renascence, and deducing from his idealization no end
of excellences in their works. When have I ever been guilty
of such professorial folly? I simply go and look at their works,
and after that you may talk to me until you go black in the
face about their being such wonderful fellows: I know by my
senses that they were as bad artists, and as arrant intellect-
mongers, as need be. And what can you say to a man who,

after pitting his philosophy against Wagner's with refreshing ingenuity and force, proceeds to hold up as the masterpiece of modern dramatic music, blazing with the merits which the Wagnerian music dramas lack—guess what! *Don Giovanni*, perhaps, or *Orfeo*, or *Fidelio*? Not at all: *Carmen*, no less. Yes, as I live by bread, as I made that bread for many a year by listening to music, Georges Bizet's *Carmen*. After this one is not surprised to find Nietzsche blundering over politics, and social organization and administration in a way that would be impossible to a man who had ever served on a genuine working committee long enough—say ten minutes—to find out how very little attention the exigencies of practical action can be made to pay to our theories when we have to get things done, one way or another. To him modern Democracy, Pauline Christianity, Socialism, and so on are deliberate plots hatched by malignant philosophers to frustrate the evolution of the human race and mass the stupidity and brute force of the many weak against the beneficial tyranny of the few strong. This is not even a point of view: it is an absolutely fictitious hypothesis: it would not be worth reading were it not that there is almost as much evidence for it as if it were true, and that it leads Nietzsche to produce some new and very striking and suggestive combinations of ideas. In short, his sallie, petulant and impossible as some of them are, are the work of a rare spirit and are pregnant with its vitality. It is notable that Nietzsche does not write in chapters or treatises: he writes leading articles, leaderettes, occasional notes, and epigrams. He recognizes that humanity, having tasted the art of the journalist, will no longer suffer men to inflict books on it. And he simplifies matters, quite in the manner of the leading article writer, by ignoring things as they are, and dealing with things as it is easiest, with our prejudices and training, to think they are, except that he supplies the training and instils the prejudices himself as he goes along, instead of picking up those that lie about the street as one does in writing leaders for the daily press.

There are two reasons why I can say no more than this about Nietzsche. The first is that I am lying on a hillside in the sun, basking, not working. The second is that I must reserve some space for [Irish playwright] Miss Clo[tilde] Graves's [1863–1932] *Mother of Three* at the Comedy, which has plucked me up from that hillside by the roots...

G.B.S.

5. "Hyndman," *The Nation*, 21 October, 1911.

[Review of The Record of an Adventurous Life, *by Henry Mayers Hyndman (London: Macmillan, 1911). This piece of criticism indirectly illustrates Shaw's stance towards the emerging socialist movement in Britain, as well the role of the Fabian Society in relation to other associations and political parties within the same ideological spectrum. The description of the author, intertwined with the appraisal of his work, is another major example of Shavian satire at its best.]*

Not many men living have impressed themselves on the consciousness of the political world in such a fashion that, in a political and literary review of picked circulation, one can drop the Mister in heading an article about them. We say [English writer and politician Henry Mayers] Hyndman [1842–1921] as who should say [Prussian statesman Otto von] Bismarck [1815–1898], or [Italian occultist and adventurer Count Alessandro di] Cagliostro [1743–1795], or Garibaldi, or [Italian Dominican friar Girolamo] Savonarola [1452–1498], or Aristotle, or Columbus. A mysterious quality this, when it exists in anyone but a poet. Poets are entitled to it in all the arts: there is nothing in calling Raphael Raphael instead of Messer Sanzio, or Beethoven Beethoven, or Shakespear

Shakespear. But why should Hyndman be Hyndman and not Mr Hyndman; or, still worse, *a* Mr Hyndman? Though he is a remarkable person—one would say brilliant if that adjective were not for some reason appropriated by comparatively young men—he has done nothing that has not been done equally well by men who cannot be identified without at least a Christian name, not to mention those who carry their Misters with them to the grave. It is clearly a matter of faith and conviction, not of works, this indefinable quality of personal style that has maintained Hyndman as the figurehead of a great revolutionary movement, even when there was really no movement behind the figure-head. It is not a triumph of tact: no man has done more unpardonable things, or done them so often (within the limits of the pardonable, if you will excuse the contradiction). It is not a triumph of sagacious leadership overcoming all defects of manner: on the contrary, Hyndman has charming manners and is the worst leader that ever drove his followers into every other camp—even into the Cabinet—to escape from his leadership. It is not any item from the catalogue of accomplishments and powers Macaulay kept for advertizing his heroes. Hyndman is accomplished; but his accomplishments are not unique. It is really the man himself that imposes, Heaven knows why! [British dramatist, actor, and theatre manager] Samuel Foote [1720–1777] is said to have stopped a man of striking carnage in the street with the inquiry, "May I ask, sir, are you anybody in particular?" Had he met Hyndman, he would have had the same curiosity; but he would not have dared to ask.

Hyndman has now given us an autobiography that does not do him justice; and yet you can say of it, as you can say of so few volumes of reminiscences, that he is his own hero. He tells you much about people he has met; but he does not hide behind them. And yet he has, to an extraordinary degree, the art of telling you nothing, either about

himself or anyone else. Here, for instance, is an account of
[English journalist] George Augustus Sala's [1828–1895] quarrel with George Meredith in Hyndman's presence. He tells it
with an air of telling you everything, and yet at the end you
know absolutely nothing that you did not know from the index: namely, that Sala and Meredith quarrelled. You do not
know what it was about, or what was said, or how they took
it. What you do know is that Hyndman was there; and this,
somehow, suffices. Do not hastily conclude that the narrative is so egotistical that Hyndman has insisted on playing the
two others off the stage. On the contrary, Hyndman is more
reticent about himself than about the others. This is no book
of confessions. Confession is not a Hyndmanesque attitude.
Not only is it true that, save for a hitherto unpublished fact or
two, there is nothing in this book about Meredith, Mazzini,
Disraeli, [French statesman Georges Benjamin] Clemenceau
[1841–1929], Morris, and [British statesman Lord] Randolph
[Henry Spencer] Churchill [1849–1895] (all of whom have
chapters to themselves) that could not have been compiled
by a clever writer who had never met them; there is actually
nothing about Hyndman himself that could not have been
written, and even considerably amplified, by a constant companion. It is not a revelation of the man: it simply lets you
know Who's Who. And yet it is frank to recklessness. Never
was there a book where there was less need to read between
the lines. Except a few harmless little chuckles over successes
that were quite genuine, there is no boasting; indeed, Hyndman does not cut anything like so imposing a figure in these
pages as he did in the public eye on several occasions. In the
expression of his dislikes he is abusive and positively spite-
ful without the smallest affectation: his collection of *bêtes
noires*, headed by [English trade-unionist and politician] Mr
John Burns [1858–1943], is reviled without mercy or justice,
and, what is much less common, without hypocrisy or any
pretence of superiority to hearty ill-will; whilst, on the other

hand, his more congenial friends and faithful followers are praised with equally unscrupulous generosity. Consequently, some of his swans are geese, and some of his geese are swans; but no great harm is done: you can always make allowances for the temper of a man who shews his temper fearlessly, whereas your man of good taste, who is afraid to praise and stabs only in the back, would mislead you seriously if he could lead you at all. And yet, in spite of all this openness, and of a vivacity that never flags and a touch on the pen that never bores, the fact remains that at the end of the book you see no deeper into Hyndman or his friends and contemporaries than you did at the beginning, though you have had a long and entertaining conversation about them. That is, if you already know your Marx and have got over the great Marxian change of mind—the great conversion which made a Socialist of Hyndman. If not, the book may be the beginning of a revelation to you. But if you know all that beforehand, the book will be to you a book of adventures and incidents, not a book of characters.

This will not surprise anyone who knows that there is a specific genius for politics, just as there is a specific genius for mathematics or dramatics. Hyndman is a born politician in the higher sense: that is, he is not really interested in individuals, but in societies, states, and their destinies. Apparently he did not care a rap for his own father; and it may be doubted whether he would care a rap for his own son if he had one; but he can see no faults in the Social-Democratic Federation, the ugly duckling which has well-nigh ruined him. He vituperates Mr John Burns, from whom he got no new political ideas, quite callously; but there is enthusiasm, almost tenderness, in his account of Marx, though Marx quarrelled with him, and strove far harder to injure and discredit him than Mr Burns did, even under the strongest provocation. The explanation is that Marx widened his political horizon as no other man. Hyndman began with the na-

tionalism of [Italian statesman Camillo Paolo Filippo Giulio
Benso, Count of] Cavour [1810–1861] and Mazzini: he ended
with the internationalism of Marx. After Marx there was
nothing to discover in the sphere of pure politics except
methods; and for methods Hyndman has no patience, no aptitude, and no qualifying official experience. He never went
on from the industrial revolution to the next things—to the
revolution in morals, and to the formulation and establishment of a credible and effective indigenous Western religion.
There is not a word in this book to indicate that the contemporary of Cavour and Marx was also the contemporary of
Wagner the artist-revolutionary, of Nietzsche the ethical revolutionary, of Sidney Webb the pathfinder in revolutionary
methods, or of Samuel Butler the founder of the religion of
Evolution. Hyndman played the flute and played duets with
Mrs Meredith without troubling himself about Wagner; dis-
missed popular religion as superstition and fraud, and was
too glad to be rid of it to see any need for replacing it; and
found the current morality quite good enough to furnish him
with invectives against the injustice and cruelty for which
he honorably loathed capitalistic society. His book, though
nominally brought up to 1889, really stops with the enlarge-
ment of his political conception of the world by Marx, and
with his founding of the Democratic Federation. He half
promises to bring his history up to date in a future volume;
but what has he to add, except a record of his own impatience
with the Fabian Society, the Independent Labor Party, and
the other bodies and movements which took the tactics of
Socialism out of his hands, complicating and obscuring his
splendid Marxist vision with all sorts of uncongenial details,
and elbowing out his poor but devoted disciples with—as
he considered them—all sorts of uncongenial, lower-middle-
class snobs and heretics?

It is not easy to reduce so exuberant a personality as Hyndman's to a type; but, roughly, we may class him with the free-

thinking English gentlemen-republicans of the last half of the nineteenth century: with [English politician Sir Charles Wentworth] Dilke [1843–1911], [English explorer and orientalist Sir Richard Francis] Burton [1821–1890], [English politician and philosopher] Auberon [Edward William Molyneux] Herbert [1838–1906], [English writer] Wilfrid Scawen Blunt [1840–1922], [British author and diplomat] Laurence Oliphant [1829–1888]: great globe-trotters, writers, *frondeurs*, brilliant and accomplished cosmopolitans as far as their various abilities permitted, all more interested in the world than in themselves, and in themselves than in official decorations; consequently unpurchasable, their price being too high for any modern commercial Government to pay. On their worst side they were petulant rich men, with perhaps a touch of the romantic vanity of the operatic tenor; and, as the combination of petulant rich man with ignorant poor one is perhaps the most desperately unworkable on the political chess-board, none of their attempts to found revolutionary societies for the advancement of their views came to much. One of the things Hyndman has never understood is the enormous advantage the founders of the Fabian Society had in their homogeneity of class and age. There were no illiterate working-men among them; there were no born rich men among them; there were no born poor men; there was not five years' difference between the oldest and the youngest. To Hyndman the acceptance and maintenance of such homogeneity still seems mere snobbery. He took up the democratic burden (as he regarded it) of working with men and women not of his generation, not of his class, not of his speed of mind and educational equipment. When the Fabians refused to involve themselves in that hopeless mess, he despised them. He even says, wildly, that they killed Morris by their refusal, just as the Unionists say Mr [Herbert Henry] Asquith [1852–1928] killed Edward VII. The Labor men knew better. They did not join the Fabian Society; but they made good use of it.

Still, the struggle with incongruity and impossibility on which Hyndman entered in 1881, though it has involved a fearful waste of his talent and energy, had something generous and heroic in it. In the Labor movement the experienced men will allow Hyndman no public virtue save this, that he has kept the flag flying—the red flag. And there are so many men who have every public virtue except this, that the exception suffices. Hyndman is still Hyndman, still, head aloft and beard abroad, carrying that flag with such high conviction that the smallest and silliest rabble at his heels becomes "the revolution." And outside that rabble there are still some friends, though he himself cares for nobody and nothing but the last act of the tragedy of capitalism.

G. B. S.

6. "Chesterton on Eugenics, and Shaw on Chesterton," *The Nation and The Athenaeum*, 11 March, 1922.

[Review of Eugenics, and Other Evils, *by G. K. Chesterton (London: Cassell & Co., 1922). This review brings together several of the most crucial areas of interest for Shaw. First, the theory of evolution and its implications for the reproduction of the human race. This gave rise to a heated public debate on eugenics and, in the political sphere, to the Mental Deficiency Act of 1913. Also, the ideas that Chesterton explores in his book come to grips with certain aspects of Shaw's Fabian socialism. Finally, there is a personal element that pervades the whole text; an element that responds to the ideological tension among luminaries like Shaw, William Morris, Sidney Webb, and Chesterton himself, among others.]*

A criticism of Mr Chesterton is in the nature of a bulletin as to the mental condition of a prophet. Mr Chesterton has disciples. I do not blame him: I have some myself. So has Mr

Wells. All sorts of people have disciples, from osteopaths to tipsters. But most of them do not get into our way politically. Mr Chesterton's do. Therefore it is important that his pulse should be felt, and his condition reported on; for if he were to go—well, may I say, for the sake of alliteration, off his chump?—the consequences might be serious. He has many magical arts and gifts at his command. He can make anything that can be made with a pen, from a conspectus of human history to a lethal jibe at the Lord Chancellor; and to utilize this practically boundless technical equipment he has enormous humor, imagination, intellect, and common sense.

Now in respect of the humor and imagination, his integrity can be depended on; but when you come to the intellect and common sense, you have to be careful, because his intellect is fantastic and his common sense impatient. That is because his humor and imagination will creep in. It is such fun to take some impossibly obsolete person—say a Crusader—and shew that he was right in his ideas, and that the sooner we get back to them the better for us, that no humorist ingenious enough to do it can resist it unless he has the dogged cerebral honesty of an Einstein. And here again it is so funny to *épater les savants* by arguing that Einstein, being a Jew, invented Relativity to popularize his longnosed relatives, and that Ptolemy, who thought the earth flat, was on solid ground, that the cumulative temptation sometimes strains even Chesterton's colossal shoulders. To give way is such an amiable weakness too! When he does it I am always amused; and I am never taken in: at least if I am I do not know it, otherwise, of course, I should not be taken in. But other people may be. Besides, Mr Chesterton may take himself in. He may stray up an intellectual blind alley to amuse himself; for it is the greatest mistake to suppose that there is nothing interesting or useful to be picked up in blind alleys before you run your head into the *cul de sac*. A man like Mr Chesterton finds more diamonds in such an alley than an ordinary man walks over pebbles in the clearest logical fairway. By stopping to pick the diamonds up, like [Greek mythological huntress] Atalanta, he may not get far enough to discover that the alley is blind. Even if he does, he may find a way out by pretending that he has found one, as the mathematician overcomes an intellectually insuperable difficulty by pretending that there is such a quantity as minus x. Searchlights in blind alleys have illuminated the whole heavens at times; and men have found courage and insight within their limits after finding nothing but terror and bewilderment in the open desert.

Thus Mr Chesterton, who once lived near the Home for Lost Dogs in Battersea, has a whimsical tendency to set up Homes For Lost Causes, in competition with Oxford University, in his half-explored blind alleys. Like the Home in Battersea, they are not popular with the lost ones; for the final hospitality offered is that of the lethal chamber. The Lost Causes like their last ditches well camouflaged. Mr Chesterton scorns concealment: he stands on the parapet, effulgent by his own light, roaring defiance at a foe who would only too willingly look the other way and pretend not to notice. Even the Lost Causes which are still mighty prefer their own methods of fighting. The Vatican never seems so shaky as when G. K. C. hoists it on his shoulders like Atlas, and proceeds to play football with the skulls of the sceptics. [American Prohibition advocate William Eugene Johnson, known as] Pussyfoot's chances of drying the British Isles seldom seem so rosy as they do the morning after Mr Chesterton has cracked the brainpans of a thousand teetotallers with raps from Gargantuan flagons waved by him in an ecstasy in which he seems to have ten pairs of hands, like an Indian god.

Nature compensates the danger of his defence by the benefit of his assault. He went to Jerusalem to destroy Zionism; and immediately the spirit of Nehemiah entered into him, and there arose from his pages such a wonderful vision of

Jerusalem that our hearts bled for the captivity, and all the rival claimants, past and present, silly Crusader and squalid Bedouin in one red burial blent, perished from our imaginations, and left the chosen people of God to inherit the holy city. He attacks divorce with an idealization of marriage so superhuman (without extraordinary luck) that all his readers who have not yet committed themselves swear that nothing will induce them to put their heads into the noose of that golden cord. He stated the case for giving votes to women so simply and splendidly that when he proceeded to give his verdict against the evidence it passed as a misprint. Really a wonderful man, this Chesterton; but with something of Balaam in him, and something of that other who went whither he would not.

His latest book is called *Eugenics, and Other Evils*. It is a graver, harder book than its forerunners. Something—perhaps the youthful sense of immortality, commonly called exuberance—has lifted a little and left him scanning the grey horizon with more sense that the wind is biting and the event doubtful; but there is plenty of compensating gain; for this book is practically all to the good. The title suggests the old intellectual carelessness: it seems mere nonsense: he might as well write Obstetrics and Other Evils, or Dietetics or Esthetics or Peripatetics or Optics or Mathematics and Other Evils. But when you read you find that he knows what he is about. The use of the word Eugenics implies that the breeding of the human race is an art founded on an ascertained science. Now when men claim scientific authority for their ignorance, and police support for their aggressive presumption, it is time for Mr Chesterton and all other men of sense to withstand them sturdily. Mr Chesterton takes the word as a convenient symbol for current attempts at legislative bodysnatching – live-bodysnatching – to provide subjects for professors and faddists to experiment on when pursuing all sorts of questionable, ridiculous, and even vicious theories of how to pro-

duce perfect babies and rear them into perfect adults. At the
very first blow he enlists me on his side by coming to my own
position and reaffirming it trenchantly. "Sexual selection, or
what Christians call falling in love," he says, "is a part of man
which in the large and in the long run can be trusted." Why
after reproducing my conclusion so exactly he should almost
immediately allege that "Plato was only a Bernard Shaw who
unfortunately made his jokes in Greek," I cannot guess; for it
is impossible to understand what the word "only" means in
this sentence. But the conclusion is none the less sound. He
does not follow it up as I do by shewing that its political corol-
lary is the ruthless equalization of all incomes in order that
this supremely important part of man shall no longer be baffled by the pecuniary discrepancies which forbid the duchess
to marry the coalheaver, and divorce King Cophetua from
the beggar maid even before they are married. But that will
come in a later book.

Mr Chesterton is implacable in his hostility to the Act
for dealing with the feeble-minded. How dangerous these
loose makeshift categories are when they get into the statute
book he brings out thus: "Even if I were an Eugenist, then
I should not personally elect to waste my time locking up
the feeble-minded. The people I should lock up would be the
strong-minded. I have known hardly any cases of mere mental weakness making the family a failure: I have known eight
or nine cases of violent and exaggerated force of character
making the family a hell."

This is a capital example of Mr Chesterton's knock-out
punch, which is much more deadly than Carpentier's. It is
so frightfully true, and illuminates so clearly the whole area
of unbearable possibilities opened up by this type of legislation, that it makes the reader an Anarchist for the moment.
But it does not dispose of the fact that the country has on
its hands a large number of people, including most authors,
who are incapable of fending for themselves in a competitive

capitalistic world. Many of them do quite well in the army; but when they are demobilized they are in the dock in no time. As domestic servants they are often treasures to kindly employers. Provide for them; organize for them; tell them what they must do to pay their way, and they are useful citizens, and happy ones if the tutelage is nicely done, as between gentlemen. But freedom and responsibility mean misery and ruin for them. What is to be done with them? Mr Chesterton says "Send them home." But that solution is already adopted in most of the cases in which it is possible. How about those who have no home? the old birds whose nest was scattered long ago? You cannot get rid of a difficulty by shewing that the accepted method of dealing with it is wrong. Mr Chesterton's demonstration of its danger actually increases the difficulty; for it is quite true that many of the most hopeless cases are cases not of Defectives but of Excessives. If the Prime Minister were to say to Mr Chesterton to-morrow, "You are quite right, God forgive us: the Act is a silly one: will you draft us another to deal with these people properly?" Mr Chesterton could not fall back on the eighteenth century and cry *Laissez faire*. All the king's horses and all the king's men cannot set that lazy evasion up again. If Mr Chesterton were not equal to the occasion, Mr Sidney Webb and his wife would have to be called in; for the facts will not budge; and it is cruel to abandon the helpless to a mockery of freedom that will slay them.

Mr Chesterton joins the campaign against the quackeries of preventive medicine with zest. "Prevention is not better than cure. Cutting off a man's head is not better than curing his headache: it is not even better than failing to cure it." He shews that the dread of religious superstition is itself a superstition, possible only to a Press that is a century out of date because its journalists are so hurried and huddled up in their stuffy offices that they have no time to observe or study anything, and can supply copy to the machines only by paying out any sort of old junk that has been current for a century past. He says with a sledge-hammer directness that reminds me of Handel: "The thing that is really trying to tyrannize through Government is Science. The thing that really does use the secular arm is Science. And the creed that really is levying tithes and capturing schools, the creed that really is enforced by fine and imprisonment, the creed that really is proclaimed not in sermons but in statutes, and spread not by pilgrims but by policemen—that creed is the great but disputed system of thought which began with Evolution and has ended in Eugenics. Materialism is really our established Church; for the Government will really help to persecute its heretics. Vaccination, in its hundred years of experiment, has been disputed almost as much as baptism in its approximate two thousand. But it seems quite natural to our politicians to enforce vaccination; and it would seem to them madness to enforce baptism."

This, except for the slip by which the essentially religious doctrine of Evolution is confused with the essentially devilish doctrine of Natural Selection, is undeniable, whether you believe in vaccination or not; and it is well that we should be made sharply aware of it, and also of the fact that as much hypocrisy, venality, cruelty, mendacity, bigotry and folly are using Science (a very sacred thing) as a cloak for their greed and ambition as ever made the same use of Religion. Indeed this is an understatement as far as the mendacity is concerned; for what priest ever lied about the efficacy of baptism as doctors have lied, and are still lying, about such shallow and disastrous blunders as [British surgeon Joseph] Lister's [1827–1912] antiseptic surgery, or have laid hands on children and gouged out the insides of their noses and throats in the spirit of the Spanish grandee who admired the works of God, but thought that if he had been consulted a considerable improvement might have been effected?

But we must not let our indignation run away with us. Let us contemplate a typical actual case. Scene: a school clinic. Present: a doctor, a snuffling child, and its mother. A dramatic situation has just been created by the verdict of the doctor: "This kid has adenoids." The mother is not in the least in a Chestertonian attitude. Far from objecting to State surgery, she holds that her child has a right to it in virtue of the doctor being paid to be there; and she is determined to insist on that right in spite of what she considers the natural disposition of all men, including doctors, to shirk their duties to the poor if they can. Far from crying, "Hands off my darling: who but his mother should succor him and know what is good for him?" she demands, "Ain't nothing to be done for him, poor child?" The doctor says, "Yes: the adenoids had better be cut out."

Now this may not be the proper remedy. It is on the face of it a violent, desperate, dangerous, and injurious remedy, characteristic of the African stage of civilization in which British surgery and therapy still languish. A better remedy may be one of the formulas of Christian Science, or the prayer and anointing of St James and the Peculiar People, or that the child should say every morning between sleeping and waking, "My nose is getting clearer and clearer," twenty-five times over. A million to one the real remedy is half a dozen serviceable handkerchiefs, a little instruction in how to use the nose in speaking and singing, with, above all, better food, lodging, and clothing. The mother does not "hold with" the mystical remedies. Of the two which are not mystical, the last mentioned means spending more money on the child; and she has none to spend, as the doctor very well knows: else, perhaps, he would honestly press it on her. Thus there is nothing for it but the knife. The hospital will cost the mother nothing; and it will be rather a treat for the child. She does not consider the hospital a disgrace like the workhouse: on the contrary, all her human instincts and social traditions

make her feel that she is entitled to help in case of sickness,
for which her very scanty household money does not provide. Accordingly, the interior of the unfortunate infant's
nose is gouged out; and possibly his tonsils are extirpated at
the same time, lest he should be overburdened with tissues
which surgeons consider superfluous because they have not
yet discovered what they are there for.

Now observe that here the mother does not protest: she
insists. The doctor operates because there is no money to
pay for sane natural treatment. The alternatives are to do
nothing, or to throw the mother back on some quack who
would promise to cure the child for a few shillings. All the responsible parties, the mother, the doctor, the schoolmaster,
and presumably Mr Chesterton, are against doing nothing.
What, then, is Mr Chesterton protesting against? He is
protesting against adapting the treatment of the child to the
low wages of its parents instead of adapting the wages of the
parents to the proper treatment for the child. And he is quite
right. From the point of view of the welfare of the community the decision of the doctor can be compared only to that
of [Swiss clown Charles Adrien Wettach, known as] Grock
[1880–1959], the French clown, who, when he finds that the piano stool is not close enough to the piano, moves the piano to
the stool instead of the stool to the piano. We have managed
to bedevil our social arrangements so absurdly that it is actually easier for our Parliamentary Grocks to move the piano
to the stool. But nobody laughs at them. Only exceptionally
deep men like Mr Chesterton even swear at them.

Mr Chesterton is, however, too able a man to suppose that
swearing at the Government is any use. All Governments
are open to Shakespear's description of them as playing such
fantastic tricks before high heaven as make the angels weep,
just as all men who undertake the direction of other men
are open to William Morris's objection that no man is good
enough to be another man's master. But when a job has to be

done, it is no use saying that no man is good enough to do it. Somebody must try, and do the best he can. If war were declared against us we could not surrender at discretion merely because the best general we could lay hands on might as likely as not be rather a doubtful bargain as a sergeant. Or let us take a problem which arises every day. We are confronted with the children of three mothers: the first a model of maternal wisdom and kindness, the second helpless by herself but quite effective if she is told what to do occasionally, and the third an impossible creature who will bring up her sons to be thieves and her daughters to be prostitutes. How are we to deal with them? It is no use to pretend that the first sort of mother is the only sort of mother, and abandon the children of the others to their fate: the only sane thing to do is to take the third woman's children from her and pay the other two to bring them up, giving the second one the counsel and direction she needs for the purpose. Of course you can put the children into an institution; only, if you do, you had better be aware that the most perfectly equipped institution of the kind in the world (it is in Berlin) acts as a lethal chamber, whilst in the mud-floored cabins of Connaught bare-legged children with a single garment, and not too much of that, are immortal. You have to do something; and since the job is too big for private charity (which is abominable, tyrannical and humiliating: in fact everything that raises Mr Chesterton's gorge in public maternity centres and school clinics and the like is a tradition from the evil days of private charity) it must be organized publicly; and its organizers must be taught manners by Mr Chesterton and the few others who know that insolence to the poor, though compulsory in our public services, acts like sand in an engine bearing.

But it remains true that as most people do not become "problems" until they become either poor or rich, most of the bad mothers and fathers and sons and daughters could be made passably good by simply giving them as much money as

their neighbors, and no more. I am not so much concerned
about their freedom as Mr Chesterton; for it is plain to me
that our civilization is being destroyed by the monstrously
excessive freedom we allow to individuals. They may idle;
they may waste; when they have to work they may make
fortunes as sweaters by the degradation, starvation, demor-
alization, criminalization, and tuberculization of their fellow
citizens, or as financial rogues and vagabonds by swindling
widows out of their portions, orphans out of their inheri-
tances, and unsuspecting honest men out of their savings.
They may play the silliest tricks with the community's wealth
even after their deaths by ridiculous wills. They may conta-
minate one another with hideous diseases; they may kill us
with poisons advertised as elixirs; they may corrupt children
by teaching them bloodthirsty idolatries; they may goad nations to war by false witness; they may do a hundred things
a thousand times worse than the prisoners in our gaols have
done; and yet Mr Chesterton blames me because I do not
want more liberty for them. I am by nature as unruly a man
as ever lived; but if Mr Chesterton could guess only half the
inhibitions I would add to the statute book, and enforce by
ruthless extermination of all recalcitrants, he would plunge a
carving knife into my ribs, and rush through the streets waving its dripping blade and shouting *Sic semper tyrannis*. I see
in the papers that a lady in America has been told that if she
does not stop smoking cigarettes her child will be taken from
her. This must make Mr Chesterton's blood boil; for he tells
us with horror that when he was in America, people were
admitting that tobacco needs defending. "In other words,"
he adds, "they were quietly going mad." But the truth, I rejoice to say, seems to be that they have given up the defence.
What right has a woman to smoke when she is mothering?
She would not be allowed to smoke if she were conducting a
bus or selling apples or handkerchiefs. A man should be able

to turn away in disgust from a railway smoking carriage without being reminded of his mother.

But unless I tear myself away from this book I shall never stop. If, as Mr Chesterton seems to insist, I am to regard it as another round in the exhibition spar with Mr Sidney Webb which he continues through all his books, I must give the verdict to Mr Webb, because the positive man always beats the negative man when things will not stay put. As long as Mr Webb produces solutions and Mr Chesterton provides only criticisms of the solutions, Mr Webb will win hands down, because Nature abhors a vacuum. Mr Chesterton never seems to ask himself what are the alternatives of Mr Webb's remedies. He is content with a declaration that the destruction of the poor is their poverty, and that if you would only give each of them the security and independence conferred by a small property on its owner (when he is capable of administering it) your problems would vanish or be privately settled. Nobody is likely to deny this: least of all Mr Sidney Webb. But Mr Chesterton's Distributive State, which is to bring about this result by simply making us all dukes on a small scale, would not produce that result even if its method were practicable. To many men—possibly to the majority of men, property is ruinous: what they need and desire is honorable service. They need also a homestead; and though for some of them the ideal homestead is a flat in Piccadilly, others want a house in the country, with a garden and a bit of pleasure ground. That is what Mr Chesterton enjoys; but if you were to offer him these things as industrial property, and ask him to turn his garden into a dirty little allotment and make money out of it, he would promptly sell himself as a slave to anyone who would employ him honorably in writing. So would I: so would Mr Belloc: so would Mr Webb. In short, this distribution of property of which Mr Chesterton tries to dream, but to which he has never been able to give his mind seriously for a moment, so loathsome is it, would be an abom-

inable slavery for the flower of the human race. Every Man his
Own Capitalist is the least inspiring political cry I know; and
when Mr Chesterton raises it my consolation is that it cannot
be realized. I urge Mr Chesterton to go on thundering against
the tyranny of Socialistic regulation without Socialistic distribution (the Servile State) to his heart's content; but I warn
him that if he persists in threatening us with the double curse
of peasantry and property as an alternative, he will give the
most fantastic extremes of doctrinaire Eugenics an air of millennial freedom and happiness by mere force of contrast.

G. B. S.

7. "The Testament of Wells," *Tribune*, 27 March, 1942.

[Review of The Outlook for Homo Sapiens, *by H. G. Wells
(London: Secker & Warburg, 1942). Wells is another of the prominent figures of Shaw's lifetime who exchanged textual blows with
a wide range of intellectuals at home and abroad, which is only
natural given Wells's personality and his professional interest (as a
fiction writer and social commentator) in controversial topics such
as science, religion, and politics. His ideas are particularly relevant
because they help to understand a crucial period in history—and
become even more so insomuch as they contrast with Shaw's.]*

Here, under the title of *The Outlook for Homo Sapiens*, is the
Testament which Herbert George Wells has bequeathed to
the world in 287 pages (say 130,000 words) for eight and six-
pence, or for the asking at the nearest public library. It is well
worth the money if you have any; and if you are in the TRI-
BUNE reader class you must read it because it is indispensable political news. And when H. G. is the writer, reading is a
treat and not a labor. Anyhow, you must read it.

The last sixty years have seen the rise of two new sects, the Wellsians and the Shavians, with a large overlap. The overlap may suggest that as our doctrine must be the same, our mental machinery must be the same also. But in fact no two machines for doing the same work could be more different than our respective brains. Ecologically (H.G's favourite word) and intellectually I am a seventeenth century Protestant Irishman using the mental processes and technical craft of [Irish-born author and cleric Jonathan] Swift [1667–1745] and Voltaire, whilst Wells is an intensely English nineteenth century suburban cockney, thinking anyhow, writing anyhow, and always doing both uncommonly well. The doctrine in my hands is a structure on a basis of dispassionate economic and biological theory: in his it is a furious revolt against unbearable facts and exasperating follies visible as such to his immense vision and intelligence where the ordinary Briton sees nothing wrong but a few cases that are dealt with by the police. He has neither time nor patience for theorizing, and probably agrees with that bishop whose diocese I forget, but who said very acutely that I would never reach the Celestial City because I would not venture beyond the limits of a logical map. These differences between us are very fortunate; for our sermons complement instead of repeating one another: you must read us both to become a complete Wellshavian.

When Wells burst on England there were no Wellshavians; but there were Webbshavians, alias Fabians, who had the start of him by ten years, and had the advantage of having been caught by the literature of Socialism when they were just the right age for it: that is to say in their mid-twenties, when he was in his teens, too young to take it in to its full depth.

At first the ten years were all to the bad. Wells, throwing himself into the Fabian movement to reform everything that was wrong in the world as well as the economic system,

found himself confronted by a disillusioned Old Gang of
wily committee men and practised speakers whose policy it
was to keep the Fabian Society to the economic point and
head off all excursions into religious controversy, party controversy, and sex controversy. Against this policy Wells
hurled himself furiously, smashing down its compromises
and platform tricks with a one-man artillery barrage of vituperation, reckless of whether he contradicted himself in
every second sentence or even in the same sentence. He
called for a society of millions of members and an expenditure of hundreds of thousands of pounds. It was a glorious
episode in the history of the Society; but the Old Gang, with
their ten years' experience and hard training, knew the possibilities only too well; and H.G. shook its dust off his feet after
kicking up a prodigious cloud of it, leaving the Old Gang in
possession.

He never thereafter worked with any existing Society of
practising politicians or became a committee man with committee manners, broken-in to accept the greatest common
measure of a council of colleagues as the limit to which
things could for the moment be carried, and with an eye always on the jury. He would not fit himself into any movement
or party, though he raged through them all, playing for his
own hand and leaving his mark wherever there was stuff plastic enough to take an impression. Far from keeping an eye
on the jury he no sooner took up a question than he forgot
everything and everybody else and charged into it, kicking
out of his way everyone, friend and foe, who obstructed him
for a moment, and always being forgiven and getting away
with it. He insulted all his friends and never lost them, and
made no enemies except the simpletons whose enmity hall-
marks its object as a friend of humanity. He obeyed no rules
of conduct except his own, and scattered invective in all directions as an R.A.F. pilot scatters bombs; but nobody has
ever accused him of doing a malicious injury or being capable

of it. He is the most ungovernable man of his rank in ability in England; but his fundamentally noble and generous nature keeps his halo undimmed all the time. And he is the best of good company: one of the few writers of whom it can be said that if his conversation could have been reported and all his books destroyed, the gain to his reputation might have been greater than the loss.

***

Wells, as a very English Englishman, is subject to attacks of a sort of mental gout or Berserkeritis which the Elizabethans called the spleen, the symptoms of which are in war reckless violence and in peace wild vituperation. When he sickens in this way, woe to the individual whom he dislikes and selects as whipping boy for his educational campaigns. Now it happens most unfortunately and quite unaccountably that his pet aversion is Karl Marx. The story of that famous exile is so pitiable that it hardly bears thinking of by any humane person. Marx's first beloved children died of slow starvation, which wrecked his health and shortened his own life. His two youngest daughters committed suicide. His wife was driven almost crazy by domestic worry. And yet he managed to write a book which changed the mind of the world in favor of Wells and nerved Lenin and Stalin to establish a new civilisation, largely Wellsian, in Russia. Yet Wells, when the fit is on him, loses his head and pursues this unhappy great man with a hatred so foreign to his own nature that one has to laugh it off as brain fever. Mention Marx to him and with the ink still wet on his chapters on the Class War and the woes of "the unpropertied," he will deny that there is any class war or any such thing as a proletariat, both being Marxian lies. He will belittle the Russian revolution and declare that the vital issue between experimenting with Socialism in a single country and waiting for an impossible world revolution

was only a wretched personal squabble between Stalin and
Trotsky.

Happily, after raving like this for pages and pages, he comes
out at last on the perfectly sound ground that it is England's
business not only to make the same inevitable revolution in
its own way in its own country (Stalinism) but to make an
equally successful job of it without any of the mistakes and
violences that would have wrecked Bolshevism had not we
and the other western powers rallied all Russia to its side by
senselessly attacking it and making its leaders national conquerors and saviours as well as international Communists.
Which is excellent Fabianism.

If H. G. in the next edition of his Testament will stick to his
conclusion and drop his vituperation of Marx with a handsome apology, asking himself what would have become of
him and of me if we, luckier than Marx, had not chanced to
possess a lucrative knack of writing novels and plays, he will,
I think, gain in authority and consistency.

There are moments too when our Protestant anti-clerical
habits get the better of Wells's Socialism. He is at the top
of his form when he shews that the Reformation is still only
half finished; but he is a bit hard on the Roman Catholic
Church when he blames it alone for the poverty and ignorance that have made civilisation a disease and that none
of the Churches have been able to cure. It is true that the
Roman Catholic Church, in desperation, has made a merit
of "holy poverty" and pleaded that without it we should be
without the virtue of charity, whilst the Protestants have on
the contrary made a supreme merit of prosperity ("holy
riches"). But both persuasions are equally helpless against the
economic consequences of private property. Without an economic Reformation none of the attempts to realise the ideal
of a Catholic Church, which has never yet existed in Rome
or Geneva or Moscow or anywhere else, will succeed. Mean-

while the Ulster slogan "To Hell with the Pope!" is only a red herring across the trail of Socialism.

I suppose I must honestly conclude by warning readers that my opinion of any work by Wells is so prejudiced in his favor by my personal liking for him that I do not myself know how much it is worth. Anyhow, his books have to be read, and not merely read about.

8. "More About Morris," *Observer*, 6 November, 1949.

[Review of William Morris, Prophet of England's New Order, *by Lloyd Eric Grey (London: Cassell, 1949). A biography of one of Shaw's closest friends, and one of the men who had a strongest influence in him.]*

Great men are fabulous monsters, like unicorns, griffins, dragons, and heraldic lions. But "this side idolatry," as Jonson put it, William Morris was great not only among little men but among great ones. All who knew him declared that he was the greatest man they had ever known. Scores of books will be written about him; but whatever record leap to light he never shall be debunked.

So far the most authoritative biography of him is [Scottish man of letters John William] Mackail's [1859–1945]. But Mackail regarded his Socialism as a deplorable aberration, and even in my presence was unable to quite conceal his opinion of me as Morris's most undesirable associate. From his point of view Morris took to Socialism as Poe took to drink.

The latest biographer, Mr Lloyd Eric Grey [American author Lloyd Wendell Eshleman, b. 1902], is free from this prejudice. He does his utmost to appreciate Morris's political acumen, prophetic farsight, and eminence not only as poet, artist, and craftsman, but as a philosopher. His book, illustrated by a superb portrait of Morris by [British artist] Cosmo

Rowe [1877–1952], and by Burne-Jones's funny drawings, has
no taint of academic snobbery. His hero worship is pushed
to the limit, as it should be. The more widely it is read, the
better.

***

It has, of course, trifling faults as well as deep qualities. It
labours overmuch to determine Morris's place in literature.
This is waste of time: Morris was no schoolman. He read
everything that did not bore him, and, like Molière, took his
goods where he could find them. He knew about Poe and
Browning and Tennyson and Swinburne as all literary people know about them; but the only poets who influenced his
beginnings were Chaucer and Rossetti. Being a born storyteller his pet modern authors were Dickens and Dumas. One
day, when he had been desperately uncomfortable at a police court, going bail for some of the comrades, I found him
rubbing it all off by reading *The Three Musketeers* for the hun-
dredth time or so. On one such occasion his co-bailsman
was Bradlaugh, and he envied the assurance with which that
platform athlete ordered everyone about and dominated the
police staff as if he had been the Home Secretary. He was
nothing of a bully in spite of his pathological temper, and
when physical courage came under discussion said: "I am a
funkster; but I have one good blow in me."

Mr Grey is wrong about the famous outbursts of temper:
he thinks that Morris laughed at himself for them. They were
eclampsias, and left him shaken as men are shaken after a fit.
The worst sorrow of his life was when his daughter Jenny
became a hopeless epileptic, and he knew that it was an inheritance from himself. Mr Grey, in one passage, suggests that
he was lonely and affection-starved at Lechlade because Mrs
Morris neglected him for Rossetti, who never tired of painting her. This is a mistake. Morris adored Jenny. He could

not sit in the same room without his arm round her waist. His voice changed when he spoke to her as it changed to no one else. His wife was beautiful, and knew that to be so was part of her household business. His was to do all the talking. Their harmony seemed to me to be perfect. In his set, beauty in women was a cult: Morris had no more reason to be jealous of Rossetti than Mrs Morris of the gloriously beautiful [British painter] Mrs [Marie Euphrosyne] Spartali [1844–1927], or of Lady Burne-Jones, whose memoir of her husband shows that Morris was her hero.

Like Hyndman, Morris had something of the petulance of the born rich, though he could not endure the society of average ladies and gentlemen. I have said from clinical observation that his rages were pathological. I go farther, and believe that his lack of physical control when he was crossed or annoyed was also congenital and not quite sane. No two human beings could be less like one another than he and H. G. Wells; yet neither of them could be depended on to behave always sensibly. Being a great man, Morris could face and bear great trials; but on some utterly negligible provocation anything might happen, from plucking hairs out of his moustache and growling "Damned fool, damned fool," to kicking a panel out of a door.

I ask Mr Grey to reconsider his estimate of *The House of the Wolfings* as more advanced than *News From Nowhere*. The *Wolfings* is, like all Morris's tales, lovely as a tissue of musical prose; but it is only his first attempt to restore Don Quixote's destroyed library, full of impossible sword fights and Dulcinea, and a very biased contrast between Roman and "barbarian" society. *News From Nowhere* is a picture of a possible future, with no fights and forlorn maids rescued from enchanters. Mr Grey writes that it is unreal because there are no crimes in it. He forgets: there is a murder in it. There are even motor-boats in it.

When I went through Morris's Merton factory with him,
I dared to say, "You should get a machine to do that." He
replied, "I've ordered one."

Sources and Further Reading

[For comprehensive and up-to-date bibliographies and other important research aids for work on Bernard Shaw in electronic and print forms see the Research Aids section on the website of the International Shaw Society: www.shawsociety.org. The selection here focuses on Shaw's views on literature and his activity as a literary critic.]

Autobiography

An Autobiography. Selected from His Writings by Stanley Weintraub. 2 vols. New York: Weybright and Talley, 1970.

The Diaries 1885–1897. Ed. Stanley Weintraub. 2 vols. University Park: Pennsylvania State University Press, 1986.

Sixteen Self Sketches. London: Constable, 1949.

Biography

Colbourne, Maurice. *The Real Bernard Shaw.* London: Dent & Sons, 1949.

Gibbs, A. M. *Bernard Shaw: A Life.* Gainesville: University Press of Florida, 2005.

———. *A Bernard Shaw Chronology.* Basingstoke: Palgrave, 2001.

Henderson, Archibald. *Bernard Shaw: Man of the Century.* New York: Appleton-Century-Crofts, 1956.

Holroyd, Michael. *Bernard Shaw.* 5 vols. London: Chatto & Windus, 1988–92.

———. *Bernard Shaw: The One-Volume Definitive Edition.* New York: Random House, 1997.

Pearson, Hesketh. *George Bernard Shaw: A Biography.* London: Macdonald and Jane's, 1975.

Letters

Agitations. Letters to the Press 1875–1950. Eds. Dan H. Laurence and James Rambeau. New York: Frederick Ungar, 1985.

Bernard Shaw: Collected Letters. Ed. Dan H. Laurence. 4 vols. New York: Viking Penguin, 1965–88.

Bernard Shaw's Letters to Siegfried Trebitsch. Ed. Samuel Weiss. Stanford: Stanford University Press, 1986.

Selected Correspondence of Bernard Shaw. Series Editors J. Percy Smith and L. W. Conolly. Toronto: University of Toronto Press, 1995– [ongoing]. *Bernard Shaw Theatrics*, ed. Dan H. Laurence, 1995; *Bernard Shaw and H.G. Wells*, ed. J. Percy Smith, 1995; *Bernard Shaw and Gabriel Pascal*, ed. Bernard F. Dukore, 1996; *Bernard Shaw and Barry Jackson*, ed. L. W. Conolly, 2002; *Bernard Shaw and the Webbs*, eds. Alex C. Michalos and Deborah C. Poff, 2002; *Bernard Shaw and Nancy Astor*, ed. J.P. Wearing, 2005; *Bernard Shaw and His Publishers*, ed. Michel W. Pharand, 2009; *Bernard Shaw and Gilbert Murray*, ed. Charles A. Carpenter, 2014.

Plays and Prefaces

The Bodley Head Bernard Shaw. Collected Plays with their Prefaces. Under the editorial supervision of Dan H. Laurence. 7 vols. London: Max Reinhardt, the Bodley Head, 1970–74.

Novels and Other Fiction

The Black Girl in Search of God and Some Lesser Tales. London: Constable, 1954.

Cashel Byron's Profession. London: Constable, 1950.

Immaturity. London: Constable, 1950.

The Irrational Knot. London: Constable, 1950.

Love Among the Artists. London: Constable, 1950.

An Unsocial Socialist. London: Constable, 1950.

Literary Essays

Bernard Shaw: Platform and Pulpit. Ed. Dan H. Laurence. London: Rupert Hart-Davis, 1962.

Bernard Shaw: The Drama Observed. 4 vols. Ed. Bernard F. Dukore. University Park, PA: Penn State University Press, 1993.

Bernard Shaw's Book Reviews, Originally Published in the Pall Mall Gazette *from 1885 to 1888.* Ed. Bryan Tyson. University Park, PA: Penn State University Press, 1991.

Bernard Shaw's Book Reviews, Volume 2: 1884–1950. Ed. Bryan Tyson. University Park, PA: Penn State University Press, 1996.

Bernard Shaw's Nondramatic Literary Criticism. Ed. Stanley Weintraub. Lincoln: University of Nebraska Press, 1972.

George Bernard Shaw on Language. Ed. Abraham Tauber. New York: Philosophical Library, 1963.

Major Critical Essays: The Quintessence of Ibsenism. The Perfect Wagnerite. The Sanity of Art. London: Constable, 1932. See also the edition with an introduction by Michael Holroyd (London: Penguin, 1989).

Plays and Players: Essays on the Theatre. Ed. A. C. Ward. London: Oxford University Press, 1952.

"Reviewing Reviewed: A Symposium," *The Author* 43 (Summer 1943): 65–74.

Shaw, Bernard. *Music in London 1890–94.* Vol. III. London: Constable, 1950.

Shaw on Dickens. Eds. Dan H. Laurence and Martin Quinn. New York: Frederik Ungar, 1985.

Shaw on Shakespeare: An Anthology of Bernard Shaw's Writings on the Plays and Production of Shakespeare. Ed. Edwin Wilson. New York: Dutton, 1961.

Shaw on Theatre. Ed. E. J. West. New York: Hill and Wang, 1958.

Criticism

Barr, Allan P. "Diabolonian Pundit: G. B. S. as Critic," *Shaw Review* 11 (1968): 11–23.

Baylen, Joseph O. "The 'New Journalism' in Late Victorian Britain," *Australian Journal of Politics and History* 18.3 (1972): 367–385.

Cary, Richard. "Shaw Reviews Satan the Waster," *Colby Library Quarterly* 9.6 (1971): 335–347.

Crawford, Fred D. "Bernard Shaw's Theory of Literary Art," *The Journal of General Education* 34.1 (1982): 20–34.

— — —, ed. *Shaw Offstage: The Nondramatic Writings. SHAW: The Annual of Bernard Shaw Studies.* Volume 9. University Park: The Pennsylvania State University Press, 1989.

Dietrich, Richard F. *Bernard Shaw's Novels: Portraits of the Artist as Man and Superman.* Gainesville: University Press of Florida, 1996.

Fromm, Harold. *Bernard Shaw and the Theater in the Nineties: A Study of Shaw's Dramatic Criticism.* Lawrence: University of Kansas Press, 1967.

Gerould, Daniel Charles. "George Bernard Shaw's Criticism of Ibsen," *Comparative Literature* 15.2 (1963): 130–145.

Gibbs, A.M., ed. *Shaw: Interviews and Recollections.* Iowa City: University of Iowa Press, 1990.

Hogan Jr., Patrick G., and Joseph O. Baylen. "G. Bernard Shaw and W. T. Stead: An Unexplored Relationship," *Studies in English Literature, 1500–1900* 1.4 (1961): 123–147.

Hugo, Leon. *Bernard Shaw's The Black Girl in Search of God: The Story behind the Story.* Gainesville: University Press of Florida, 2003.

Innes, Christopher, ed. *The Cambridge Companion to George Bernard Shaw.* Cambridge: Cambridge University Press, 1998.

Kent, Brad, ed. *George Bernard Shaw in Context.* Cambridge: Cambridge University Press, 2015.

King, Carlyle. "G. B. Shaw on Literature: The Author as Critic," *Queen's Quarterly* 66 (1959): 135–145.

Laurence, Dan H. "Bernard Shaw and the *Pall Mall Gazette*: An Identification of His Unsigned Contributions," *Bulletin of the Shaw Society of America* 5 (1954): 1–7.

Laurence, Dan H., and Margot Peters, eds. *Unpublished Shaw. SHAW: The Annual of Bernard Shaw Studies.* Volume 16. University Park: The Pennsylvania State University Press, 1996.

Ohmann, Richard M. *Shaw: The Style and the Man.* Middletown: Wesleyan University Press, 1962.

Palmer, John. *George Bernard Shaw: Harlequin or Patriot?* New York: The Century Co., 1915.

Silverman, Albert H. "Bernard Shaw's Shakespeare Criticism," *PMLA* 72.4 (1957): 722–736.